SECURITY AND DEFENCE
IN THE TERRORIST ERA

FOREIGN POLICY, SECURITY AND STRATEGIC STUDIES
Editors: Alex Macleod and Charles-Philippe David

The Foreign Policy, Security and Strategic Studies Series seeks to promote analysis of the transformation and adaptation of foreign and security policies in the post Cold War era. The series welcomes manuscripts offering innovative interpretations or new theoretical approaches to these questions, whether dealing with specific strategic or policy issues or with the evolving concept of security itself.

Canada, Latin America, and the New Internationalism
A Foreign Policy Analysis, 1968–1990
Brian J.R. Stevenson

Power vs Prudence
Why Nations Forgo Nuclear Weapons
T.V. Paul

From Peacekeeping to Peacemaking
Canada's Response to the Yugoslav Crisis
Nicholas Gammer

Canadian Policy toward Krushchev's Soviet Union
Jamie Glazov

The Revolution in Military Affairs
Implications for Canada and NATO
Elinor Sloan

Inauspicious Beginnings
Principal Powers and International Security Institutions after the Cold War, 1989–1999
Edited by Onnig Beylerian and Jacques Lévesque

Security and Defence in the Terrorist Era
Canada and North America
Elinor Sloan

Towards a Francophone Community
Canada's Relations with France and French Africa, 1945–1968
Robin S. Gendron

PROCEEDINS
The Future of NATO
Enlargement, Russia, and European Security
Edited by Charles-Philippe David and Jacques Lévesque

Security and Defence
in the Terrorist Era

Canada and the
United States Homeland

SECOND EDITION

Elinor C. Sloan

McGill-Queen's University Press
Montreal & Kingston • London • Ithaca

© McGill-Queen's University Press 2010
ISBN 978-0-7735-3679-1 (cloth)
ISBN 978-0-7735-3694-4 (paper)

Legal deposit first quarter 2010
Bibliothèque nationale du Québec

Printed in Canada on acid-free paper that is 100% ancient forest free
(100% post-consumer recycled), processed chlorine free

McGill-Queen's University Press acknowledges the support of the Canada
Council for the Arts for our publishing program. We also acknowledge
the financial support of the Government of Canada through the Book
Publishing Industry Development Program (BPIDP) for our publishing
activities.

Library and Archives Canada Cataloguing in Publication

Sloan, Elinor C. (Elinor Camille), 1965–
 Security and defence in the terrorist era: Canada and the United States Homeland /
 Elinor C. Sloan. – 2nd ed.

 Includes bibliographical references and index.
 ISBN 978-0-7735-3679-1 (bnd)
 ISBN 978-0-7735-3694-4 (pbk)

 1. National security – Canada. 2. National security – United States.
 3. Canada – Defenses. 4. United States – Defenses. I. Title.

 UA22 S56 2010   355'.033071   C2009-906545-2

This book was typeset by Interscript in 10.5/13 Sabon.

Contents

SECURITY AND DEFENCE
IN THE TERRORIST ERA

Introduction

No responsibility is more fundamental to a federal government than providing for the security of citizens. Since World War II modern, democratic governments have progressively taken on a multitude of responsibilities with respect to their country's citizens, each meant in some way to better their daily lives. But, in the final analysis, these pale in comparison with the original and most fundamental element of the social contract between the individual and the state: that people give up a certain measure of freedom in return for government-provided security.

"Security," here, is the absence of threat to a particular set of values. What this set of values includes differs among countries and could even differ between peoples within a country. Nonetheless, it can be argued that Canadians generally agree on a common set of values that must be guaranteed. National security, Canada's National Defence College argues, "includes freedom from military attack or coercion, freedom from internal subversion and freedom from the erosion of the political, economic and social values which are essential to our quality of life."[1] Freedom from military attack and internal subversion, in turn, can be elaborated to include the physical security of our national territory, our territorial integrity, the safety of our nation's citizens, and the protection of our critical infrastructures. Those political, economic, and social values that are essential to the quality of our lives include national sovereignty and control over our territory, democracy and the rule of law, individual rights and freedoms, and a certain measure of economic well-being or prosperity.

In principle, there could be any number of threats to national security – that is, threats to those values I have listed. To provide the analytic boundaries necessary for any meaningful policy prescription, we must ascribe some sort of timeframe to the concept of threat. In this context, a threat to national security can be seen as an action or sequence of events that threatens drastically and over a relatively brief span of time to degrade one or more of the values Canadians deem essential to their way of life.[2] A national security strategy involves measures designed to guard against these threats. Both military and non-military instruments will be involved; defence policy is a derivative of security policy in that it is meant to address the specific range of threats against which military force is perceived to be a necessary or primary instrument of action.[3] In theory, security policy serves as a bridge between defence policy and a country's broader foreign policy.[4]

Any Canadian government seeking to guarantee the security of its citizens is faced with two broad choices. It can take measures overseas in an attempt to address threats as far away from North American shores as possible, an approach that is captured in the phrase "a good defence is a good offence" and is sometimes referred to as the "away game." Or it can focus on shoring up security and defence measures in and around the North American continent – that is, it can focus on the "home game." The two approaches are not mutually exclusive; any prudent government will place a certain degree of emphasis on each. Rather, the central decision lies in what balance the government should find between measures abroad and those at home in allocating scarce resources.

Surrounded by oceans and faced throughout the Cold War with a direct threat to its territory against which there was no effective defence (i.e., nuclear-armed ballistic missiles), Canada has historically looked primarily overseas to address potential threats to the country, with the possible exception of the government of Pierre Elliott Trudeau in the early 1970s. This remained the predominant approach in the 1990s, when Canada and it allies focused their attention on addressing civil strife and intrastate war abroad. Not until 11 September 2001 was the frame of North America's "fireproof house" truly fractured. This event, combined with the onward march of climate change and the melting Arctic icecap, has raised new questions about Canadian security. How can the Canadian government best provide for the security of Canadians in the contemporary era? What balance should it find between measures abroad and those at home in guaranteeing the security of its citizens? What are the associated military capability requirements? These are the questions that this book seeks to answer.

Canadian security and defence requirements of the future can be roughly divided into four categories: military responses at home (homeland defence); civilian responses at home (homeland security); military responses abroad (warfighting and stabilization operations); and civilian responses abroad (e.g., development aid and diplomacy). This book centres on the first three quadrants of responses and where the Canadian government could best place its emphasis. The fourth quadrant, civilian responses abroad, falls squarely in the realm of foreign policy and will be addressed only insofar as it pertains directly to Canadian security.

Chapter 1 places Canadian security and defence policy into context, providing an overview of its evolution from the early post–World War II period to the Conservative governments of Prime Minster Stephen Harper. Chapter 2 examines the nature of the contemporary threat to North America, a central factor in finding the appropriate balance between measures abroad and those at home. Chapter 3 highlights the evolution of US thinking about threats to the North American continent during the first post–Cold War decade, thereby providing the context for post-9/11 developments. Chapters 4 and 5, respectively, discuss the numerous homeland security and homeland defence initiatives that have been taken jointly or separately by the United States and Canada since the 9/11 attacks, while chapter 6 addresses a specific aspect of the homeland defence debate: space and ballistic missile defence. Chapter 7 examines military requirements for addressing threats to North America overseas, before they reach our shores, and looks at Canadian military capabilities in these areas. The final chapter gives guidance on what balance Canada should find in providing for its security offensively abroad or defensively at home, and it concludes with a window on the broader civilian and diplomatic activities that are necessary if the Canadian government is to guarantee the security of its citizens.

The Evolution of Canadian Security and Defence Policy since World War II

Contemporary decision makers seeking the balance Canada should strike between measures abroad and those at home in guaranteeing the security of its citizens can benefit from a knowledge of the evolution of Canadian security and defence policy since World War II. It was during this conflict that Canada most definitively matured as an independent nation, and in the war's aftermath it was clear to observers that the country had "won" a place on the international stage.[1] Since that time, successive federal governments have responded to the changing global threat environment with varying approaches to promoting the security of Canadians. Examining these reveals a broad consistency in the components of Canadian security and defence policy over the years and decades. It also brings to light the degree to which past elements of Canadian security and defence policy hold resonance with contemporary circumstances. Early ideas on how to guarantee Canadian security have re-emerged with greater relevance today, a decade into the new millennium.

In their 1995 volume on Canada's International Security Policy, David Dewitt and David Leyton-Brown point out that up until that time Canada had never had an explicitly stated international security policy – that is, a statement of how it could best "guarantee" the security of its citizens. This contrasts with, for example, the United States, which issues a formal *National Security Strategy of the United States* roughly every four years. But the fact that Canada had not explicitly put anything to paper – until the 2004 National Security Policy,[2] issued by Prime Minister Paul Martin – did not mean that Canada had no policy or approach to national security.

Rather, the policy was implicit in the actions and statements of the various governments over the years.

THE ST LAURENT-PEARSON ERA

It was Secretary of State for External Affairs Louis St Laurent who best expressed the security policy of Prime Minister William Lyon Mackenzie-King's postwar government. In a January 1947 speech, the Gray Lecture at the University of Toronto, St Laurent focused on bilateral relations with Canada's key postwar allies, the United States, Britain, and France, as well as on collective security through the United Nations (UN) as the key areas of activity in Canadian foreign and security policy.[3] In this latter area St Laurent stressed that Canada had emerged from the war with international responsibilities and that these responsibilities would be carried out primarily through the support of the United Nations.[4] Thus, at this early stage, St Laurent established the "internationalist" perspective on, or approach to, guaranteeing Canadian security, under which threats to Canadian security are addressed "over there," as far from Canadian shores as possible.

Yet this internationalist perspective was not the central focus of Canada's defence policy statement released only six months later. Unlike in the case of security policy, since the end of World War II Canada *has* had a tradition of explicitly stating its defence policy – albeit haphazardly and with no set timeframe in terms of years between the statements. The first of what have now been seven postwar statements was *Canada's Defence 1947*, included as part of the Department of National Defence's estimates to Parliament in July of that year. In this statement, Canada's defence minister, Brooke Claxton, highlighted Canada's defence "needs": "Canada's defence forces may be required: (1) to defend Canada against aggression; (2) to assist the civil power in maintaining law and order within Canada; (3) to carry out any undertakings which by our own voluntary act we may assume in cooperation with friendly nations or under any effective plan of collective action under the United Nations."[5]

Although not stated as such, the list may be read as one that indicates priorities, with the first and second priorities clearly centred on defence measures at home. Douglas Bland has referred to these as "defence imperatives" in Canadian defence policy,[6] to which would be added, in subsequent years, defending North America in cooperation with the United States. At this early stage, however, there was as yet no direct threat to Canadian territory. Although the Soviet T-4 bomber – capable of reaching Canada and the United States from the Soviet Union – first appeared in 1947, not until 1952 did the United States consider the USSR to have enough bombers to present a critical threat to North America.[7]

Only with his third priority does Claxton move to activities abroad under UN auspices, a centrepiece of St Laurent's vision but a "strategic choice" from a purely defence perspective.[8] In the first months of 1947 the Soviet threat still presented itself primarily in political and diplomatic terms; concrete military expression did not come until the June 1950 North Korean invasion of South Korea. Moreover, Canada was in the midst of a postwar drawdown in military forces and was seeking to reduce defence expenditures. The combined result was that notwithstanding the overseas emphasis in St Laurent's Gray Lecture, Canada's first postwar defence statement did not place a high priority on Canadian operations abroad.

Within a year the global threat environment had changed dramatically. The clear deterioration of East-West relations (by late 1947), the Berlin airlift (starting in 1948), the Soviet detonation of an atomic bomb (1949), and finally the North Korean invasion of South Korea (1950) precipitated the conclusion of progressively more substantial initiatives for international cooperation among Western countries, including the Western Union (1948), the North Atlantic Treaty (1949), and the North Atlantic Treaty Organization (NATO) (1950). As it became apparent the East-West standoff would prevent the UN from carrying out its originally envisaged collective security role, the internationalist perspective of Louis St Laurent, now prime minister, and his secretary of state for external affairs, Lester B. Pearson, came to encompass and focus on NATO and collective defence.

Despite these developments, the Claxton statement of defence priorities was broad enough to remain relevant throughout the 1950s. Indeed, its opening pages presaged the impetus behind the best-known Canadian foreign and defence policy development of this time period: Pearson's negotiation of a UN interpositionary force to resolve the 1956 Suez Crisis. The introductory statement to *Canada's Defence 1947* notes, "The object of Canadian policy is to do all that we can to prevent the outbreak of another world war."[9]

More than half a century after the invention of peacekeeping, which can be dated either to the creation of the United Nations Truce Supervision Organization in 1948 or to the first United Nations Emergency Force in 1956, it is easy to forget that Cold War peacekeeping missions were rooted not in altruism or humanitarianism but in the stark interest of peace between the Great Powers. A conflict between the Cold War superpowers would have been harmful for Canadian national security, to say the least. To the extent that the interposition of a peacekeeping force between parties allied with one side or the other could prevent a crisis from escalating to a Great Power conflict, peacekeeping became an important component of Canadian security and defence policy.

Thus in these early days the deployment of peacekeeping forces was best characterized as a defence imperative for Canada; only later did it become more of a strategic choice. In the 1950s and 1960s Canada was also particularly well suited to be a peacekeeping nation. Canada had emerged from World War II with one of the largest militaries in the world, but the force had been drawn down in the immediate postwar years. The outbreak of war on the Korean peninsula in June 1950, and the subsequent creation of NATO (putting the "O" into the North Atlantic Treaty) a few months later, precipitated a significant conventional force build-up on the part of Canada and her allies. But the United States (and the Soviet Union) could not be seen as impartial, which was a key requirement – along with consent of the parties and use of force only in self-defence – for what are now termed "traditional" peacekeeping operations. At the same time, other countries with strong military forces, like France and Britain, were saddled with a colonial/imperial history. Canada faced neither encumbrance. Canada's unique combination of strong military forces and a relatively impartial stance on the international stage made it the ideal peacekeeper of the era.

THE DIEFENBAKER YEARS

Even as Canada burnished its internationalist credentials, it was at the same time developing an increasingly "continentalist" perspective on guaranteeing the security of its citizens. Canada's overall approach to its foreign and security policy has been described as being like a pendulum in nature,[10] sometimes leaning abroad (the internationalist approach, or "away game") and sometimes leaning toward

North America (the continentalist approach, or "home game"). The election of Prime Minister John Diefenbaker marked the first post-war swing in the continentalist direction. While remaining committed to NATO and collective defence and to the UN and collective security, the government centred its concrete defence efforts on North America and defence relations with the United States. During the 1950s the direct Soviet threat to Canada and North America progressively increased as the Soviet Union built more and more nuclear-armed long-range bombers capable of reaching Canadian and US airspace. The two countries responded to growing vulnerability with a series of radar sites across Canada, including the Pine-tree line of radar stations at the 50th parallel, the Mid-Canada line at the 54th parallel, and finally the Distant Early Warning (DEW) line at the 70th parallel. They also sought to institutionalize the co-ordination of a growing number of fighter aircraft on both sides of the border that would be used to combat any Soviet aircraft detected by the radar lines. This was achieved by signing the North American Air Defence Agreement (NORAD) in 1957.[11]

The United States and Canada had cooperated for the defence of North America for some two decades prior to the creation of NORAD. In August 1938 US president Franklin Roosevelt, meeting his Canadian counterpart at Kingston, Ontario, stated in a speech that the United States would "not stand idly by if domination of Canadian soil is threatened by any other empire," to which Mackenzie King responded a few days later that Canada would ensure no enemy forces could "pursue their way either by land, sea or air, to the United States across Canadian territory."[12] This informal commitment proved only a prelude to a more formal arrangement. Under the terms of the 1940 Ogdensburg Agreement, so named because of their meeting place in upper New York State, the two leaders affirmed that continental security was indivisible, pledged mutual assistance in the event of hostilities, and established a Permanent Joint Board on Defence (PJBD). As the first institutional reflection of Canada-US defence cooperation, the PJBD was charged with drawing up a Canada-US Basic Defence Plan, and it continues to meet twice a year at both the diplomatic and military levels to consider important Canada-US security and defence questions. A subordinate organization, the Military Cooperation Committee (MCC) created by the PJBD in 1945 to update the Basic Defence Plan after the war, also continues to meet and update what is now called the Canada-US Basic Security Plan.

Apart from the creation of NORAD, in the security and defence realm the Diefenbaker government is most remembered for three issues: its cancellation of the Avro Arrow, its failure to arm the Bomarc missile with nuclear warheads, and its reaction to the Cuban Missile Crisis. The well-known story of the Avro Arrow centres on Canada's effort to indigenously produce a supersonic fighter aircraft to replace the CF-100 fighters, which, by the mid-1950s, were too slow to outrun the ever-faster Soviet bombers threatening North America. A centrepiece of Canada's attempt to develop a Canadian defence industrial base to support the country's military needs, the Arrow fell victim to the rising costs of producing military platforms and a dramatic change in the security environment that rendered fighter aircraft less relevant to North American security. Ironically, the first of the Avro Arrow aircraft – which did not go through the usual prototype stage of development – was officially rolled out for flight-testing on the same day that the Soviet Union launched its Sputnik satellite, 4 October 1957. Although a satellite and not a missile, Sputnik marked the definitive beginning of the missile age because it revealed to the world that the Soviet Union had the capability to develop an intercontinental ballistic missile that could reach US territory. As a platform designed to combat what was suddenly yesterday's threat – manned bombers – the Avro Arrow was immediately at risk; in early 1959 the program was cancelled altogether. What Arrow enthusiasts remember is not so much that the program was cancelled, which probably made sense in light of increasing costs and the changed security environment, but rather the sudden and wholesale manner in which it was carried out: for reasons that are still disputed, the Canadian government chose to shut down the entire factory and ensure that all completed aircraft were destroyed.

Meanwhile, and before the emphasis shifted to countering ballistic missiles, the United States decided to establish a defence against Soviet long-range bombers using a series of eight surface-to-air Bomarc missile sites across the centre of North America. The unreliable accuracy of a missile shot into the air meant that the Bomarcs could be effective only if they were armed with a nuclear warhead. In 1958 the fledgling Diefenbaker government agreed to house and operate two Bomarc missile sites on Canadian soil. Production delays meant that the missiles were not ready for deployment until 1962, but in the meantime an increasingly unpopular Diefenbaker government, faced with a growing peace movement in the early 1960s, became unwilling to accept the nuclear warheads. The decision only exacerbated an already tense Canada-US relationship that was characterized by mutual dislike between Diefenbaker and US president John F. Kennedy. It also created turmoil in the governing party, contributing in part to the government's fall in 1963. Reversing its earlier opposition to the warheads, the new Liberal government under Pearson accepted the warheads, which were installed in 1964, and then embarked on a renegotiation process that led to the Bomarcs' deactivation in 1972. The Pearson government also accepted nuclear-tipped Genie missiles, the armament for the American-built CF-101 Voodoo aircraft that Canada ultimately acquired in 1961 to replace the CF-100s. These aircraft stayed in service until they were replaced in the early 1980s by Canada's present, conventionally armed CF-18 fighter aircraft.[13]

Diefenbaker's nuclear dithering meant that both the Voodoo aircraft and Bomarc missiles on Canadian soil were unarmed when the most serious crisis of the Cold War, the Cuban Missile Crisis, broke in October 1962. Here, the issue was in part one of indecision as the Diefenbaker Cabinet debated for two days – a lifetime in terms of nuclear crisis management – whether to place Canada's military forces on high alert. This was necessary if US fighters were to deploy to Canadian dispersal sites and if the Canadian naval contribution to antisubmarine warfare was to increase around North America. But the crisis also raised concerns about government control of the military because the defence minister secretly placed Canada's NORAD forces on full alert, while the navy commander on the east coast sent Canada's ships to sea to relieve US ships needed further south for the blockade around Cuba. Not surprisingly, civilian control of the military figured centrally in the next defence white paper.

PEARSON AS PRIME MINISTER

When Pearson came to power as prime minister, Canada returned to the familiar internationalist approach to security. The government strongly supported the United Nations and NATO, sought to repair relations with key allies like the United States (although Canada increasingly disagreed with America on its policy in Vietnam), and saw no real direct threat to Canada, at least not one against which it was possible to defend. The March 1964 *White Paper on Defence*, the first explicit statement of Canadian defence policy in almost a generation, and the first such document to be released in standalone form and be termed a "white paper," reflected the Pearsonian perspective. The opening section states the objectives of Canadian defence policy as being collective defence, meaning NATO; participation in international organizations, meaning collective security through the UN; and the protection and surveillance of Canadian territory, air space, and coastal waters. Any mention of the United States and North America is curiously absent, but in the next breath the document highlights "four parallel methods" by which Canadian defence policy had been pursued in the postwar period: (1) *Collective Measures* as embodied in the UN Charter; (2) *Collective Defence* as embodied in the North Atlantic Treaty; (3) *Partnership with the United States* to defend North America; and (4) *National Measures* to protect Canada[14] – thereby implying that this was the more complete list of Canadian defence policy priorities.

The 1964 *White Paper on Defence* bears the strong imprint of Pearson's minister of national defence, Paul Hellyer, who had some firmly held, sometimes controversial, and in many ways prophetic ideas about Canada's military forces. Notably, the white paper introduced several ideas that resonate with the military requirements of the contemporary security environment. One was the notion of a "range of conflict." Canada's military forces were not necessary solely for responding to an East-West warfighting scenario, the document argued; rather, they had to be prepared for a range, or spectrum, of conflict situations extending "from the possibility of all-out thermonuclear war, through large-scale limited war, to insurrection, guerrilla activity and political upheaval."[15] Today, and indeed ever since the end of the Cold War, it has been commonplace in the security and defence field to speak of a range, or spectrum, of conflict against which military forces must be able to respond.

A second idea relevant to today was the saliency of mobile forces. When it came to peacekeeping, the white paper argued, there was "likely to be a need for highly mobile forces for ground observation, air surveillance, rapid transportation and reliable communications."[16] As for NATO, increased air transport would "make it possible to move units to the European flanks, if and when required, from bases in Canada and the United States."[17] In terms of force structure this meant that two of Canada's five brigades would be re-equipped and retrained as mobile forces. Force Mobile Command was created at a base just south of Montreal in 1968, encompassing two of five Canadian Mechanized Brigade Groups (CMBGs): 1 CMBG based in Edmonton and 5 CMBGs based in Val Cartier. Re-equipping these brigades to achieve "maximum flexibility" and mobility, the paper argued, would enable them to be effectively deployed in "circumstances ranging from service to the European theatre to United Nations peacekeeping operations."[18] Like the "spectrum of conflict," the notion of flexibility/mobility – which raised concerns in the Department of External Affairs because it suggested Canada's commitment to NATO may be scaled back – was an idea before its time. Today, it is well accepted that military forces must be configured and equipped for rapid deployment to theatre and be highly mobile in theatre if they are to respond effectively to the range of contingency operations.

Finally, the white paper highlighted the importance of the three military services being able to work together in operations. "Doubts ... have been raised in all countries in recent years about the traditional pattern of organization by individual services," the paper argued. "Combined operations have become commonplace, and the services have found a growing area of overlap in the tasks with which they are charged."[19] The practical implications of these observations was the decision to "integrate the Armed Forces of Canada under a single Chief of Defence Staff and a single Defence Staff" as a "first step toward a single unified defence force for Canada."[20]

Integration was driven by the need to rationalize overhead, create coordinated policy positions, and above all, "strengthen civilian control of the military in the aftermath of the turbulent Diefenbaker government years and the Cuban Missile Crisis."[21] Previously, policies had been coordinated in a Chiefs of Staff Committee, comprising a chairman and the heads of the three services, each of who had direct access to the minister. Under the new system one four-star chief of defence staff (CDS) position was created, reporting to the minister. The service chiefs would now report to the CDS, thereby ensuring policy positions were integrated rather than merely coordinated (with varying degrees of success, depending on the personalities involved). Moreover, the integration of the command structure would permeate the command chain such that there would be one deputy chief of defence staff in charge of operations, one vice chief of defence staff in charge of budgets, one joint staff, one pay office, one procurement organization, one recruiting system, one medical system, and so on.

What created greater controversy, and the resignation of more than a few senior officers, was the sister idea of "unification." This involved eliminating the Royal Canadian Air Force, the Royal Canadian Navy, and the Canadian Army as separate entities and creating in their place, on 1 February 1968, one Canadian Forces (CF). The most visible manifestation of unification was the replacement of the different service uniforms with a common CF uniform. But the original intention was for unification to go so far as to encompass common training and operations. Over the years, training was unified to a significant extent in the trades of combat support (e.g., communications, engineers, military police) and combat service support (e.g., logistics and administration), but in the combat trades joint training was more difficult to achieve. Training exercises remained largely distinct, with Canada's army conducting operations with the German Army, and Canada's navy and air force working closely with their American counterparts. Only in the 1990s, for example, did the navy attempt to integrate elements from all three services into their Maritime Coordinated Operational Training (MARCOT) exercises; and only after 9/11 did the air force begin to focus on joint operations with the army in their Exercise Maple Flag.

Overall, unification is something that went largely unachieved, a fact that was reflected in the return to distinct service uniforms in the mid-1980s. But the underlying rationale – an increased ability of Canada's three military services to work together – has only increased in relevancy. Today, it is captured in the term "jointness," something most, if not all, Western military forces consider central to conducting effective military operations both at home and abroad.[22] The requirement for increased jointness is a recurring theme, with the most recent organizational push in Canada coming from the creation of a new CF command structure in 2006 (see chapter 5).

THE TRUDEAU ERA

The election of Pierre Elliott Trudeau in 1968 marked a change in Canada's approach to guaranteeing its security. The new prime minister questioned the Pearsonian internationalist tenets of collective defence through NATO and collective security through the United Nations. He cut Canada's military commitment to Europe in half, from 10,000 to 5,000 troops, and was less than convinced of the value of UN peacekeeping. But this did not mean that Trudeau was not internationalist in nature; rather, he was looking beyond the traditional multinational organizations that had been established in the early post–World War II era. The government placed significant stock in the process of détente, or a relaxation in relations between East and West, which began in the late 1960s, and it strongly supported the Conference on Security and Cooperation in Europe, a Soviet initiative for increased East-West dialogue that began in the early 1970s and led to the 1975 Helsinki Accords.

Unlike some of his predecessors and his immediate successor, Trudeau did not conceive of Canadian security as including a close Canada-US bilateral dimension. In the economic realm, the government sought to reduce Canada's dependence on the United States by choosing a "Third Way" to economic security. Given a choice of keeping the status quo, increasing economic integration with the United States, or attempting to develop closer ties with other regions of the world as a means of guarding against the twitches and turns of the southern "elephant," the government opted for the latter, or third, option. In the defence realm, not only did Trudeau reduce Canada's force level commitment to NATO, a US-dominated organization, but, influenced by the unannounced transit of the US oil tanker *Manhattan* through the Northwest Passage in September 1969, he also gave rhetorical emphasis to the need for increased Canadian military independence at home.

Defence in the 70s, the white paper on defence that was released in August 1971 by Minister of National Defence Donald Macdonald, drew out many of these themes. In the global dimension, it noted that the optimism that had greeted peacekeeping ten years earlier had not been matched with success in resolving conflicts in areas ranging from the Middle East to Cyprus to Indo-China. Regionally, it was felt that the countries of western Europe, now prosperous and cooperating closely, could do more for their own defence, so the reduction in CF force levels, which by this time had already been effected, made good military sense. Continentally, this white paper conceded that cooperation with the United States for the defence of North America would "remain essential so long as our joint security depends on stability in the strategic balance."[23] But it was on Canada and safeguarding Canada's sovereignty and independence that the document placed its greatest emphasis, arguing in its opening section that "The first concern of defence policy is the national aim of ensuring Canada should continue secure as an independent entity."[24] The Canadian Forces was to have a major role to play in this endeavour, and to this end, "The provision of adequate Canadian defence resources for this purpose ... [was] a matter of first priority."[25]

The defence policy priorities of *Defence in the 70s* reflected this perspective of the world. Arguing there was a need to adjust the balance between Canadian defence activities abroad and those at home, the document enunciated a list of priorities that exactly reversed those of the 1964 *White Paper on Defence* and also included some notable qualifications regarding CF activity abroad. Canada's defence priorities were: (1) the surveillance of Canada's territory and the protection of its sovereignty; (2) the defence of North America in cooperation with the United States; (3) the fulfilment of NATO commitments – qualified by "as may be agreed upon"; and (4) international peacekeeping roles – qualified by "as we may from time to time assume."[26] Like the 1964 *White Paper on Defence*, *Defence in the 70s* contains ideas that resonate strongly with the contemporary security environment. In a paragraph that could have been written today, the document highlights potential external challenges in Canada's North, including increased activity/traffic and a growing commercial interest in the area's natural resources, notably oil and gas. Written in the wake of the October Crisis of 1970, precipitated by the actions of the Front de libération du Québec (FLQ), the white paper also stressed Canada's internal, domestic security environment and the requirement that the CF be able to provide aid to the civil power if so required. The focus on both the Arctic and CF assistance to civilian authorities at home – now to address terrorism and weapons of mass destruction – are issues that figure centrally in current Canadian defence policy.

Over the expanse of his roughly fifteen years in power, Trudeau's security and defence policies proved less revolutionary than was originally anticipated. Détente deteriorated over the course of the 1970s and definitively broke down when the Soviet Union invaded Afghanistan in 1979. The superpower standoff re-emerged, revealing as wishful thinking the 1971 white paper's assertion that the bipolar international system was loosening in favour of a multipolar world. UN peacekeeping forces could be needed again to stop a local crisis from escalating to war between East and West. And a focus on the military value of Canada's force commitment to NATO had missed the broader necessity of demonstrating political solidarity. Canada actually increased its stated commitments to NATO in the 1970s, adding a Canadian Air-Sea Transportable (CAST) brigade group based in Canada but ready to deploy to Norway if necessary. In 1979 it also agreed, along with other NATO countries, to spend 3 per cent of its gross domestic product (GDP) on defence, a level that has not been reached since. But Canada's overall military capability deteriorated under Trudeau as a result of reduced budgets in earlier years, and much of the 1979 increase went to personnel costs. Meanwhile, the Third Way economic option floundered in the face of the inexorable pull of the American market; the percentage of Canadian exports going to the United States continued to increase. As for Canada and the North, little attempt (the acquisition of Aurora long range patrol aircraft under Trudeau being a notable exception) was made to back up the sovereignty and independence rhetoric with actual military capabilities or even civilian assets like a new icebreaker. Ironically, Trudeau left office demonstrating a mindset as incongruous as when he arrived, promoting East-West dialogue and cooperation during a farewell peace tour even as the underlying Cold War structure stubbornly persisted.

THE MULRONEY YEARS

When Brian Mulroney was elected prime minister in September 1984, the "second Cold War" remained firmly in place. Mikhail Gorbachev would not become general secretary of the Communist Party of the Soviet Union for another six months, and it would be about two more years before Gorbachev's new approach to the West would become apparent. The Mulroney government's response to this security environment was a mixture of internationalism and continentalism. The government supported traditional multilateral commitments to the United Nations, NATO, the Commonwealth, and La Francophonie. It also campaigned in part on a platform of rebuilding the Canadian Forces after years of neglect and of honouring Canada's commitments to its allies. At the same time, and uniquely among Canada's post–World War II prime ministers, the Mulroney government placed significant and explicit emphasis on close bilateral relations with the United States. Under Mulroney, Canada sought to guarantee Canadian economic security not by diversifying trading partners but by cementing its access to the American market. The centrepiece of this effort, it goes without saying, was the Canada-US Free Trade Agreement, signed when Mulroney returned to power after the so-called free trade election of 1988.

The military component of the Mulroney government's international security policy was expressed in *Challenge and Commitment: A Defence Policy for Canada*, commonly referred to as the *1987 Defence White Paper*. The document begins by pointing out that the great hopes of the early 1970s, captured by the word "détente," had not been realized. The world had not grown multipolar, superpower tensions had not decreased, and the central fact of international life remained the confrontation and rivalry between East and West. Alongside a picture of Soviet tanks in front of a large red banner with Vladimir Lenin's portrait, the white paper notes that since the end of World War II the Soviet Union had persistently expanded its military power. Soviet bombers, ballistic missiles, and cruise missiles threatened North America and therefore Canadian interests directly, while the Soviet Union's numerically superior conventional forces threatened Canadian interests indirectly in Europe.

In its section on Canadian defence policy, the document indicates priorities that accord with this assessment. The first task mentioned is contributing to "strategic deterrence" – that is, the defence of North America in cooperation with the United States, largely through NORAD. The second is "conventional defence," meaning collective defence measures through NATO in the European theatre. The white paper's third priority, sovereignty, which in the Canadian context can be equated to the word "Arctic," is the one that the Department of National Defence in the 1970s had placed first on its list, while the paper's fourth and fifth priorities are peaceful settlement of international disputes through peacekeeping and arms control.

The paper's section on peacekeeping is useful because it sets out the rationale for such missions and the criteria for Canadian participation. Although Canada had, by this time, been involved in international peacekeeping missions for almost forty years, no Canadian defence policy document had included so detailed a discussion. The *1987 Defence White Paper* states that peacekeeping missions were necessary to hold in place smaller conflicts that engaged the interests of the superpowers so that these conflicts did not lead to war between the superpowers. It further elaborated that government decisions on participation in a peacekeeping mission would be based on seven criteria: (1) whether there is a clear and enforceable mandate; (2) whether the parties to the conflict agree to a ceasefire and to Canada's participation; (3) whether the arrangements will likely lead to peace in the long run; (4) whether the size and composition of the force is appropriate for the mandate; (5) whether Canada's participation will compromise other (i.e., NATO) commitments; (6) whether there is an authority (i.e., the UN) to support the operation; and (7) whether the mission is adequately funded.

A notable aspect of this white paper is the marked disjuncture between its introductory chapters, focusing on the East-West confrontation, and its prescriptions later on for "the way ahead." More specifically, although sovereignty appears third on the defence policy priority list, and is not raised at all in the paper's opening sections, the requirements for ensuring Canadian sovereignty in the North dominate decisions on how to re-equip the CF and address the widening commitment-capability gap. For the latter, the government decided "to alter some commitments to bring them more into line with resources, while improving the effectiveness with which the remaining commitments are carried out."[27] Altering commitments meant eliminating the CAST commitment to Europe and consolidating the Canadian effort in Germany at its base in Lahr. In practical terms, this meant a reduction in the number of CF personnel committed to the conventional battle in western Europe. Improving the effectiveness of how remaining commitments were carried out, as its happens, was a reference almost entirely to increasing Canada's ability to conduct the surveillance of its east, west, and especially northern approaches. "The Arctic Ocean, lying between the superpowers, is ... an area of growing strategic importance," the white paper argues. "Technology is making the Arctic more accessible. Canadians cannot ignore that what was once a buffer could become a battleground."[28]

In terms of military requirements, addressing the perceived Soviet threat in the North dovetailed with responding to renewed sovereignty concerns. These had been raised, once again, in the summer of 1985 when the Polar Sea, a US Coast Guard ship, transited the Northwest Passage without first asking for Canadian authorization, much as the USS Manhattan had done sixteen years earlier, sparking the Trudeau government's focus on sovereignty in the North. Soon thereafter the Mulroney government had announced it would build a

Polar 8 icebreaker, and this was reiterated in the 1987 white paper. *Challenge and Commitment* also announced the government would continue on with previous decisions to replace the old DEW line with a new North Warning System of radars (still at the 70th parallel) and build Forward Operating Locations as dispersal locations for its CF-18 fighter aircraft. But the centrepiece of the paper's acquisition plan was a "vigorous naval modernization program" to include six additional frigates, six more long-range patrol aircraft, and most controversially, between ten and twelve nuclear-propelled submarines. The key to a three-ocean navy, such submarines were considered "essential to meet ... long-range ocean surveillance and control requirements in the Atlantic and the Pacific as well as in the Arctic."[29]

The rationale presented for the submarines, and indeed the paper as a whole, surprised observers because it seemed rooted in the darkest days of the Cold War. In many ways, the *1987 Defence White Paper* was the document the Trudeau government should have released when it returned to power after Joe Clark's brief tenure as prime minister in 1979–80. At that time, the Soviet Union had only recently invaded Afghanistan, and hard-line communists continued to dominate Soviet politics. But by June 1987, when the paper was tabled in the House of Commons, East-West tensions had palpably begun to thaw. Driven by a bottom-up process that had begun more than two years earlier, when the international security environment was much different, the white paper that was finally released under Defence Minister Perrin Beatty (who, due to ministerial scandals, was Mulroney's third defence minister in as many years) seemed detached from overall political and perhaps economic reality. Remarkably, a follow-on document, the March 1988 Defence Update, found that "events since the tabling of the White Paper have demonstrated that the principles on which it is founded remain sound."[30] Yet well before the Berlin Wall fell in November 1989, questions were raised about the validity of the assumptions behind the white paper's proposals.

The sudden end of the Cold War soon rendered *Challenge and Commitment* obsolete. The second Mulroney government released a Defence Update in 1992 that gave an accounting of security and defence developments around the world and announced the major elements of Canada's response. These included a reduction in the size of the CF and the withdrawal of its permanently stationed forces in Germany, a move that provoked significant outcry from

European members, who feared it was the first step in a general North American (i.e., United States) force withdrawal from Europe. But at this early stage, as Defence Minister Marcel Masse put it, "the number of certainties" continued to be "far outweighed by the number of uncertainties."[31] Not until the dust had further settled and a new government was in place would there be a full elaboration of a post–Cold War Canadian defence policy.

THE CHRÉTIEN ERA

The era of Jean Chrétien marked a return to a relatively more internationalist approach to guaranteeing Canadian security. In signing the North American Free Trade Agreement (NAFTA), which had been negotiated under Mulroney and which extended to Mexico the original Canada-US Free Trade Agreement, the government implicitly supported economic integration with the United States as the best means of securing economic prosperity. But it also sought a degree of independence from the political pull of America. This was demonstrated most vividly in the policies and approach of Lloyd Axworthy, Canada's minister of foreign affairs from 1996 to 2000. At a time when Canada, like many countries, was still struggling to define what sort of new world order had replaced the familiar framework of the Cold War, Axworthy put forward "human security" as the appropriate organizing principle. The idea was to focus on the security of the individual during conflict, and it came with a particular agenda, not all of it to America's liking. Key elements included the Anti-Personnel Landmines Convention of 1997, the creation of the International Criminal Court, a protocol on child soldiers, and addressing small-arms proliferation.

Human security was not the only idea proposed in the 1990s as a means of responding to the new security environment. A second idea was "cooperative security," put forward by various scholars in the 1990s and also promoted early on, in 1990, by Joe Clark when he was Canada's secretary of state for external affairs. Unlike human security, which answered the question of "whose security" (the individual rather than the state), cooperative security focused on the method: multilateral means. The idea was to include both friends and adversaries in "habits of dialogue" around a range of military and non-military security concerns, with the hope that such a process would eventually transform existing institutions or create new multilateral ones.[32] These internationalist views formed the overall context of the Chrétien government's approach to security and defence in the almost eight years.it was in office before the terrorist attacks of 11 September 2001. In essence, it was a move from the hard power of military capability to the soft power of diplomacy, negotiation, and the promotion of values, and with this shift came a de-emphasis on the role of the military in Canadian security policy.

At first glance, this was not the perspective presented by official Canadian defence policy, which appeared quite robust in military terms. The Chrétien government moved more quickly to define a new defence policy for Canada than had any government since Pearson's Liberals were elected in 1963. After its landslide win in the fall of 1993, the new Liberal government established two special joint committees of the Senate and House of Commons, one each for foreign and defence policy. The Special Joint Committee on Defence solicited informed views from across the country about the future of the military, hearing perspectives that ranged from focusing on overseas development assistance and undertaking low-risk UN peacekeeping activities to developing "niche" combat capabilities and maintaining a multipurpose, combat-capable force that could participate in high-intensity warfighting missions. The Special Joint Committee recommended the latter and gave a force level of 70,000 personnel as the minimum necessary for Canada to play a meaningful role in the world.

"Virtually all [of the Special Joint Committee's] recommendations," Defence Minister David Collenette notes in the introduction to the 1994 *Defence White Paper,* "are reflected in this White Paper."[33] And indeed this is true. The white paper opens by painting a picture of an international security environment that, although safer than during the Cold War, was still characterized by pockets of chaos and instability that would continue to threaten international peace and security. In such an environment, the paper argued, the maintenance of multipurpose, combat-capable forces was in the national interest. These forces had to be able to carry out a range of operations from preventative peacekeeping, traditional peacekeeping, and postconflict peacebuilding to collective security, enforcing the will of the international community, and the collective defence of allies. The white paper does not contain an explicit list of defence policy priorities, but these are implicit in the ordering of its chapters: "The Protection of Canada," "Canada-United States Defence Cooperation," and "Contributing to International Security."

A notable aspect of the *1994 Defence White Paper* is that for the first time since Brooke Claxton's defence statement of 1947, before NATO was created, there was no section devoted to NATO. Rather, Canada's contribution to the alliance is detailed in the chapter on contributing to international security, along with other organizations like the United Nations and the Organization for Security and Cooperation in Europe. The paper thus implicitly places collective security and the United Nations at the heart of Canadian defence policy, and this impression is reinforced by the fact that specific force levels are designated for strengthening the United Nations (but not NATO), including up to 10,000 contingency forces for UN operations and a UN stand-by force commitment of up to 4,000 personnel. Ironically, only a year later CF participation in multinational operations turned in precisely the opposite direction. Beginning with the NATO-led Implementation Force launched in Bosnia in late 1995, followed by the Stabilization Force also in Bosnia, and now the ongoing International Security Assistance Force in Afghanistan, almost all CF participation in overseas operations has been under NATO leadership. No more than a few hundred Canadian troops are scattered on UN missions around the world, leading some commentators to lament the decline of Canadian participation in peacekeeping – a misplaced critique that fails to account for post–Cold War changes in the international security environment.

Even as it put forward the need for a strong military force, the pages of the *1994 Defence White Paper* revealed that the government's robust rhetoric would not be matched with resources. This was evident in three areas: force levels, budget, and capital acquisitions. From a level of 75,000 regular force personnel when Mulroney left power – itself a reduction of almost 10,000 from when the 1987 white paper was released – the CF fell to an established level of 60,000 under the terms of the *1994 Defence White Paper*, much lower than what the Standing Joint Committee had recommended. In subsequent years the CF's effective strength would continue to decrease, eventually settling around 52,000 by the late 1990s. At the same time, in a chapter on "domestic considerations," the white paper set out the rationale for a substantial cut in the defence budget. This was necessary, it argued, to help reduce the federal deficit, which had grown substantially during the Mulroney years. Between 1993 and 1998 the Department of National Defence's budget fell by some 23 per cent in nominal terms and by 30 per cent in terms of real purchasing power. Finally, the white paper minced no words when it came to capital acquisitions. Whereas previous policy statements had announced plans for new CF equipment, the *1994 Defence White Paper* does no such thing: "The emphasis will be on extending the life of equipment ... Planned acquisitions will be cut by at least 15 billion dollars ... a large number of projects currently in plans will be eliminated, reduced or delayed."[34]

The upshot to this approach to security was a significant decline in Canada's military capability and, many would argue, in Canada's influence in international political forums during the first post–Cold War decade.[35] The defence budget did begin to inch up in 1999, but there were no significant increases during the Chretien Era. Even in the so-called "security budget" of December 2001, passed in response to the 9/11 attacks, the government (probably appropriately) allocated most of the increased funding to intelligence-gathering agencies like the Canadian Security Intelligence Service and the Communications Security Establishment, as well as to increasing the strength of Canada's special operations force, Joint Task Force 2. Beyond the security budget, the Chretien government undertook several other measures in response to the 9/11 attacks, and these will be detailed in chapters 4 and 5. But the government's response in general was piecemeal. Not until Paul Martin replaced Jean Chretien as the Liberal Party leader, and therefore as prime minister, in November 2003 did Canada begin to adopt a more comprehensive approach to national security. In Canada, one could argue, the post-9/11 era began more than two years after the terrorist attacks.

THE POST-9/11 ERA UNDER MARTIN

The government of Prime Minister Paul Martin was the first to explicitly state a national security policy for Canada, albeit one that was limited in scope. *Securing an Open Society: Canada's National Security Policy*, released in April 2004, delivers less than its title promises. It is, in effect, a homeland security document and is better equated to America's *National Strategy for Homeland Security* than to the *National Security Strategy of the United States*. Nonetheless, its existence sheds light on the Martin government's approach to Canadian security. Specifically, it points to the importance the government placed on the homeland as an organizing principle for Canadian security and defence efforts, much as the Trudeau government did in the wake of the 1970 October Crisis. But whereas the Trudeau rhetoric remained just that, the Martin effort contained concrete initiatives in the areas of intelligence, disaster management, and public health that were subsequently implemented.

Although the Martin's government's approach to national security contained an important homeland dimension, its national security policy was in fact much broader in scope. *Securing an Open Society* alluded to this in its final chapter, entitled "International Security," which promises an international policy review to elaborate on the link between international peace and security and national security interests. The outcome was *Canada's International Policy Statement* (*IPS*), released in April 2005 by a new Martin government, which had been reduced to minority status the previous summer. The *IPS* contained five parts: "Overview," "Diplomacy," "Development," "Defence," and "Commerce." Because the "Overview" has a strong security and defence emphasis, it is this component along with that of "Defence" – which soon became known as the Defence Policy Statement (DPS) – that best expressed the Martin government's international security policy.

Economics figured centrally in the Martin government's approach to security. Describing North America as Canada's "anchor" in the global economy, the "Overview" stresses the importance of Canada's economic relationship with the United States. It discusses the trilateral trade relationship with the United States and Mexico through both NAFTA and the March 2005 Security and Prosperity Partnership, placing a particular emphasis on the need to focus more directly on trade with Mexico. In an approach vaguely reminiscent of Trudeau's Third Way, it also draws out the importance of forging new ties around the world: "While our current relationships with major trading partners will remain important, large developing countries are emerging ... with implications for our own prosperity."[36] The document points especially to China, India, and Brazil, but also to Japan and the European Union, as particular areas of focus for future economic relationships.

The Martin government adopted a similarly "part-continentalist, part-internationalist" approach in other areas of its security policy. The *IPS*'s "Overview" stresses the importance of security and defence measures at home: "The first priority of the Canadian Forces will be the protection of Canada itself. North America has become a theatre of operations in its own right."[37] The DPS adds even greater weight to this theme: "The first challenge is to strike the right balance between the Canadian Forces' domestic and international roles ... The government believes ... that a greater emphasis must be placed on the defence of Canada and North America than in the past."[38] The practical implication of this argument was that the CF was reorganized into four new command structures: Canada Command, Expeditionary Forces Command, Special Operations Command, and Operational Support Command. Canada's previous structure had focused primarily on overseas operations, now the purview of Expeditionary Forces Command, so the truly unique aspect of this new structure was the creation of Canada Command. Underlining this change in focus, the IPS highlights the effects of climate change on the Arctic, while the DPS emphasizes the importance of the CF being able to operate in the North. In an apparent contradiction of the IPS's call for "revitalizing our North American Partnership,"[39] however, in February 2005 the Martin government took the sudden and poorly delivered decision that Canada would not participate in America's ballistic missile defence (BMD) system for North America.

At the same time, the IPS and DPS contain strong internationalist themes. Like many of its predecessors, the Martin government saw in multilateralism through international organizations a key means of guaranteeing the security of Canadians. "A world that is governed well," states the IPS's "Overview," "is not a soft ideal. It is a vital Canadian interest."[40] Yet, although it was generally supportive of the United Nations, the government also argued that this "foundational" institution was challenged by questions of relevance and legitimacy and that there was an emerging role for new multilateral institutions. Specifically, it put forward the notion of an "L20" comprised of the UN's Great Powers along with leaders of major developing states like Brazil and India, a reflection of changes in the power of states since 1945. The IPS notes that another foundational institution, NATO, also faces challenges in the contemporary environment but stresses the necessity of carrying out an ambitious transformation of the organization so its members can address requirements for "building a secure world," especially countering terrorism, stabilizing failed and failing states, and stemming the proliferation of weapons of mass destruction. The requirement, the IPS argues, is to increase the CF's capacity to participate with allies in conducting operations associated with these threats. Part of this involved a commitment to increase the size of the Canadian Forces, which by this time stood at about 62,000 on paper, by some 5,000 troops.

The IPS and the DPS contain strong words about the Canadian Forces' future ability to operate at home and abroad in guaranteeing Canadian security. But much like in the 1994 *Defence White Paper*, the sweeping rhetoric was not accompanied by commitments to concrete capabilities. Rather, the Department of National Defence was to "publish a paper in the coming months detailing the capabilities and force structure required to implement" the DPS,[41] a task that was not completed before the Martin government lost power in early 2006. In the 2005 budget the government announced significant increases in defence spending over five years, but most of this was not to come until near the end of that time period. To the degree that there was any policy implementation at all, beyond the organization changes, it was in the internationalist dimension as Canada significantly increased its commitment to Afghanistan beginning in the summer of 2005.

THE CONSERVATIVES UNDER HARPER

The two minority governments led by Conservative prime minister Stephen Harper did not articulate a statement comparable to the IPS by setting out a broad rationale and context for Canadian defence policies. Rather, the Harper government returned to the Canadian tradition of implicit international security policies revealed through the actions of the government. The notion of collective security through the UN as a means of contributing to Canadian security, gently questioned by the Martin government, seems far removed from the Harper government's frame of reference. The UN and other multilateral organizations, such as the Commonwealth and La Francophonie, were not mentioned in the Conservative Party's 2005–06 election platform, *Stand Up for Canada*, nor has the United Nations appeared in speeches from the throne since that time. One of the first actions the government took when elected in 2006 was to close out Canada's last remaining substantial UN peacekeeping commitment: our contribution to the UN Disengagement Observer Force on the Golan Heights. Soon thereafter the government rejected suggestions that Canada should contribute troops to any possible UN mission in Darfur, citing the substantial Canadian commitment to the NATO-led operation in Afghanistan.

Early in its mandate, the Harper government also indicated that the parameters of Canadian security interests included good bilateral relations with the United States. In stark contrast to the tense Canada-US relations of the Liberal era (with the 1997 Landmines Convention, the 2003 decision not to support the war in Iraq, and the 2005 BMD decision marking particularly low points), the Conservative government referred to the United States as "our best friend and largest trading partner" in its inaugural throne speech. Since that time the tone has remained generally positive and relations have been relatively smooth, even if the Harper government's concrete policies have been little different from those of its immediate predecessor (the Conservatives, for example, have made no attempt to reopen the BMD issue).

Taking a cue from the IPS, the Harper government's Canadian security and defence policy is a more robust advancement of themes that had been identified by the Martin government. Like the government before it, the Harper government has stressed the importance of rebuilding failed states, notably Afghanistan, as an important contributing factor to Canadian security. Within months of being elected, Harper travelled to Afghanistan to highlight Canada's commitment. Although the Liberals authorized the original deployment, the Conservatives increased Canada's force level commitment, progressively deployed additional equipment such as Leopard tanks, helicopters, and unmanned aerial vehicles to support the mission, and in 2007 steered a mandate extension to February 2011 through Parliament. To bolster Canada's ability to operate abroad, the Harper government defied the normal lengthy process of purchasing major military equipment by buying four C-17 strategic lift aircraft in the space of about eighteen months.

The Harper government also advanced his predecessor's move to increase the emphasis placed on domestic roles and the defence of Canada. The Martin government's homeland security-oriented National Security Policy of 2004 remains in place, along with most, if not all, of the initiatives associated with the document. Beyond this, the 2005–06 election campaign included Conservative Party promises to deploy territorial defence battalions in major Canadian cities in response to any terrorist use of weapons of mass destruction. More dramatically, the party put forward a number of initiatives to increase Canadian sovereignty in the North, including the construction of three armed icebreakers, a deep-water docking facility, and an Arctic training centre for the army. Midway through their first minority government, the Conservatives announced these initiatives would go ahead, with the exception that Canada would purchase a greater number of smaller and less ice-capable Arctic offshore patrol vessels in place of the armed icebreakers.

After referring for more than two years to a non-existent, or at least not formally released, *Canada First Defence Strategy*, the Harper government finally issued this document in June 2008, the most recent of Canada's seven post–World War II official defence policy documents. The strategy captured all of the government's defence-related activity since coming to power and also made a few new announcements. Its opening pages announce six core missions of the Canadian military: conduct daily domestic and continental operations, including in the Arctic and through NORAD; support a major international event in Canada, like the Olympics; respond to a major terrorist attack; support civilian authorities during a crisis in Canada like a natural disaster; lead and/or conduct a major international operation for an extended period; and deploy forces at crises elsewhere in the world for a shorter time period.[42]

A number of points emerge from this list. First, although the document states the CF must maintain the ability to carry out these core missions "at times simultaneously," their order of appearance does imply a certain prioritization. In this regard, it is notable that the first four of the six points pertain directly to Canadian territory, an indication that the Harper Conservatives, even more so than the Martin Liberals, consider a certain rebalancing between the "away game" and the "home game" to be important for future Canadian security. Second, "responding to a terrorist attack," presumably on Canadian soil, is separated out from other homeland scenarios where the CF would support civilian authorities, an implicit recognition that such a situation would likely escalate to the requirement for a CF-led role in relatively short order. And finally, once the list turns to overseas operations, the commitment is very ambitious – "*lead* a major international operation" (emphasis added) – indicating the government continues to see actions abroad as central to Canadian security.

For the Harper government, increasing Canada's military capability is an important aspect of Canadian security policy. In the 2005–06 election it campaigned on the issue of increased defence spending, and once elected, it maintained and augmented the budgetary measures announced by Martin. Like the Martin government, however, it also allocated the most significant increases to the final year of a five-year window. In the 2008 budget the government announced further increases, and these became the basis of the *Canada First Defence Strategy* (CFDS). The CFDS sets out a budgetary plan to spend $490 billion on defence over a twenty-year period to 2028, about $60 billion of which is to be spent on capital equipment acquisitions. The plan includes a list of things that had already been announced and also states a force level ambition of 70,000 troops, although no target date for completion is given. As for the strategy's new announcements, the document highlights some major new fleet replacements planned for the future, including future-generation fighter aircraft, combined destroyers and frigates, and land combat vehicles and systems. These are things that had been discussed for years within the defence community but had never been part of an official government announcement.

For all the rhetoric surrounding the Harper government's support of rebuilding the Canadian Forces and placing a greater emphasis on Canada and the North, there have not been many concrete changes. The only major equipment purchase that has actually taken place is that of the C-17s. Other promises remain stuck in the procurement process, some years behind schedule. Funding is to be spread over twenty years, during which there will be many changes in government, and the global economic crisis that came to the fore in 2008 could impact even short-term promises of defence budget increases, despite assurances to the contrary.[43] Meanwhile, CF activity remains overwhelmingly "away" in Afghanistan, not close to the shores of North America.

Viewing Canadian security and defence policy over the expanse of the post–World War II period reveals a slight yet discernible change of course, as ideas expressed in previous decades have re-emerged with greater relevance today. The salient question for policymakers is: what is the appropriate balance between measures abroad and those at home in the short to medium term? If the object of Canadian security and defence policy is to guarantee the security of Canadians, then the starting point must be an identification and examination of possible threats to Canada's national security.

2

Threats to National Security

The starting point for determining the relative emphasis to be placed on activities abroad and those at home for guaranteeing Canadian security is an appreciation of the nature of the threat to North America. This chapter begins with an overall look at the threat to the United States and Canada and then examines in more detail the strategic options, motives, and capabilities that make up this threat assessment. It concludes that policy changes cannot eliminate the threat in the short to medium term and that ultimately Canadian security will depend on finding and implementing the most appropriate balance of military and civilian measures at home and abroad.

THE THREAT TO AMERICA

International Terrorism

Almost a decade after the 9/11 attacks, US officials continue to characterize international terrorism as posing the most significant threat to the United States. In early 2007 the director of national intelligence (DNI) stated in his *Annual Threat Assessment* that al-Qaeda posed "the greatest threat to US interests, including the Homeland."[1] The thwarted attempt to use liquid explosives to blow up airliners out of Heathrow Airport in August 2006 had provided concrete recent evidence of terrorist intent: intelligence officials determined that the plan involved exploding the airliners over US cities, rather than the Atlantic, to maximize the loss of life in America.[2] For terrorism experts, this case indicated that Islamic extremists remained focused on attacking the United States directly on

US soil and in spectacular fashion.[3] A summer 2007 *National Intelligence Estimate* of the terrorist threat to the US assessed that "Al-Qa'ida is and will remain the most serious terrorist threat to the Homeland" and that "its central leadership continues to plan high-impact plots [against the United States]."[4] The 2008 annual DNI assessment stated that "Al-Qa'ida and its terrorist affiliates continue to pose significant threats to the United States at home" and that its "Homeland plotting" is focused on prominent political, economic, and infrastructure targets designed to produce mass casualties.[5] In his 2009 testimony before Congress, Dennis Blair, the first DNI of Barack Obama's administration, reiterated this perspective.[6]

Athough al-Qaeda clearly has the intent to target America again, views on whether it actually has the capacity to do so have undergone a subtle change in recent years. Central to a capability determination is, as the 2007 estimate of the terrorist threat to the US homeland put it, a determination of the degree to which al-Qaeda has "protected or regenerated key elements of its Homeland attack capability"[7] since being routed from Afghanistan in late 2001. By the middle of the decade, it was clear that al-Qaeda had been able to regenerate core operational capabilities by establishing a safe haven, or base of operations, within the Federally Administered Tribal Areas (FATA) of Pakistan. Moreover, beginning in 2006 there was an influx of new Western recruits into the FATA – potential operatives to infiltrate the United States and plot attacks. But in the last months of 2008, US precision strikes against terrorists in the FATA using unmanned drones became increasingly accurate, eliminating many key leaders, including the mastermind of the 2006 airliner plot. At the same time, it is thought that tension between members of al-Qaeda and their tribal hosts has increased. In early 2009 then director of the Central Intelligence Agency (CIA) Michael Hayden stated that al-Qaeda was feeling a backlash from Pakistani tribes and was under strain because of the loss of senior leaders.[8] A month later, the new DNI argued that a "succession of blows" against al-Qaeda in the tribal areas had led to a significant loss in al-Qaeda's command structure "as damaging to the group as any since the fall of the Taliban in late 2001."[9]

Generally speaking, over the past several years there has been a debate among terrorism experts over whether al-Qaeda is "on the march" or "on the run," with the open literature leaning most recently toward the "on the run" sentiment.[10] A November 2008 assessment captures the essence of this debate and recent trend. *Global Trends 2025* notes, "most experts assert that the struggle against [al-Qaeda] will continue indefinitely, the so-called 'long war,'" whereas other experts who study "waves" of terrorist activity see al-Qaeda as at the start of the "ebb" phase of a normal forty-year terrorist cycle, having already gone through the "rise" and "floodtide of violence" phases.[11] The document implicitly supports the "wave" perspective, noting that although "terrorism is unlikely to disappear by 2025 ... support for terrorist networks in the Muslim world appears to be declining."[12] It suggests al-Qaeda could "decay" sooner than expected because of "unachievable strategic objectives, inability to attract broad-based support, and self-destructive actions."[13]

Overall, the various intelligence assessments point to cautious optimism with regard to the international terrorist threat to the United States, drawing out recent successes but warning of a continuing threat in the short to medium term. The 2007 *National Intelligence Estimate* noted that worldwide counterterrorism efforts had constrained al-Qaeda's ability to attack the US homeland;[14] the 2008 DNI assessment referred to "the setbacks the violent extremist networks are experiencing";[15] and the DNI's 2009 testimony notes, "Sustained pressure against al-Qa'ida in the FATA has the potential to further degrade its organizational cohesion and diminish the threat it poses."[16] Yet at the same time, the DNI is quick to point out "al-Qai'da and its affiliates and allies remain dangerous and adaptive enemies,"[17] while US counterterrorism officials have stressed al-Qaeda remains a major threat to US assets and the US mainland.[18] In one of his final speeches as outgoing secretary of homeland security, Michael Chertoff stated categorically: "This threat has not evaporated, and we can't turn the page on it."[19]

Weapons of Mass Destruction

Although the 11 September attacks were conducted using conventional weapons, one of the US intelligence community's biggest concerns is that the "next" terrorist attack on American soil could involve weapons of mass destruction (WMD) – that is, chemical, biological, radiological, or even nuclear weapons. This prospect has been raised consistently as a grave concern by US intelligence and outside experts for more than a decade. Harvard University's Richard

Falkenrath was one of the first to argue, in the late 1990s, that "future acts of NBC [nuclear, biological, chemical] terrorism should be regarded as likely enough to place this threat among the most serious national security challenges faced by modern liberal democracies."[20] Closely linked to this assessment was a marked change in the nature of terrorism after the end of the Cold War. "Old terrorism," noted the *Economist* in a survey published soon after the 1998 terrorist bombings of American embassies in Africa, generally had a specific political objective, such as the overthrow of a colonial power. Perpetrators of the "old terrorism" were careful to keep casualties to a minimum so as to maintain their group's political legitimacy and increase its chances of achieving its goal.[21] Limited political aims, a strategy of controlled violence for achieving them, and an interest in self-preservation were the hallmarks of terrorist activity throughout the Cold War period.[22]

By the mid-1990s it was clear that the "old terrorism" had begun to break down. New groups had emerged with vague objectives, using violence for its own sake rather than to advance an explicit political agenda, demonstrating no overriding concern for self-preservation, and most ominously, seeking to produce an ever-greater number of casualties. The increase in the number of casualties per incident, combined with the sarin gas attack in Tokyo in 1995, gave rise to the view that terrorists could seek mass casualties through the use of weapons of mass destruction. "Long before 11 September," one terrorism expert has pointed out, "there was concern that international terrorism might be entering a new, more dangerous phase."[23]

The attacks themselves heightened concerns about the use of WMD. Soon after 9/11 former secretary of defense William Perry argued, "Nuclear or biological weapons in the hands of terrorists constitute the single greatest danger to American security, and a threat that is becoming increasingly less remote."[24] Five years later the DNI stated that although a terrorist attack using conventional explosives was the most probable scenario, al-Qaeda remained interested in acquiring WMD to attack the United States.[25] The 2008 DNI assessment echoed this judgment,[26] while *Global Trends 2025* confirmed, "One of our greatest concerns continues to be that terrorist ... groups might acquire and employ biological agents, or less likely, a nuclear device, to create mass casualties."[27] A high-level Congressional commission reporting in December 2008 found that unless the world community acts decisively, "it is more likely than not that a weapon of mass destruction will be used in a terrorist attack somewhere in the world by the end of 2013."[28] In his 2009 testimony before Congress, the new DNI specified that even as conventional weapons will continue to be the most likely terrorist instrument, over the coming years the US homeland will face a "substantial threat" from terrorists attempting to acquire biological, chemical, and possibly nuclear weapons to conduct large-scale attacks.[29]

Homegrown Terrorism

A notable feature of the past few years has been the rise in domestic terrorism against Western states, perpetrated by citizens of the targeted country – in some cases, by people who have been born in that country. The Madrid and London transit attacks of 2004 and 2005 respectively are the most obvious examples, but there have also been many thwarted plots in Western countries, including in the United States. American-born Muslim converts charged in 2005 with a suspected plot to target military facilities[30] as well as American citizens charged with plotting attacks in Miami and Chicago in 2006[31] are just two of several open-source examples. In another case, American citizens met in Canada to discuss a plot against the United States,[32] a sign, perhaps, that Islamists view the United States and Canada as "one strategic arena for operations."[33] These trends led the director of the Federal Bureau of Investigation (FBI) to assess in 2008 that "the principal terrorist threat within the United States [is] self-radicalized individuals with no contact with any foreign terrorist leaders."[34]

Experts argue the United States is less susceptible to domestic terrorism than are European countries. Explanations offered include that America has a professionally employed and upwardly mobile Muslim population, that it allows for a greater acceptance of publicly displayed religion, and that it is a land of immigrants. By contrast, European Muslims tend to be poor, non-professional, and isolated in ethnic enclaves, and their religion threatens secular values.[35] The US intelligence community judges that homegrown extremists in the United States do not yet rise to the numerical level of western Europe.[36] Nonetheless, the FBI under the Obama administration has voiced concerns about pockets of possible radicals among the melting-pot communities of the United States.[37]

Rogue States

In the years immediately after 9/11, America's intelligence agencies also stated the possibility that certain so-called rogue states, also referred to as "states of concern," presented a direct threat to North America. A "rogue state" is defined in the September 2002 *National Security Strategy of the United States* as being one that brutalizes its own people and squanders its national resources for the personal gain of its rulers, threatens its neighbours and violates international treaties to which it is party, attempts to acquire weapons of mass destruction to achieve its aggressive designs, sponsors terrorism around the globe, and rejects basic human values.[38] In his worldwide threat briefing of 2003, the then director of central intelligence (DCI) argued that in addition to the longstanding threats from Russian and Chinese missile forces, the United States faced a near-term intercontinental ballistic missile threat from North Korea and potentially a similar threat from Iran.[39] More recent threat assessments also focus on North Korea and Iran, but these assessments do not state so explicitly a direct threat to the US homeland, even as the capabilities of these nations to launch such an attack have increased (see below). The DNI assessed in 2009 that Pyongyang "probably would not attempt to use nuclear weapons against US forces or territory unless it perceived the regime to be on the verge of military defeat."[40]

Cyber Threats

A possible direct attack on the United States could come in the form of a computer network attack. The dependence of Western societies on computer systems and networks has created significant vulnerabilities that can be exploited. Critical infrastructures at risk of a cyber-war attack include those of transportation, oil and gas production and storage, water supply, emergency services, banking and finance, electrical power, and information and communications. Part of the threat may come from international terrorists. Early post-9/11 evidence suggested that al-Qaeda had spent considerable time mapping US vulnerabilities in cyberspace.[41] At the end of the decade, the US intelligence community continued to point to the expressed desire of terrorist groups like al-Qaeda, Hamas, and Hezbollah to use cyber means to target the United States.[42] The US

Department of Homeland Security has argued Islamic terrorists, including al-Qaeda, would like to conduct cyber attacks but currently lack the capability to do so.[43]

The more immediate cyber threat may be one posed by state actors. US intelligence has assessed that "a number of nations, including Russia and China, have the technical capabilities to target and disrupt elements of the US information infrastructure."[44] In a likely reference to Russia's targeting of Estonia in 2007, the DNI points out in his 2009 testimony that "over the past several years we have seen cyber attacks against critical infrastructures abroad, and many of our own infrastructures are as vulnerable as their foreign counterparts."[45] China is thought to pose a particular cyber threat to the United States; in recent years, numerous computer network attacks against US government systems have been traced to the People's Republic of China.[46]

THE THREAT TO CANADA

International Terrorism

Reports by the Canadian Security Intelligence Service (CSIS) also indicate that the primary threat to the physical security and safety of Canadian citizens, as well as to the country's critical infrastructures, is international terrorism. In its *2001 Public Report*, published in 2002, CSIS determined that Canada was at risk of being targeted directly or indirectly by Sunni Islamic terrorists.[47] More than two years later, the view of the Department of National Defence remained that the most serious, direct threat faced by Canada was terrorism.[48] In 2002 Osama bin Laden had named six Western countries, including Canada, as targets of retribution because of their military support for the war on terrorism in Afghanistan.[49] Since that time, al-Qaeda has included Canada on its list of target countries on two additional occasions. In 2006 then director of CSIS Jim Judd argued it was possible Canada could be spared major terrorist attacks like those that had hit other Western countries;[50] nonetheless, he continued to place international terrorism first on a list of risks to Canada.[51] CSIS's *2007–2008 Public Report*, tabled in Parliament in 2009, states that the threat of terrorism from groups and individuals inspired by al-Qaeda – the "Al Qaeda phenomenon" – continues to pose the primary threat to Canada and its interests.[52]

Although Canada does not have the exposure of the United States, Canadians have a number of things to fear from terrorism. Canada's close ties to America, the openness of its society to the movement of people and money, and its multiethnic population make it attractive to terrorists as a safe haven. Experts have argued that from the terrorists' point of view, Canada is one of the pillars of Western society, and it is regarded as a close ally of the United States.[53] Moreover, as CSIS's 2007–2008 *Public Report* notes, Canada's combat role in Afghanistan has continued to raise its profile with al-Qaeda. Finally, there are a number of American assets in Canada that could be targeted for attack.

The proximity of Canada to the United States is an important dimension of the terrorist threat to Canada. CSIS's 2001 *Public Report* highlighted changes in the nature of terrorist activity in Canada in the 1990s, noting that Canada was no longer being used by terrorist organizations strictly for logistical or support activities and had become a staging ground for terrorist acts against the United States. The well-known and often cited case is that of Ahmed Ressam, a member of a Montreal-based terrorist cell arrested late in 1999 while trying to enter the United States for the purposes of carrying out a terrorist attack. Until then, it had been believed that Muslim radicals saw Canada mainly as a safe outpost from where they could engage in fundraising, recruitment, and other activities to support terrorist networks abroad. (In an increasingly interconnected world, the notion of a staging area is not restricted to countries bordering the United States. The DNI's 2009 intelligence assessment points out, "Al Qai'da has used Europe as a launching point for external operations against the [US] Homeland on several occasions since 9/11, and we believe the group continues to view Europe as a viable launching point."[54])

Apart from the possibility of transborder terrorist activity, such as was averted in the Ressam case, officials at the US Department of Homeland Security are concerned about terrorists targeting flights that take off and land in Canada but come close enough to US soil to be used to launch an attack.[55] In addition, homeland security experts have stressed the need to think in terms of threats to shared critical infrastructure between the two countries. Most of the northeastern United States, for example, is powered by hydroelectric plants in Quebec and would therefore make an attractive terrorist target.[56] Indeed, the security of Canada's entire energy infrastructure is an area of growing concern. "As the largest single exporter of oil and natural gas to the United States," notes a prominent Canadian terrorism and intelligence expert, "Canada and its energy infrastructure [which features numerous North-South pipelines] must figure prominently among the high-value targets for attack according to al-Qaeda operational doctrine."[57] CSIS's 2007–2008 *Public Report* specifically notes that al-Qaeda has identified Canada's oil industry as a target.

Weapons of Mass Destruction and Cyber Threats

Like US intelligence agencies, CSIS has in the past highlighted concern about the nexus of terrorism and weapons of mass destruction and about the threat of cyber attacks against critical infrastructures. "The potential use of nuclear, chemical, biological or radiological materials by a terrorist group poses an emerging threat," argued CSIS's 2001 *Public Report*. "Of concern is the desire of some groups to use techniques which could cause large-scale damage to governments ... they consider as opposed to or offending their beliefs." The report also stressed that Canada's increasing reliance on critical information infrastructures had created "new and ambiguous vulnerabilities from cyberterrorists, foreign intelligence services or extremists," making the protection of these networks increasingly a matter of national security. Such concerns were reiterated in CSIS's 2002 *Public Report*, released in 2003. More recent reports give less detail about the threat but continue to cite the proliferation of weapons of mass destruction as a persistent concern and safeguarding critical infrastructure as a key priority.[58]

Homegrown Terrorism

Like the United States, Canada is not assessed to be at as great a risk from homegrown terrorism as its Western allies in Europe. Factors such as "the lack of a colonial history, our non-participation in the Iraq conflict, a generally moderate foreign policy, and our relative success in accommodating new immigrants to Canada" are thought to work in Canada's favour.[59] Nonetheless, the arrest in Toronto in June 2006 of more than a dozen individuals – all of them Canadian citizens or residents – on terrorism charges, including plots to strike Canadian targets, provided clear evidence of a homegrown terrorist threat to Canada. Since that time the Royal Canadian Mounted Police (RCMP) has uncovered numerous terrorist plots by second- or third-generation immigrants.[60] CSIS has highlighted radicalization of citizens as a key focus of its operations,[61] and the Privy Council Office has placed radicalization and homegrown terrorism first on a list of national security concerns, just ahead of threats from abroad.[62] "Historically, it's always been the threat from somewhere else in the world coming over here," the RCMP's top national security officer stated in 2009, "but it's no secret to anyone that a larger part of the threat is the so-called homegrown threat."[63]

ASSESSING THE THREAT

Thus statements of the threat to North America above and below the 49th parallel centre on the threat of international terrorism, the concern about a possible terrorist attack using weapons of mass destruction, and the risk of information warfare. An indirect rogue-state threat to North America also figures in recent US assessments. (Early post-9/11 CSIS reports mentioned the rogue-state threat, at one point raising the possibility of a state hostile to Canadian interests striking Canada directly,[64] but such ideas are absent from more recent reports.) These assessments, in turn, are a product of changing strategic options and motives in the two decades since the end of the Cold War. The literature on this is vast, and the purpose here is merely to highlight the range of salient explanatory points as a basis for charting the way forward.

Strategic Options

International terrorism, the use of weapons of mass destruction, information warfare, and limited ballistic missile strikes by rogue states are often collectively termed "asymmetric threats." Asymmetric threats, as defined by the Joint Chiefs of Staff, are those that target US weaknesses or vulnerabilities and do not operate according to conventional modes of behaviour. Incentives for US adversaries to seek asymmetrical approaches centre on the overwhelming superiority of America's conventional military capabilities, first displayed during the 1991 Gulf War and demonstrated more recently in Kosovo (1999), Afghanistan (2001), and Iraq (2003). These capabilities have convinced potential adversaries, nonstate and state, that they cannot contest American power on the conventional battlefield and must seek alternative strategic options. Notes one post-9/11 assessment, "The overwhelming disparity between US forces and those of any potential rival drives terrorist adversaries to the extremes of warfare – toward 'the suicide bomber or the nuclear device' as the best way to confront the United States."[65] In the state-actor arena, notes another, ever "Since the Persian Gulf War and Operation Allied Force (1999), PLA [People's Liberation Army] military strategists have emphasized using asymmetric approaches to level the playing field against technically superior opponents."[66]

For nonstate actors, the strategic appeal of conducting asymmetric warfare emerged at a time when adversarial groups were presented with increased options for where to establish their base of operations. The demise of the Soviet Union and the end of the Cold War brought to a halt superpower support of many Third World regimes, inadvertently contributing to the emergence of the "failed state" phenomenon. Whereas previously such states were viewed as a humanitarian tragedy, 9/11 also revealed their potential to create major national security problems. In 2003 the then DCI, George Tenet, captured the prevailing sentiment when he argued, "We know from the events of September 11th that we can never again ignore a specific type of country: a country unable to control its own borders and internal territory, lacking the capacity to govern ... Such countries offer extremists a place to congregate in relative safety."[67] He drew attention especially to places like Somalia and Afghanistan. A high-level bipartisan study concluded the following year that weak states – stretching in a broad band from Central America to Africa to South and Central Asia – posed one of the biggest twenty-first-century threats to the United States.[68]

Since that time, such sweeping statements have been fine-tuned by more detailed analysis. In 2008 a US think-tank developed an index of state weakness, according to which Somalia and Afghanistan were found to be "failed" states.[69] But of the other places identified by the US State Department as havens for international terrorists – including Yemen; parts of Pakistan, Colombia, and Lebanon; and the triborder area between Brazil, Argentina, and Paraguay – "none were ranked as particularly weak. Conversely, many of the most wretched places in the world – Congo, Burundi, Zimbabwe, Haiti,

Myanmar and North Korea – are not known as havens for international terrorists."[70] Thus although "Failed states always cause misery ... only sometimes are they a global threat."[71] In fact, some experts argue that international terrorists do not find the world's most failed states to be particularly attractive; rather, extremists prefer "weak but moderately functional" states.[72]

Motives

Although the notion of asymmetric warfare and, in some cases, the existence of failed states may point US toward strategic options, understanding current assessments of the threat to North America must go deeper to include an examination of possible motives and sources of grievances. Here, there are a multitude, some dating back to recent years and decades and others originating in past centuries. The most broadly conceived perspective on the international terrorist threat to the United States, and indeed to the Western world in general, places it in the context of the historic confrontation between the Muslim and Christian religions. The struggle between Islam and Christendom, argues Princeton's Bernard Lewis, "has now lasted for some fourteen centuries. It began with the advent of Islam, in the seventh century ... and has consisted of a long series of attacks and counterattacks ... For the first thousand years Islam was advancing, Christendom in retreat and under threat. For the past three hundred years Islam has been on the defensive ... For some time now there has been a rising tide of rebellion against this Western paramountcy."[73] In this conceptualization, the West and Islam are locked in a prolonged struggle, defined over centuries; and the contemporary era, marked as it is by Western domination, constitutes the darkest era in the history of Islam.[74] With the demise of Communism and the ascendance of US power and culture in the post–Cold War era, the Western way of life arguably poses the most significant challenge to the alternative presented by Islam.

The historical context has also been framed in the context of the collapse of the Ottoman Empire at the end of World War I. At that time, the Arabic-speaking peoples who had been part of the Turkish-ruled empire sought to establish an independent Arab state, but instead the region was divided up into British and French colonial possessions. "The absorption of virtually the whole Muslim world

into various European empires in the early 20th century," argues
the *Economist*, "is not a good neighborly story."[75] After World War
II the state of Israel was created, further driving a wedge between
the Arab states. The result is that for the better part of a century,
Arabs and Muslims have been humiliated – the most humiliating
moment of all being the Israeli defeat of the Arab nations in the
1967 Six-Day War.[76]

Other explanations date to contemporary policies of the West in
general and the United States in particular. The 1991 Gulf War is an
important benchmark not so much because of the conflict itself but
because in its aftermath a large number of Western – especially US –
military forces were stationed in the region to enforce the no-fly
zones over Iraq. Thus Osama bin Laden's February 1998 declaration of jihad stated as a key grievance: "For more than seven years
the United States is occupying the lands of Islam in the holiest of its
territories, Arabia."[77] Al-Qaeda wants the United States, and the
West more generally, out of the Persian Gulf and the Middle East.[78]
Territorial concerns are the centerpiece of Robert Pape's explanation of the strategic logic of suicide terrorism. He argues that the
terrorist elites who organize such attacks seek to achieve specific
territorial goals, most often the withdrawal of the target state's military forces from what the terrorists see as their national homeland.[79] (The United States withdrew most of its military forces from
Saudi Arabia immediately after the war in Iraq in 2003.)

A second contemporary explanation focuses on the Israeli-Palestinian conflict and the view that the United States has unduly supported Israel at the expense of the suffering Palestinian people.
Although many Arab and Islamic leaders were quick to condemn the
9/11 attacks, Arab and Muslim opinion has remained sharply
critical of US policy in the Middle East and of America's perceived
one-sided approach to the conflict.[80] Yet when it comes to al-Qaeda
itself, the grievance does not appear to be a longstanding one. In his
1998 statement, bin Laden did not devote significant attention to the
conflict, and not until October 2001 did he focus his verbal wrath
on Israel's occupation of Palestinian lands.[81] Moreover, experts have
argued that certain historical discrepancies make it difficult to pinpoint American support for Israel as the single, simple cause of terrorist activity against the US. Soon after the founding of Israel, the
Soviet Union granted immediate *de jure* recognition and support,
yet there seems to have been no great ill will toward the Soviets

for this.[82] Nonetheless, it is certainly true that the ongoing Israeli-Palestinian conflict forms one of bin Laden's principal arguments for claiming that Western nations are aligned against Muslims.[83]

It is also possible that policies have little to do with the sources of terrorism. The tangible record, argues one scholar, demonstrates that America's policies in the Middle East have been remarkably pro-Arab and pro-Muslim over the years, including in the post–Cold War era. America has supported Muslims in Afghanistan against the Soviet Union, in Kuwait and Saudi Arabia against Iraq, in Bosnia against Serbia, in Pakistan against India, and in Turkey against Greece. At the same time, although Islam and Christendom have clashed for centuries, there is little in the essence of Islam that predetermines its adherents to violent conflict with the West.[84] Of the civilizations listed by Samuel Huntington,[85] the Islamic and Western appear to have more in common with one another than with many of the others.[86]

A key source of international terrorism is seen to lie in the lack of representative governments in the Arab world, which produces, proportionally, by far the greatest number of terrorists among Islamic countries. Some argue that oligarchic regimes portray US policy as anti-Arab in order to divert their subjects' attention from the internal weaknesses that are their real problem. "Thus, rather than pushing for greater privatization, equality for women, democracy, civil society, freedom of speech [and] due process of law, the public focuses instead on hating the United States."[87] In this conceptualization, the basic reason for the prevalence of anti-Americanism is that it has been a useful tool for radical rulers, revolutionaries, and even moderate regimes to build domestic support.

Others see an indirect causal link in which the lack of democracy facilitates terrorism by inhibiting economic development and stemming alternative means of political expression. A 2002 United Nations Development Program (UNDP) report found that for the previous twenty years, income per capita in the twenty-two Arab countries was lower than anywhere else in the world, with the exception of Sub-Saharan Africa. The UNDP blamed the high level of poverty on the survival of absolute autocracies, the holding of bogus elections, confusion between the executive and the judiciary, constraints on the media, and an intolerant social environment.[88] Poverty itself is not a source of terrorism; rather, it is a facilitating factor. The causal link is the discontent created when those living in a situation of economic deprivation are also politically oppressed and have no legitimate venue for voicing their views on their own affairs. "Opponents of today's rulers have few, if any, ways to participate in the existing political system," notes *The 9/11 Commission Report* in an assessment of the foundation of the new terrorism. "They are thus a ready audience for calls to Muslims to purify their society [and] reject unwelcome modernization."[89]

A related source of Islamic fundamentalist terrorism against the Western world may be globalization and its impact on traditional societies. Scholar Michael Mousseau draws a distinction between traditional economies and the market economies that are associated with modernization.[90] Traditional economies involve implied and long-enduring obligations, reciprocity, gift giving, social linkages, ethnicity, and kinship; they naturally lend themselves to the creation of in-groups and out-groups. Market economies are based on explicit contracts and statements of self-interest; they naturally lend themselves to the liberal values of individualism, universalism, tolerance, equity, the rule of law, and democracy. Terrorism can emerge, he argues, when traditional economies are bombarded with, but cannot adapt quickly enough to, the market forces of globalization.

Mousseau's analysis is supported by that of others who implicitly or explicitly find the broad underlying source of contemporary terrorism to be people responding to, or coming to grips with, accelerated globalization and/or modernization. *The 9/11 Commission Report* argues that Osama bin Laden "appeals to people disoriented by cyclonic change as they confront modernity and globalization."[91] One scholar argues the current phase of terrorism is characterized by participants who "feel powerless and left behind in a globalizing world."[92] Another describes the dominant feature of the contemporary environment as being "a saga of individuals, freed from the constraints of tradition ... finding their place in a changing, globalizing world."[93] Explaining future conflict, American defence analyst Thomas Barnett argues, "globalization empowers the individual at the expense of the collective, and that very American transformation of culture is quite scary for traditional societies."[94]

Capabilities

STATE ACTORS The threat to North America reflects not only the motives and circumstances of various actors but also increased means to present a significant danger. Weapons of mass destruction have proliferated among state actors over the past several years. For half a century, weapon-design information and the technology for producing fissile material for nuclear weapons was the purview of only a few countries. But in 1998 India and Pakistan detonated nuclear bombs, in 2006 and 2009 North Korea conducted nuclear tests, and there continue to be strong concerns that Iran is developing nuclear weapons. Although Iran is not thought to possess a nuclear weapon yet, it is keeping the option open to develop one by pursuing uranium enrichment technology.[95] Indeed, high-ranking Pentagon officials believe Iran already has enough fissile material to build a nuclear weapon.[96] The United States has indicated that several other countries in addition to North Korea and Iran may be trying to develop nuclear weapons, but it has not revealed which ones.[97]

A major factor impacting nuclear proliferation was the demise of the Soviet Union, which resulted in looser controls on nuclear materials and created a large pool of unemployed scientists willing to sell their nuclear knowledge to other countries. Equally if not more damaging were the actions of Abdul Qadeer Khan, the father of Pakistan's nuclear program. In 2004 it came to light that for a decade and a half he had run an underground network that supplied nuclear technology to countries like Iran, Libya, and North Korea. The head of the International Atomic Energy Agency has stated in the past that up to forty countries are capable of manufacturing nuclear weapons within just a few months.[98]

Meanwhile, the US intelligence community estimates that about a dozen states maintain offensive biological warfare programs, as compared to the three or four that were thought to have offensive biological weapons programs when the Biological Weapons Convention entered into force in 1975. Iran, Syria, Libya, China, North Korea, Russia, Israel, Taiwan, and possibly Sudan, India, Pakistan, and Kazakhstan are all believed to possess biological weapons.[99] Prior to the 2003 war in Iraq, the US intelligence community assessed that despite the Chemical Weapons Convention, at least sixteen states continued to maintain active, clandestine chemical weapons programs.

Complicating an assessment of rogue-state WMD capabilities is the increased challenge of intelligence detection. Chemical and biological weapons programs have always been hard to detect because of the dual nature of the technology involved. But the CIA notes that it has become even more difficult to monitor maturing biological and chemical warfare programs in countries of concern, like Iran, North Korea, and Syria, because these countries are becoming less reliant on foreign suppliers. Indigenous biological warfare programs have become more technologically sophisticated as a result of a rapid growth in the field of biotechnology and the spread of information through the Internet.[100] Indeed, much of the latent ability of state and nonstate actors to develop chemical, biological, and even nuclear weapons can be explained by the impact of economic, educational, and technological progress. As Falkenrath noted over a decade ago, "The new physics that Manhattan Project scientists had to discover to make nuclear weapons possible is now standard textbook fare for young physicists and engineers."[101]

Increased means and capacities involve not only acquiring the destructive device itself but also having a delivery vehicle – generally, ballistic missile technology. Whereas only eight countries were capable of fielding ballistic missiles in 1972, that number has since grown to more than twenty-five according to the Missile Defense Agency.[102] Of greatest concern among the new entrants are Iran and North Korea. In the summer of 2008 Iran test-fired several ballistic missiles with sufficient range to strike targets in the Middle East and South Asia.[103] This prompted the DNI to note in his 2009 testimony that Iran's "development of medium-range ballistic missiles, inherently capable of delivering nuclear weapons, has continued unabated."[104]

Meanwhile, North Korea has deployed medium-range ballistic missiles capable of reaching Australia, and since the late 1990s it has been seeking to develop an intercontinental ballistic missile, the Taepodong-2. It is thought this missile could reach US military facilities in Guam, Okinawa, Japan, and possibly Alaska.[105] After a failed attempt in 2006 to launch a long-range missile, in 2009 North Korea sent a satellite into orbit on a space-launch vehicle considered "indistinguishable" from an intercontinental ballistic missile.[106] Long-range ballistic missiles are sufficiently imprecise that they do not present a significant danger in the hands of a hostile force unless the missile has a nuclear or biological warhead.[107] For this reason, it is imperative to identify those actors seeking to acquire both long-range missiles and a WMD capability. North Korea could soon enter this category of actors. Experts believe it does not yet have the capability to miniaturize a nuclear weapon enough to fit on a ballistic missile, but its 2009 nuclear test may have furthered its ability to achieve this goal.[108]

Just as ballistic missile technology is proliferating, so are other methods of delivering weapons of mass destruction becoming apparent. State and nonstate actors are no longer limited to traditional methods, such as bombers and sophisticated ballistic missiles. They can now transport highly destructive devices in small trucks, cargo containers, boats, and airplanes. Thus weapons of mass destruction, and especially nuclear and biological weapons, can be dangerous even in the absence of ballistic missiles.

TERRORISTS There is significant evidence that terrorist organizations are attempting to acquire weapons of mass destruction. As early as 1998, bin Laden publicly declared that acquiring unconventional weapons was "a religious duty."[109] Documents recovered from al-Qaeda facilities in Afghanistan in the fall of 2001 revealed that al-Qaeda's search for WMD had been even more determined, and had progressed even further, than was previously believed. Al-Qaeda was pursuing a sophisticated biological weapons research program focused on a number of agents, including anthrax. The concrete evidence that has emerged since that time (in the open literature) on al-Qaeda's attempts to acquire WMD includes: two Pakistani nuclear scientists met with Osama bin Laden in 2001;[110] documents seized in Pakistan in March 2003 revealed al-Qaeda had acquired the necessary materials for producing biological and chemical weapons;[111] that same year Osama bin Laden received fresh approval from a Saudi cleric for the use of a nuclear weapon against the United States, considered a significant milestone;[112] specific intelligence received by US agencies in 2004 indicated al-Qaeda planned to conduct an attack using a radiological bomb;[113] captured al-Qaeda leaders have confessed to the CIA their attempts to smuggle a radioactive device into the United States;[114] in 2006 a British Muslim admitted to plotting a series of coordinated terrorist attacks in Britain, including one involving a radioactive dirty bomb;[115] and in 2009 US counterterrorism officials authenticated a video by an al-Qaeda recruiter threatening to smuggle a biological weapon into the United States through tunnels from Mexico.[116] Al-Qaeda has also made its own (unconfirmed) claims that it has acquired briefcase nuclear weapons.[117]

These indicators have been reflected in the broad statements of national agencies and international organizations. America's Department of Homeland Security has argued that al-Qaeda is aggressively pursuing a WMD capability and that the acquisition, production, or theft of such weapons remains a top al-Qaeda objective.[118] Canada's CSIS has concluded that whether or not al-Qaeda actually has "briefcase-sized" nuclear weapons, there is no doubt that the terrorist network is intent on acquiring nuclear capabilities.[119] A United Nations panel has concluded that the al-Qaeda network would like to use chemical and biological weapons but does not yet have the technological expertise to do so.[120] The head of the International Atomic Energy Agency has bluntly warned of the imminent danger of terrorists acquiring nuclear materials.[121] And the former head of the FBI has asserted that it is only a matter of time before terrorist organizations are able to purchase nuclear weapons on the black market.[122]

Although WMD terrorism has dominated the post-9/11 debate in academic and official circles over threats to North America, it is important to put the threat in perspective. In the first instance, there are significant technical difficulties involved in conducting terrorist attacks with chemical and biological weapons. It takes massive amounts of a chemical agent to produce significant casualties, and the agent itself, being highly susceptible to wind patterns, is hard to disseminate with any precision. Meanwhile, for biological agents to produce massive fatalities, lethal doses must be inhaled, and the particles involved must be of a particular size (not too small to be exhaled and not too large to be blocked before reaching the lungs).[123] Finally, acquiring enough fissile material for a nuclear weapon remains a challenging task – expert estimates of the probability of terrorists obtaining a nuclear device have ranged from 50 per cent to 1 per cent – and it may also be technically difficult to successfully denote a nuclear weapon.[124]

The relative difficulty of deploying chemical and biological weapons, and of acquiring nuclear material, indicates that in the majority of cases terrorists will likely continue to choose conventional weapons for their attacks. Nonetheless, it is the one attack of this nature that officials fear the most. Studies have shown, for example, that a single airplane delivering one hundred kilograms of anthrax spores by aerosol on a clear, calm night over Washington, DC, could cause more than a million casualties.[125] Moreover, "even a small-scale

[WMD] attack with little or no casualties would achieve the psychological impact desired by such groups."[126] WMD terrorism is a high-consequence, low-probability threat that, based on the character of contemporary terrorism, remains the most significant threat facing North America.

CONCLUSION

An assessment of the threat to North America points to the strategic option of asymmetric warfare, the vast range of plausible sources and motivations behind such activity, and the growing capabilities of the actors involved. The list of issues is no doubt partial and the discussion admittedly cursory. But it does reveal a crucial aspect of the threat to North America: although it may be possible to reduce the threat through policy adjustments or changes in approach, in the final analysis it cannot be eliminated in the short to medium term. The world has become more religious, religious expression has generally become more assertive, and apocalyptic thinking has become more prominent. Weapons of mass destruction, well suited to calamitous war, are becoming more widely available.[127] Ultimately, Canada and the United States will need to defend themselves through some combination of civilian and military measures against the primary threat of international terrorism, as well as against other threats. The challenge is to determine the necessary balance of activities at home and abroad. But first it is useful to take a step back and examine America's understanding of, and approach to, the threat to North America as it emerged in the first post–Cold War decade.

The Evolution of US Security and Defence Policy in the Post–Cold War Era

The essence of an asymmetric threat is the notion of using unconventional means, such as terrorism and/or weapons of mass destruction, to target the perceived vulnerabilities and weaknesses of a more powerful actor. Although US military forces and civilian facilities overseas do face asymmetric threats, throughout the 1990s defence analysts within and outside the US government increasingly voiced their concern that a key area of weakness was the nation's ability to protect itself at home. A tragic validation of this argument occurred on 11 September 2001.

This chapter traces the evolution of the US government's understanding of the asymmetric threat in the post–Cold War era by examining America's key security and defence policy statements, as well as reports by high-level bipartisan commissions, during the administrations of Bill Clinton and George W. Bush. What emerges is a picture of officials making increasingly prophetic predictions of the calamity to come. Moreover, it becomes apparent that despite the dramatic change in the North American security environment, US security strategy remains as firmly rooted in the overseas dimension of protecting American soil as it was during the Cold War.

THE CLINTON ADMINISTRATION

Bottom-Up Review

The first full post–Cold War statement of US defence policy was the Clinton Administration's *Bottom-Up Review* (*BUR*), released in May 1993. Although the term "asymmetric warfare" did not appear in it, the review did cover aspects of the security environment that would later be associated with the asymmetric threat to North America. The BUR noted that the most striking aspect of the transition from the Cold War to the post–Cold War era was the dramatic shift in the nature of the dangers to America's interests. The previous global threat from massive Soviet nuclear and conventional forces had been replaced, it argued, by myriad smaller "dangers." Number one on the list was the dangers posed by nuclear weapons and other weapons of mass destruction, including those associated with the proliferation of nuclear, biological, and chemical weapons and with the large stockpiles of these weapons remaining in the former Soviet Union.

Beyond this brief mention of proliferation and WMD in the opening section of the BUR, however, there was no further elaboration. There was no discussion of how US military strategy might be adjusted in light of these threats, nor was there any attempt to place the proliferation of WMD in the context of threats to the US homeland. The focus was on the need to project power into regions important to US interests and to defeat two potentially hostile regional powers, such as North Korea and Iraq, in overlapping timeframes. In the BUR defending the United States remained very much something that was done overseas. The idea that threats might arise from within the continent was beyond its conceptual boundaries, as was any notion of viewing such threats collectively in terms of their asymmetric nature.

Quadrennial Defense Review *of 1997*

The 1997 *Quadrennial Defense Review* (QDR) was the first post–Cold War US defence policy document to mesh the idea of asymmetric warfare with threats to North America. In its opening discussion of the global security environment, the review highlighted a range of significant challenges to US security in the period to 2015. These included regional dangers, like rogue states, and the proliferation of weapons of mass destruction, which could destabilize regions and increase the number of adversaries with significant military capabilities. In a departure from the *Bottom-Up Review*, the 1997 *Quadrennial Defense Review* also drew attention to the phenomena of failed states and the role they could play in creating instability, as well as to transnational dangers like the illegal drug trade, international organized crime, and terrorism. "Increasingly capable and violent terrorists," the QDR argued, "will continue to directly threaten the lives of American citizens [overseas] and try to undermine US policies and alliances." The review's final observation about the global security environment was that although the United States was "dramatically safer than during the Cold War, the US homeland is not free from external threats." This referred in part to the latent threat posed by the strategic nuclear arsenals of Russia and China. In addition, "other unconventional means of attack, such as terrorism, are no longer just threats to our diplomats and military forces overseas, but will threaten Americans at home in the years to come."[1]

Thus the QDR of 1997 went directly to the notion of asymmetric threats to the US homeland. This was a completely new area of focus for official US defence policy in the post–Cold War era. The QDR argued that US dominance in the conventional military arena could encourage adversaries to use "asymmetric" means – defined in the document as "unconventional approaches to circumvent or undermine our strengths while exploiting our vulnerabilities" – to attack forces and interests overseas and Americans at home. "Strategically," the review went on to explain, "an aggressor may seek to avoid direct military confrontation with the United States, using means such as terrorism, NBC [nuclear, biological, chemical] threats, information warfare, or environmental sabotage instead in order to achieve its goals."[2]

Although the 1997 QDR identified the asymmetric threat to the US homeland, it made no attempt to determine how the United States might respond to it. The review pointed out that US forces overseas were also likely to face asymmetric threats and that dealing with such asymmetric challenges should be an important part of US defence strategy, from fielding new capabilities to changing how US forces operate in future contingencies. Yet it did not address how the US military might deal with asymmetric threats to the homeland. The major force-sizing framework contained in the 1997 QDR continued to be what was established in the *Bottom-Up Review* – namely, the ability to "deter and defeat large-scale, cross-border aggression in two distant theatres in overlapping time frames."[3]

National Defense Panel

Developing a homeland response to asymmetric threats was one of the key gaps in analysis that was identified in a December 1997 report by a bipartisan commission of experts called the National Defense Panel. Created by Congress in 1996 to give a parallel and independent assessment of the ongoing QDR, the panel put forward a number of ideas that proved to be remarkably prescient and remain highly relevant today. Its report, entitled *Transforming Defense: National Security in the 21st Century*, was the first high-level US defence and security policy document in the post–Cold War era to highlight and emphasize the need to take measures to defend the US homeland from asymmetric threats. "We can assume that our enemies and our adversaries have learned from the Gulf War," the report stated. "They are unlikely to confront us conventionally ... [Rather] they will look for ways to match their strengths against our weaknesses. In short, we can expect those opposed to our interests to confront us at home and abroad – possibly in both places at once – with asymmetrical responses to our traditional strengths."[4]

This is not to say that the report focused entirely on the US homeland – far from it. It also stressed the overseas dimension of protecting the United States, and one of its key criticisms of the 1997 QDR was that the review did not adequately address the need to transform US military forces for the power projection requirements of the future. As well, the report dealt at length with the nature of the asymmetric threat to military forces abroad – such as enemies blocking US access to overseas ports by threatening to use (or actually deploying) weapons of mass destruction.

But *Transforming Defense* was a trailblazing document in that it gave at least equal weight to the asymmetric threat to the homeland and the role of the military in confronting that threat. The panel predicted that enemies would use terror as a weapon against America's will and that terrorist attacks would compel the US to divert assets to protect critical infrastructures and populations at home. Weapons of mass destruction, especially, were identified by the panel as a serious and growing threat to the people of the United States. Examples included chemical and biological weapons used on mass-transportation systems and small nuclear devices smuggled into population centres. These developments, the report argues, would require a military response. "Just as deployments abroad are key to a stable international environment, an adequate defensive structure at home is crucial to the safety of [US] citizens ... One of the salient features of US security in 2010–2020 will be a much larger role for homeland defense than exists today."[5]

Transforming Defense ranked homeland defence as America's number-one national security challenge – above regional stability and power projection – in the period to 2020. Besides an ongoing need to deter a strategic nuclear attack, it argued, the United States had a need to defend itself against terrorism, information warfare, weapons of mass destruction, ballistic and cruise missiles, and other transnational threats to its sovereign territory. In many cases, civilian agencies would have to take the lead in responding to an asymmetric homeland threat, but the US military would also play a key role in some missions. Moreover, the military had to be prepared to play an active role in supporting the civilian agencies.

Among the National Defense Panel's recommendations were:

- an America's Command be created to address the challenges of homeland defence (today we see this in the new Northern Command);
- a missile defence system be deployed that is capable of defeating limited ballistic missile attacks;
- passive and active defence measures be developed against the use of WMD;
- National Guard units – although kept as an overseas reserve – be given additional specific training to assist in responding to civil emergencies, including the WMD threat and information warfare;
- military capabilities be called upon to assist in protecting the nation from threats such as cyber terrorism on America's information or economic infrastructures;
- changes be made to the intelligence structure to eliminate artificial bureaucratic boundaries that prevent the timely sharing of information; and
- the entire US national security structure, which dates from 1947, be re-examined. (Coordination gaps among US government agencies, the report argued, would impede US domestic-crisis response capabilities.)

It is evident from this list that the panel proposed changes that pertained not only to the US military but also to the entire US security structure and key civilian agencies within that structure. The panel anticipated many of the problems that were exposed by 9/11, and elements of many of its recommendations have been or are in the process of being implemented.

National Security Strategy for a New Century

The National Defense Panel's strong emphasis on threats to the US homeland was partially reflected in the next major US security policy document, *National Security Strategy for a New Century*, released by the White House National Security Council in October 1998. The strategy's three core objectives were to enhance US security, to bolster America's economic prosperity, and to promote democracy abroad. To these ends, it encompassed a wide range of initiatives, like expanding NATO, working with Ukraine and Russia, promoting free trade through the World Trade Organization, promoting arms control regimes, and developing multinational coalitions to combat terrorism. Surprisingly, measures to increase homeland security and defence were entirely absent from this opening list. Only later, after mentioning things like "renewing a commitment to America's diplomacy," did the document state, "Protecting U.S. citizens and critical infrastructures at home is an essential element of U.S. strategy."[6]

The document's discussion of threats to US interests gives greater attention to homeland threats. Second on the list after regional or state-centred threats was transnational threats, including the possibility that terrorists could target the US homeland directly with weapons of mass destruction or target US infrastructure with an information warfare attack. *National Security Strategy for a New-Century* highlighted a number of initiatives that were underway at that time to address the increased asymmetric threat to the homeland:

- Presidential Decision Directive 62 on combating terrorism was signed in May 1998. It established an overarching policy and assigned responsibilities for responding to terrorist acts on US soil involving WMD.
- Under the Domestic Terrorism Program, the Department of Defense (DOD) was building a capability in 120 major US cities for first-responders to deal with WMD incidents.
- The president announced a comprehensive strategy to protect the civilian population from biological weapons, including upgrading the public health and medical surveillance systems, training first-responders, stockpiling vaccines, and increasing research and development of new vaccines and medicines.

- Presidential Decision Directive 63 on critical infrastructure protection, also signed in May 1998, made it US policy to take all necessary measures to eliminate significant vulnerabilities to physical or information attacks on US critical infrastructures, especially information systems.
- The directive provided for the creation of a national organizational structure to handle the cyber threat, including sector coordinators to promote cooperation within industry, lead agencies to serve as conduits from government to each sector, and the Office of National Infrastructure Assurance, associated with the National Security Council.
- Beyond this, the attorney general/FBI had established the National Infrastructure Protection Center to integrate information from federal, state, and local government entities, as well as the private sector, on possible threats to national infrastructures.

Despite this flurry of activity, America's ability to cope with a threat to the US homeland did not appreciably increase. Experts faulted the government for having no coherent national strategy for combating terrorism and for having a multitude of programs that were fragmented, uncoordinated, and politically unaccountable. The result was the creation in 1999 of another high-level commission: the U.S. Commission on National Security/21st Century. Led by Senators Gary Hart and Warren Rudman, the commission met for two years and produced three reports. It sounded even louder alarm bells than did the National Defense Panel, and it produced even more prescient conclusions.

US Commission on National Security/21st Century

The commission's number-one conclusion in its phase 1 report of September 1999, entitled *New World Coming*, was that America would "become increasingly vulnerable to hostile attack on its homeland" and that US military superiority could not fully protect the country from such attack. "American influence will increasingly be both embraced and resented abroad," it argued, "as US cultural, economic, and political power persists. States, terrorists, and other disaffected groups will acquire weapons of mass destruction and mass disruption, and some will use them. *Americans will likely die on American soil, possibly in large numbers.*"[7]

Based on this new security environment, the commission's phase 2 report, *Seeking a National Strategy*, released in April 2000, attempted to set out a coherent national security strategy for dealing with the dangers ahead. It began by pointing out that ten years after the fall of the Berlin Wall, US national security strategy continued to be derived largely from the measures drawn up shortly after World War II to contain Soviet Communism. The structure had not been altered because the United States had been victorious in the Cold War, and serious reform rarely takes place in countries that have not suffered a major defeat. Yet "Americans are less secure than they believe themselves to be. The time for re-examination is now, before the American people find themselves shocked by events they never anticipated."[8]

The first objective of a new national security strategy, the commission argued, should be to take measures to defend the United States and ensure that it is safe from the dangers of a new era – particularly those arising from the proliferation of weapons of mass destruction and terrorism. To this end, it stated, key policy aims should include:

- building national defences against a limited ballistic missile attack;
- developing methods to defend against other, covert means of attacking the United States with weapons of mass destruction and disruption (that is, information warfare);
- considering carefully the means and circumstances of pre-emption; and
- augmenting US public health capabilities to deal medically and psychologically with potentially large losses of American life in attacks against the American homeland.

The commission's third report, *Road Map for National Security*, released early in 2001, outlined the concrete organizational changes required to fulfil the proposed national security strategy. Not surprisingly, measures to secure the national homeland are first and foremost. "The combination of unconventional weapons proliferation with the persistence of international terrorism will end the relative invulnerability of the US homeland to catastrophic attack," the report argues. "A direct attack against American citizens *on American soil* is likely over the next quarter century."[9] The commission therefore recommended the creation of an independent National Homeland Security Agency with responsibility for planning, coordinating, and integrating various US government activities related to homeland security. The agency would be built upon the Federal Emergency Management Agency, which had primary responsibility for the consequence management of any WMD attack. The three organizations on the front line of border security – the Coast Guard, the Customs Service, and the Border Patrol – would be transferred to the new agency. Dismissed as overly ambitious in early 2001, all of these recommendations have now been implemented in the context of the Department of Homeland Security, created in 2003.

THE BUSH ADMINISTRATION

Quadrennial Defense Review *of 2001*

The next major security policy statement released in the United States was the 2001 *Quadrennial Defense Review*, issued at the end of September 2001, about two and a half weeks after the terrorist attacks. The timing of the document's release, which had been set months in advance, necessitated many hasty revisions that could only partially accommodate the dramatic change in the international security environment. The section on defence strategy outlines four defence policy goals that are meant to provide "a new strategic framework to defend the nation and secure a viable peace."[10] Focused on the overseas element of defending the homeland, these goals include assuring allies and friends, dissuading future military competition, deterring threats and coercion against US interests, and, if deterrence fails, decisively defeating any adversary.

The force-planning priorities of the 2001 QDR are more directly reflective of the post-9/11 security environment. Appropriately titled "Paradigm Shift in Force Planning," this section of the document replaced the longstanding requirement to respond to two major regional contingencies with the less ambitious goal of achieving decisive victory in one regional conflict while containing another. More notable for our purposes here, however, the new force-sizing framework also specifically stated the need to shape forces to defend the United States. This was number one on the defence planning list, followed by deterring regional aggression, defeating regional aggression, and conducting smaller-scale contingency operations. In this way, the framework, rhetorically at least, "place[d] new emphasis on the unique operational demands associated with the defense of the United States and restore[d] the defense of the United States as the Department's primary mission."[11] Thus, although it was not stated as a defence policy goal, the direct defence of the United States figured prominently in the review's force-planning section. "The highest priority of the US military," stated the 2001 *QDR*, "is to defend the Nation from all enemies."[12] To this end, the United States would maintain sufficient military forces to protect the US domestic population, its territory, and its critical defence-related infrastructure against attacks emanating from outside its borders.

National Security Strategy of the United States *of 2002*

Released in September 2002, the Bush administration's *National Security Strategy of the United States* placed a greater emphasis on the US homeland than did any previous official US defence or security policy document of the post–Cold War era. "Enemies in the past," President Bush pointed out in his opening letter, "needed great armies and great industrial capabilities to endanger America. Now, shadowy networks of individuals can bring great chaos and suffering to our shores for less than it costs to purchase a single tank."[13] To defeat this threat, Bush continued, the United States had to make use of every tool in its arsenal: military power, better homeland defences, law enforcement, intelligence, and vigorous efforts to cut off terrorist financing. Several of these clearly centred on the homeland element of bringing security to America. The strategy also emphasized the need to strengthen America's intelligence on threats emanating from within the country that are inspired by foreign governments and groups.

Beyond these points, however, America's 2002 *National Security Strategy* remained rooted in the overseas dimension of guaranteeing security for the US homeland. Although it recognized the need to increase America's homeland security in order to protect against and deter attack, the strategy took as its basic starting point the notion that the "best defence is a good offence." The overseas-oriented defence policy goals of the 2001 *QDR* were reiterated verbatim, and the bulk of the *National Security Strategy* centred on things like:

- strengthening alliances to defeat global terrorism;
- identifying and destroying the terrorist threat before it reaches America's borders;

- investing time and resources in building international relationships;
- developing cooperative agendas with other main centres of global power; and
- stopping rogue states before they can threaten the United States and its allies with WMD.

Regarding military responses to the threat, the *National Security Strategy* raised two possibilities: deterrence and pre-emptive action. The former was quickly dismissed as not being a viable option. The nature of the threat, the document argued, has fundamentally changed in the post–Cold War era, especially since 9/11. During the Cold War the United States faced a generally status quo, risk-adverse opponent. "But deterrence based only on the threat of retaliation is less likely to work against leaders of rogue states more willing to take risks, gambling with the lives of their people."[14] The *National Security Strategy* went on to note that during the Cold War, weapons of mass destruction were considered weapons of last resort that could destroy those who used them. Yet today they may be considered weapons of choice in the face of overwhelming US conventional superiority. Moreover, if traditional concepts of deterrence do not work on rogue regimes, then they are even less applicable to international terrorists who have no state or territory to defend and who include suicide as an operational strategy.

If not deterrence, then what? The *National Security Strategy*'s answer was pre-emptive military action. The document noted that for centuries, legal scholars conditioned the legitimacy of pre-emption on the existence of an imminent threat, most often a visible mobilization of armies, navies, and air forces in preparation for an attack. But the nature of the threat today – involving rogue states, terrorists, and weapons that can be easily concealed, delivered covertly, and used without warning – is such that there can be an imminent threat without visible warning. Moreover, the weapons involved may be weapons of mass destruction. Therefore, "as a matter of common sense and self-defense, America will act against such emerging threats before they are fully formed."[15] Although the strategy referred to this idea as the pre-emptive use of force (against an imminent or proximate threat), in fact the more accurate term when describing an emerging threat is "preventive war" (against a non-imminent or non-proximate threat).[16]

Relaxing the traditional requirements of necessity and imminence creates a potentially destabilizing precedent by making it possible for powerful countries to intervene wherever and whenever they choose. Yet we must recognize that today the threats are very different from what they were when international law on pre-emptive war was first developed.[17] The law was sufficient when the context was conventional threats against states; however, in an era when the primary concern is the terrorist use of WMD, waiting until the threat is apparent will not generally allow enough time to mobilize an effective defence.

In its 2004 report of the High-Level Panel on Threats, Challenges and Change, the United Nations attempted to adapt the concept of imminent threat to contemporary circumstances. Taking its cue from the doctrine of just war, not only did the report reaffirm the right of pre-emptive use of force, but it also expanded the right of anticipatory self-defence to include preventive war, as long as it is authorized by the UN Security Council (under article 42 of the UN Charter) and as long as certain conditions are met. These include proper purpose (or right intention), last resort, proportional means, and balance of consequences (or reasonable prospect of success).

But the crucial, and perhaps most intangible, criterion is seriousness of the threat. "Is the threatened harm to the State of a kind, and sufficiently clear and serious, to justify prima facie the use of military force?"[18] In other words, is there a just cause? Establishing even broad thresholds for this question would have gone to the heart of determining when it is legitimate to act against today's perceived potential threats; unfortunately, the UN did not attempt to do so. "It may be that there is nothing much to be gained by attempts at further refinement," one of the report's principal authors argued in a scholarly piece; "what matters is that the question be asked, and given a rational and credible answer."[19] In any case, the High Level Panel's approach proved controversial enough to elude consensus at the UN's World Summit in 2005. The General Assembly's *World Summit Outcome* document contained none of the High Level Panel's criteria for authorizing preventive war, confining itself to reaffirming that "the relevant provisions of the Charter are sufficient to address the full range of threats to international peace and security."[20]

National Security Strategy of the United States *of 2006*

Notwithstanding efforts to establish some rigour around the decision to wage preventive war, the Bush administration's approach remained unchanged. "When the consequence of an attack with

WMD are potentially so devastating, we cannot afford to stand idly by as grave dangers materialize," states the 2006 version of America's *National Security Strategy*. "This is the principle and logic of preemption. *The place of preemption in our national security strategy remains the same.*"[21]

So too does the overall emphasis on measures abroad to guarantee US security remain unchanged in the 2006 *National Security Strategy*. Indeed the document, which in many ways is simply an update of the 2002 version, arguably focuses even more on activity "over there" than did its predecessor. The president's opening section contains none of the more balanced rhetoric of using a range of tools to address the threat, including those that pertain to measures at home. Rather, America's strategy is stated to rest on two very overseas-oriented and somewhat redundant pillars: promoting effective democracies and leading a growing community of democracies.

The most significant references to the homeland come in its closing section on transforming America's national security institutions, which highlights the changes that have been made in US intelligence-gathering and homeland security structures (see chapter 4) and argues for "sustaining the transformation already underway."[22] Moreover, it goes beyond the 2002 document by giving more detailed guidance to the Department of Defense. The US military, the strategy states, must prepare for four categories of challenges: traditional, meaning states using conventional arms; irregular, referring to state and nonstate actors using methods like terrorism and insurgency; catastrophic, involving WMD, including biological pandemics; and disruptive, like cyber and space operations to counter America's technological advantage. These four security challenges were also listed and elaborated in the 2005 *National Defense Strategy of the United States*, which provided the strategic foundation for work surrounding the 2006 QDR. It is left to the QDR itself, released a month before the 2006 *National Security Strategy*, to "operationalize" the four categories of challenges first enunciated in the *National Defense Strategy*.[23]

Quadrennial Defense Review *of 2006*[24]

The QDR of 2006 begins by arguing that the United States is engaged in what will be a Long War. Whereas the Cold War was a standoff between two conventionally armed camps of nation-states that never went hot, the Long War went hot some time ago and is characterized by traditional states facing irregular forces of dispersed, global terrorist networks. Just as the Cold War was with us for decades, the Long War can be expected to last at least one, if not two, generations. The QDR operationalizes the security challenges identified in both the *National Defense Strategy* of 2005 and the *National Security Strategy* of 2006 by identifying four priorities for the US military: defeating terrorist networks, defending the homeland in depth, shaping the choices of countries at a strategic crossroads, and preventing hostile states and nonstate actors from acquiring or using WMD.

The first two priorities are interrelated. The QDR places a strong emphasis on "relentlessly finding, attacking and disrupting terrorist networks"[25] – implicitly emphasizing overseas activity. Doing so, in turn, is part of "defending the homeland in depth,"[26] which refers in part to the need to be able to defeat threats at as great a distance as possible from the United States. But it also encompasses defensive measures if threats reach US shores. These are divided into three roles: those where the Department of Defense takes the lead, notably defending US airspace and air and maritime approaches; those where the Pentagon acts in support of other government departments, as was the case with Hurricanes Katrina and Rita; and those where the US military enables other departments to respond to threats to the homeland but does not actually take part. The overall goal, notes the QDR, is "to maintain a deterrent posture [that] persuade[s] potential aggressors that their objectives in attacking would be denied and that any attack on US territory ... could result in overwhelming response [abroad]."[27]

The priority of shaping the choices of countries at a strategic crossroads centres on the challenges and possible threat posed by major and emerging powers. Major powers include Russia and, most notably, China, which is the country the Pentagon singles out as possessing the greatest potential to compete militarily with the United States. Emerging powers include India but also countries in the Middle East, Central Asia, and Latin America. The goal of preventing hostile states and nonstate actors from acquiring or using WMD cuts across the priorities of defeating terrorist networks and shaping the choices of countries. States like Iran (identified as an emerging power) and North Korea could pose a direct threat to the United States, or they may pose an indirect threat by transferring

WMD to a terrorist organization. The QDR talks about preventative measures to stop the proliferation of WMD and, if preventative measures fail, responding with diplomacy and, when necessary, with the use of force. These "WMD elimination operations"[28] may involve, among other things, special operations forces, persistent surveillance capabilities, and interdiction operations to stop air, ground, and maritime shipments of WMD.

CONCLUSION

An examination of major American security statements from the 1990s reveals a growing and almost prophetic anticipation of the nature of events to come, particularly on the part of the independent, bipartisan commissions. Early documents from the 1990s made almost no reference to the US homeland, whereas those appearing later in the decade increasingly focused on the asymmetric threat to America at home. Nonetheless, the change in the nature of the threat has not appreciably altered America's approach to addressing threats. Although there has been a greater emphasis on defensive measures, particularly in the wake of 9/11, official US policy remains almost as firmly entrenched in the overseas dimension of defending North America as it was during the Cold War.

Is this an appropriate emphasis? "Because of its geography the United States has become accustomed to defending its borders offensively abroad," one scholar has argued. "But in this battle the defensive will loom equally large, if not larger."[29] Finding the right balance between offence and defence necessarily involves a closer look at the civilian and military components, both at home and abroad, of guaranteeing North American security. The next chapter examines the first part of this four-part framework: civilian measures at home – that is, homeland security.

4

Homeland Security

Under the administration of George W. Bush, the United States defined "homeland security" as "a concerted national effort to prevent terrorist attacks within the United States, reduce America's vulnerabilities to terrorism, and minimize the damage and recover from attacks that do occur."[1] Unquestionably, addressing terrorist threats to the US homeland is a central requirement in the post-9/11 era. But Hurricane Katrina demonstrated that natural disasters can also be devastating; therefore, it is important to view homeland security in more encompassing terms. In this context, homeland security can be broadly understood as civilian-led measures to protect the people, property, and systems of a country.

In enacting these measures, the military could play a supporting role to a civilian agency, or it could play no role at all. "Homeland defence" is a subset of the overarching homeland security concept and refers to military-led measures to defend a national territory. This chapter provides an overview of the numerous homeland security initiatives that have been taken jointly or separately by the United States and Canada since 11 September 2001, while chapter 5 focuses on homeland defence issues. Both chapters examine areas of ongoing contention or debate and propose some solutions.

HOMELAND SECURITY IN THE UNITED STATES

The Patriot Act

One of the Bush administration's first steps to promote homeland security in the wake of the 9/11 attacks was to draft legislation for the Patriot Act. Enacted by Congress in October 2001, the Patriot Act has as its goal enhancing the ability of federal agents to gather information on possible terrorist activity in the United States. When the legislation was passed, it included an expanded federal ability to secretly tap phones, obtain library and bank records, and search the homes of terrorist suspects. It also gave government agencies the authority to detain immigrants thought to be supporting terrorism for up to a week without being legally charged with a crime or an immigration violation as well as to deport foreigners who raise money for terrorist groups. The Patriot Act came under attack for concerns about the impact on civil liberties. Nonetheless, it was renewed in 2005, and although the new legislation incorporated some additional safeguards, it made permanent almost all of the Act's original provisions.[2]

Institutional Change

Even as the Bush administration was negotiating the Patriot Act, it was apparent that homeland security in the United States would also require institutional changes. At the time, there were a multitude of US departments and agencies that played some role in various aspects of homeland security; the 11 September attacks highlighted the need to integrate these functions. Within a month of the attacks, this task was assigned to a newly created Cabinet-level Office of Homeland Security under the leadership of former Pennsylvania governor (and later the first US secretary of homeland security) Tom Ridge. But because it lacked a budget and direct resources, the Office of Homeland Security proved incapable of coordinating the agencies. Under the Homeland Security Act of 2002, the office was renamed the Homeland Security Council and established as a parallel entity to the National Security Council in the White House. Rather than coordinating agencies, the Homeland Security Council was given the more specific mandate of advising the president on homeland security issues, a mandate that remained in place throughout the Bush years. Under Barack Obama's administration, there have been further organizational changes related to the Homeland Security Council. To reduce overlapping bureaucracy, and in accordance with a recommendation of The 9/11 Commission Report, the council has been merged into the National Security Council; its members now report to the national security advisor.

Throughout the winter and spring of 2002, Congressional pressure increased on former president Bush to create a department of homeland security. The response was a draft blueprint for such a department released in June 2002. Although Congressional-presidential wrangling over the details prevented any final decisions from being made until after the November 2002 midterm elections, the end product closely followed the president's original blueprint.

The Department of Homeland Security

In December 2002 former president Bush signed into law legislation to fold 170,000 employees and twenty-two agencies into the Department of Homeland Security (DHS). The creation of the department, which formally came into existence in March 2003, represented the biggest US government reorganization since 1947. DHS was established in March 2003 with four major directorates: Border and Transportation Security, Emergency Preparedness and Response, Science and Technology, and Information Analysis and Infrastructure Protection.

In the area of borders and transportation, DHS was given the mandate of securing America's borders, transportation systems, and territorial waters. It assumed authority over the Customs Service and the primary enforcement unit of the Immigration and Naturalization Service, the Border Patrol, to create a new organization called Customs and Border Protection (CBP). It also assumed control over the Animal and Plant Health Inspection Service and the Transportation Security Administration, the latter of which had been created after 9/11 as a component of the Department of Transport to ensure the security of America's transportation systems, such as airports, railways, and transit systems. The US Coast Guard, with its enforcement role in securing territorial waters, was also transferred from the Department of Transportation to the Department of Homeland Security.

In the area of emergency preparedness and response, DHS was given responsibility for ensuring that the United States is prepared for, and can recover from, a terrorist attack or natural disaster. This is often referred to as "consequence management" – dealing with the aftermath of a homeland security incident. In the event of a major incident, DHS coordinates the involvement of other federal response assets, such as the National Guard. The core of this response capability is the Federal Emergency Management Agency (FEMA). With respect to science and technology, the focus is especially on chemical, biological, radiological, and nuclear countermeasures for use in the event of a terrorist attack involving weapons of mass destruction.

Finally, in the area of information analysis and infrastructure protection, DHS was tasked with integrating intelligence and information pertaining to threats to the homeland from multiple sources, assessing this information, issuing the necessary warnings, and taking preventive measures. The sources include the Central Intelligence Agency (CIA), the Federal Bureau of Investigation (FBI), the National Security Agency, the Immigration and Naturalization Service, the Drug Enforcement Administration, the Department of Energy, and the Department of Transportation, among others. Prior to the establishment of DHS, the US government had no institution primarily dedicated to analyzing all information and intelligence on potential terrorist threats within the United States. In this regard, the department is responsible for evaluating the vulnerabilities of America's critical infrastructures – such as nuclear power plants, water facilities, and telecommunications networks – and taking the lead in coordinating federal, state, and local efforts to protect the infrastructure.

Although there can be physical threats to critical infrastructures, one of the biggest concerns is a computer-network, or cyber, attack on essential services. Therefore, DHS also unified the various cyber-security activities and initiatives previously performed by other departments, including the White House.[3] Under the Bush administration, these included the 2003 *National Strategy to Secure Cyberspace* and the 2006 *National Infrastructure Protection Plan*. More recently, President Obama has created a "cyber-security czar" position in the National Security Council. Reporting directly to the national security advisor, the occupant will have broad authority to develop a strategy to protect the nation's government-run and private computer networks.[4]

The Department of Homeland Security faced many organizational challenges in its early years. Some of the difficulties originated in the lack of clear guidelines on specific roles and mandates of organizations within the department, while others pertained to the relationship of this huge, new, federal government department to established departments like the Department of State.[5] In the summer of 2005 former DHS secretary Michael Chertoff announced a number of organizational changes aimed at integrating this "ungainly collection of 22 federal agencies" into an effectively functioning department.[6] A year after Hurricane Katrina, which was arguably an even greater instigator of measures to address America's homeland security shortcomings than 9/11, these changes were signed into law as part of the Post-Katrina Emergency Management Reform Act. In an effort to reduce bureaucratic reporting layers, the key components of the original Border and Transportation Security Directorate, such as the Transportation Security Administration, now report directly to the secretary of homeland security. Additionally, and crucially, the Emergency Preparedness and Response Directorate was separated out into two major entities: the National Protection Directorate, which focuses solely on preventive measures; and a "new" FEMA responsible for response/consequence management activities. The goal here was to give renewed focus and resources to the old FEMA, which, as only one component of a bigger directorate, had proven wholly incapable of effectively responding to the August 2005 Katrina crisis.

Intelligence Questions

Finally, and also in the vein of removing bureaucratic layers and providing renewed focus to DHS activities, the former secretary separated information analysis from infrastructure protection. A new post of chief intelligence officer, heading up a newly named Office of Intelligence and Analysis, was created to coordinate the gathering and analysis of intelligence within DHS, while cyber security and infrastructure protection were integrated into the new National Protection Directorate. The immediate impact of all these changes was to perhaps triple the number of organizations reporting directly to the secretary. The objective, Secretary Chertoff said at the time, was to make the department "nimble and decisive."[7] Whether that has been achieved remains an open question; nonetheless, the department's relatively more efficient response to hurricanes in the years after Katrina would seem to indicate that the changes are having some positive effect.

When the Department of Homeland Security was created, it faced challenges related not just to its own organizational structure but also to other government departments. Notably, although information analysis was established as one of the department's four core functions, the decision was taken to keep the main US intelligence agencies – the FBI and the CIA – separate from the Department of Homeland Security. In fact, roughly 80 per cent of the US intelligence establishment, in terms of functions and resources, was to remain located in the Department of Defense (DoD), as had historically been the case.[8] As a result, there was no guarantee that the Department of Homeland Security would receive all of the intelligence it needed to conduct its analysis.

At the same time, there was a requirement to address some of the key intelligence-related problems exposed by the 11 September attacks. In their August 2004 report, the National Commission on Terrorist Attacks upon the United States (the 9/11 Commission) found that two of the key factors behind the failure to prevent the 9/11 attacks were a lack of intelligence-sharing among government agencies and the fact that individual agencies did not rate specific information important enough to pass up the chain of command to the National Security Council.[9] These problems stemmed from the fact that there were fifteen (now sixteen) US government agencies wholly or partly involved in gathering intelligence, and that the co-ordinating function – but (significantly) not the budgetary authority – fell to the director of the CIA in his double-hatted capacity as overall director of central intelligence (DCI).[10] The 9/11 Commission found that in 1998 DCI George Tenet recognized the seriousness of the threat posed by al-Qaeda but did not have the budgetary authority to direct resources where he believed they were needed.[11] To remedy this situation, the commission recommended the creation of a director of national intelligence (DNI) position with budgetary authority over all federal government intelligence agencies. The DNI would be responsible for ensuring that the relevant organizations focused on the right threats and sent information on to those who needed it. The commission also recommended the creation of an accompanying National Counterterrorism Center (NCTC) in the White House to integrate terrorism-related intelligence from across all federal government departments.[12]

Former president Bush moved rapidly to win acceptance for the idea of a national intelligence director, and, significantly – despite concerns in the Pentagon – he also agreed to give the position power over budgets. The Intelligence Reform and Terrorism Prevention Act, signed into law at the end of 2004, created the new post of director of national intelligence with budgetary authority over all US intelligence agencies with the exception of battlefield assets, over which the Pentagon retains control. In addition, the Act codified the NCTC, created by an executive order of the US president the previous summer.[13]

For the first few years after the DNI post was created, there were concerns about whether intelligence was being coordinated any better under the new structure as compared to the old DCI framework. The intelligence reform bill was complex enough to allow for debate over the exact power of the DNI position in terms of budgetary authority. A competing directive from the Pentagon issued in November 2005 appeared to assert control over the direction of the large intelligence-gathering agencies that are part of the Defense Department, like the National Security Agency.[14] This budgetary tug-of-war continued throughout the tenure of the nation's first DNI, John D. Negroponte, but with the appointment of a new DNI in early 2007, the office began to function more effectively and along the lines originally envisioned.[15] Moreover, intelligence officials report that the creation of NCTC has done much to increase intelligence-sharing among agencies.[16]

The FBI was significantly impacted by the 9/11 terrorist attacks. Although the United States has numerous intelligence agencies, no one agency is primarily responsible for domestic intelligence-gathering, as are the Canadian Security Intelligence Service and Britain's MI5. Rather, the FBI has always been responsible for both law enforcement and domestic intelligence-gathering. Yet substantial differences exist between the relatively short-term measures necessary to arrest people involved in criminal activity and the longer-term activities designed to infiltrate terrorist groups.[17] Moreover, most FBI agents are imbued with a culture that puts law enforcement first, with the result being that the US intelligence community has historically had little knowledge of domestic vulnerabilities or potential domestic targets.[18]

A key factor behind the intelligence failures of 9/11 is seen to be that the FBI has two sometimes mutually exclusive missions: law enforcement and intelligence-gathering. These factors have led to calls over the years for the United States to create a new domestic intelligence service, but to date this has not happened. "Only the United States buries its principal domestic intelligence service in a police force (the FBI)," notes one scholarly critic.[19] The 9/11 Commission examined and rejected the creation of a domestic intelligence agency, citing concerns about possible abuses of civil liberties and the drawbacks of diverting counterterrorism efforts while the threat remains high.[20] During the 2008 election, Obama proposed creating a senior position in the executive branch that would focus specifically on coordinating domestic intelligence-gathering.[21]

Nonetheless, the FBI has reoriented its activities. The bureau no longer separates criminal and intelligence cases; all cases are now handled jointly, allowing greater access to information on terrorist suspects.[22] In addition, the FBI moved a substantial amount of its resources and manpower from traditional criminal investigative areas, like organized crime and drugs, to counterterrorism activities.[23] America's first homeland security strategy, the 2002 *National Strategy for Homeland Security*, called for a restructuring of the FBI such that it would prioritize the prevention and interdiction of terrorist activity within the United States while continuing to investigate and prosecute criminal activity.[24] The more recent 2007 *National Strategy for Homeland Security* notes that this has been accomplished, as evidenced by the creation of a new National Security Branch in the FBI to integrate intelligence and investigative operations.[25]

Homeland Security Initiatives

THE MARITIME DIMENSION Since its creation, the Department of Homeland Security has been very active in all of the sea, land, and air dimensions of homeland security. One of its biggest concerns is that a chemical, biological, or radiological weapon could be smuggled into a US port in one of the thousands of cargo containers that arrive every day. Aside from its lethal effects, the explosion of a biological, chemical, or radiological weapon in a US port could have a severe impact on the US economy. In light of this, the department undertook the Container Security Initiative, which involves US inspectors stationed at foreign ports using an automated system to analyze manifests and identify high-risk containers so that they can be more closely inspected. The first phase of the initiative centred on twenty large container ports in Europe and Asia, while the second phase focused on major seaports in selected Muslim nations.[26] As part of the initiative, vessels headed for the United States are required to transmit their cargo manifests to US authorities before they even leave the foreign port, allowing customs officials to better track high-risk cargo containers. Since 2005 Canadian border agents have also been deployed at foreign ports to help the United States search shipping containers bound for North America.[27]

Closer to home, the US Coast Guard has been assigned many homeland security tasks in the area of port protection. Before 9/11 these tasks were not very demanding; since the attacks they have absorbed some 30 per cent of the Coast Guard's operating time. This has raised questions about whether the Coast Guard can juggle the new requirement of antiterrorism activities in the form of port and coastal protection with its ongoing responsibility for environmental response and marine safety, including patrolling territorial waters and apprehending smugglers. The oil spill off San Francisco in 2007 provoked renewed "institutional soul searching" as the Coast Guard strove to find the right balance between the two mandates.[28]

To increase port security, the United States has also installed radiation monitors at all major US ports. This is an area of homeland security that has proceeded expeditiously in the period since DHS was created. In 2005, of the 20,000 containers that enter US ports every day, only about 5 per cent were inspected.[29] By the end of the decade, this figure was closer to 100 per cent in places like Charleston, South Carolina, and technological challenges like radiation sensors being set off by bananas and cat litter are in the process of being addressed. The next layer of defence will be to scan containers at overseas ports before they are even loaded on a US-bound ship. This is a much more difficult diplomatic proposition considering that, ultimately, the United States cannot force foreign ports to install and operate such equipment. Nonetheless, legislation passed by Congress in 2007 included a requirement that within five years 100 per cent of all US-bound maritime cargo must be screened for radiation before being loaded at foreign ports – although provisions were made for deadline extensions.[30]

THE LAND DIMENSION For increased security on land, much of what the United States is doing on its northern border is in the context of Canada-US cooperation, to be discussed later. Beyond this, in the period after 9/11, Customs and Border Protection tripled the number of enforcement officers assigned to the Canada-US border (including the Alaska stretch) to over 1,000 agents. Although large, this number was still far smaller than the close to 10,000 who were patrolling the US-Mexico border as of 2003.[31] The intelligence reform bill of December 2004 required the Department of Homeland Security to increase the number of border patrol agents on America's northern and southern borders by an additional 10,000 personnel over five years, the vast majority of which have been assigned to the US-Mexico border. In the interim, during the period 2006–08 some 6,000 National Guard troops were deployed along the US-Mexico border to assist CBP in interdicting drugs and deterring illegal immigration. To avoid any perception of militarization, however, their role was limited to things like operating surveillance systems and helping to install fences.

One way that the United States is seeking to improve the monitoring of its northern and southern land borders is by using unmanned aerial vehicles (UAVs). It has already allocated billions of dollars to the development of UAVs for homeland security missions along its borders and coasts. The Coast Guard plans to use UAVs to help patrol the waters around the United States, and CBP is operating UAVs along both the Mexican and Canadian borders. Five Predator UAVs patrol the Mexican border, while the first in a planned network of Predator drones is already conducting surveillance along the Canada-US border.[32] Depending on feasibility, as well as on the resolution of certain safety and privacy issues, other potential homeland missions for unmanned aerial vehicles could include monitoring oil and gas pipelines, electricity transmission lines, power plants, dams and drinking water supplies, and transportation routes for hazardous materials.[33] Indeed, in the future the Department of Homeland Security could be an even bigger customer of unmanned aerial vehicles than the Pentagon. Already, Predators have been used, for example, to monitor the progress of Red River flooding. One of the inevitable accompanying issues being addressed by the Federal Aviation Administration is the potential air traffic control problems associated with adding medium-altitude drones to private and commercial air traffic.

A major area of focus of the Department of Homeland Security is preventing and responding to a biological weapons attack. In 2003 the department launched the BioWatch system, an air-sniffing sensor network designed to detect a biological weapons attack established in more than thirty major American cities. And the department's Project Bioshield, a multibillion-dollar program to build a national stockpile of medicines and vaccines for use in the event of a biological attack, was also put in place. To bring the many programs together and give them strategic direction, in 2004 former president Bush signed a classified directive detailing the responsibilities of various agencies in preventing and responding to a biological attack.[34] Beyond this, the Department of Homeland Security has run several major exercises, in conjunction with Canadian officials, simulating WMD terrorist attacks and computer-network attacks on critical infrastructures.

THE AIR DIMENSION To increase security in the air, the Department of Homeland Security added thousands of armed agents to the federal air marshal program for monitoring commercial flights. From only 30 agents before 11 September 2001, the program ballooned within a few years to over 5,000 armed personnel.[35] The department has also explored the feasibility of outfitting commercial airliners with the type of electronic devices used by some military aircraft to protect them from missiles fired by terrorists on the ground. In 2008 the first of what are expected to be thousands of commercial airline jets were outfitted with antimissile systems.[36]

US-VISIT One of the most ambitious programs undertaken by the Department of Homeland Security is the United States Visitor and Immigration Status Indicator Technology (US-VISIT) program, which it launched at more than a dozen major US ports, over a hundred US airports, and about fifty US-Mexico border crossings in 2004. Using a combination of digital photographs, fingerprint scans, and biometrics to trace the unique physical traits of individuals, US-VISIT enables authorities to track visitors to the United States and determine who is still in the country and who has left. The program originated in the Immigration Reform Act of 1996, which was approved by Congress in 2000, but because many of the 9/11 hijackers carried expired visas, it was accelerated after the attacks and specific deadlines were included in the Patriot Act, signed in October 2001. By 2009 US-VISIT was in place at all of America's sea, land, and air ports of entry.

The US-VISIT program was originally limited to visitors who required a visa to enter the United States. But it was later expanded to encompass all those permitted to visit the United States for up to ninety days without a visa – including citizens of some of America's closest allies, like Britain and Australia. Given the unique relationship between Canada and the United States and the vast daily transborder flow of people and commerce, Canadian citizens are the only ones in the world (other than American citizens) who are not subject to the program. Although US-VISIT is primarily designed to determine which visitors to the United States have overstayed their visas, it is also meant to enable authorities to determine whether an individual should be prohibited from entering the United States in the first place. Here, the logic is more problematic because today the last terrorist act of many terrorists is also their first. That is to say, the primary threat does not come from known terrorists but rather from recruits who are groomed for suicide bombing. Clearly, determining the unique physical traits of these individuals will not help US authorities to identify threats to America.

HOMELAND SECURITY IN CANADA

The Anti-Terrorism Act and Other Legislation

As in America, one of Canada's first responses to the 9/11 attacks was to enact legislation. In December 2001 the Canadian Parliament passed Bill C-36, the Anti-Terrorism Act, which granted Canadian law enforcement agencies expanded wiretap powers and the authority to detain anyone for up to seventy-two hours without a warrant on suspicion of terrorism. With a view to protecting Canadians from terrorist acts, in its so-called "security budget" of the same month, the government also allocated several billion dollars to increasing intelligence-gathering capabilities, improving critical infrastructure protection, enhancing border security, and improving immigrant and refugee claimant screening.

Beyond this, the government of Jean Chrétien introduced legislation for a new public safety act meant to increase the government's ability to prevent terrorist attacks. Ultimately passed in 2004, the Public Safety Act allows for the collection of air-traveller information, establishes tighter controls over explosives and hazardous materials, and increases funding to port security. And in 2002 the government enacted the Immigration and Refugee Protection Act, which makes it easier for the government to deport individuals deemed a security threat, denies these individuals access to Canada's refugee determination process, and imposes harsher penalties on people-smuggling.

Institutional Change

Institutionally, the Canadian government responded to the 9/11 attacks by creating a special Cabinet Committee on Public Safety and Antiterrorism. Led by former deputy prime minister John Manley, the committee was charged with reviewing policies, legislation, regulations, and programs throughout the government to strengthen Canada's ability to fight terrorism. Manley was Canada's primary contact with Tom Ridge when he was director of the Office of Homeland Security. Today, ministers continue to engage on homeland security in a special Cabinet committee; under Prime Minister Stephen Harper, this is known as the Foreign Affairs and Security Cabinet Committee.

When the terrorists struck, Canada already had in place one agency that was dedicated to "homeland security" functions: the Office of Critical Infrastructure Protection and Emergency Preparedness (OCIPEP). The genesis of OCIPEP was preparations related to the so-called "Y2K problem," the now largely forgotten concern of the late 1990s about the potential impact of the turn of the century on the computer networks that control the vast majority of contemporary society's critical infrastructures. An additional concern at the time, based on threat assessments and growing vulnerabilities, was the possibility of a physical or computer network attack on Canada's critical infrastructures.

After millennium celebrations came and went without notable failures or interruptions, the prospect of an asymmetric attack on Canada's critical infrastructures moved to centre stage. In February 2001 the government formally created OCIPEP with two important missions: (1) to provide national leadership for a comprehensive approach to protecting Canada's critical infrastructure, including both its physical and cyber dimensions; and (2) to act as the government's primary agent for ensuring national civil-emergency preparedness for all types of emergencies, including natural disasters or those involving weapons of mass destruction.[37] The new office absorbed the old Emergency Preparedness Canada (EPC), which was roughly equivalent to America's FEMA.

Like EPC before it, OCIPEP was established as part of the Department of National Defence. Yet OCIPEP had responsibilities that cut across several government departments. This incongruity may have been a factor behind OCIPEP's inability to effectively respond to the massive electrical blackout in August 2003, which left 50 million people in Ontario and the north-eastern United States without power, some for several days. This failing, in turn, was likely a contributing factor behind the decision of Paul Martin's government to integrate OCIPEP's functions into a new department focused entirely on public safety and emergency preparedness.

Public Safety Canada

When Paul Martin became prime minister in December 2003, his government immediately announced the creation of Public Safety and Emergency Preparedness Canada (PSEPC), with Anne McLellan as minister. PSEPC, which was renamed Public Safety Canada (PSC) by the Harper government in 2006, integrates the functions of the former OCIPEP; the former Department of the Solicitor General, notably CSIS and the RCMP; and the Canada Border Services Agency (CBSA), a new agency created at the same time as PSEPC.

Public Safety Canada is charged with "ensur[ing] coordination across all federal departments and agencies responsible for national security and the safety of Canadians."[38] The core of the department's mandate is critical infrastructure protection and emergency management. The department defines "critical infrastructures" as "those physical and information technology facilities, networks, services and assets which, if disrupted or destroyed, would have a serious impact on the health, safety, security or economic well-being of Canadians or the effective functioning of governments in Canada."[39] It lists ten sectors that make up Canada's national critical infrastructure, including energy and utilities, communications and information technology, finance, healthcare, food, water, transportation, safety (such as the safety of hazardous materials), government services, and manufacturing.

Threats to Canada's critical infrastructures could come in the form of a physical attack, such as a bomb targeted at an electrical grid. But the scenario that most often comes to mind is that of a cyber attack against the computer systems on which these infrastructures are dependent. Therefore, the government has created a Canadian Cyber Incident Response Centre, responsible for monitoring threats and coordinating the national response to any cybersecurity incident.[40] In 2009 the government also announced it is developing a new cyber-security strategy in light of "repeated incursions into the country's key computer networks," often from computer locations in China.[41]

"Emergency management" is a broadly based term that encompasses disaster prevention and mitigation,[42] emergency preparedness, and the response to and recovery from an emergency situation, whether the source is a natural disaster or a terrorist incident. At the hub of Canada's emergency management system is the Government Operations Centre (GOC),[43] also created by the Martin government. Housed at an undisclosed location in Ottawa, the GOC provides the mechanism for strategic coordination and direction that was lacking during the August 2003 blackout, and indeed during the SARS crisis of March 2003. Operating twenty-four hours a day, seven days a week, it has representation from the range of federal departments and agencies that play a role in Canada's homeland security, and it also coordinates with the provinces, key allies like the United States, and international organizations like NATO.

All of the functions of the former Department of the Solicitor General are also part of PSC, including the RCMP and CSIS. Under the Security Offences Act, the RCMP has primary investigative responsibility for offences related to terrorism. In the event of a terrorist incident, the RCMP would head up the crisis response and law enforcement aspects, whereas the emergency preparedness component of PSC would coordinate the consequence management efforts. This division of responsibilities is similar to that between the FBI and FEMA in the United States.

A key agency in Canada's security and intelligence community is the Canadian Security Intelligence Service. Created in 1984, CSIS is mandated to collect security intelligence and to provide it to departments of the Government of Canada, provincial governments, and foreign governments, as required. "Security intelligence" is intelligence pertaining to threats to the security of Canada. These threats, in turn, are defined in the CSIS Act as espionage or sabotage against Canada or Canadian interests; foreign-influenced activities within, or relating to, Canada that are detrimental to its interests; activities within, or relating to, Canada in support of serious violence against people or property to achieve a political, religious, or ideological objective within Canada or a foreign state; and activities directed toward violently overthrowing the Canadian government, like espionage, sabotage, foreign-influenced activities, or politically motivated violence. CSIS can collect information related to these threats both in Canada and abroad.

CSIS has no police powers. Historically, the domestic intelligence-gathering function was carried out by the security service of the RCMP, much as domestic intelligence-gathering is a component of the hitherto primarily law-enforcement-focused FBI. But Canadian officials ultimately recognized that intelligence-gathering and law enforcement can be incompatible. As a result, with the creation of CSIS, the two functions were separated. Canada's decision to separate domestic intelligence-gathering from domestic law enforcement was a sensible one: as noted earlier, prior to the release of The 9/11 Commission Report, much of the post-9/11 failure-of-intelligence debate south of the border centred on whether the FBI's function of security intelligence-gathering should be separated out and placed in a newly created agency.

Security intelligence can be distinguished from foreign intelligence, which is broader in scope. "Foreign intelligence" refers to information on the capabilities, activities, or intentions of foreign countries, organizations, or individuals. Such intelligence serves a country's national (not just security) interests, including economic, political, military, technological, or environmental objectives.[44] The CIA and Britain's MI6 are examples of organizations dedicated to gathering foreign human – as opposed to electronic – intelligence.

Unlike many members of NATO, as well as countries such as Australia and Sweden, Canada has never had an organization dedicated to gathering foreign human intelligence. Canada collects its foreign intelligence primarily electronically, through the Communications Security Establishment (CSE), which is part of the Department of National Defence. Created in the closing days of World War II, CSE is part of a network of agencies in the United States, Britain, Australia, and New Zealand – known as the UKUSA alliance – that emerged from a successful wartime collaboration to collect signals intelligence, or SIGINT.[45] Valued for its geography, Canada was assigned SIGINT responsibilities for the northern latitudes and polar region. To this end, it established giant antennas at CFS Alert in Nunavut, CFS Masset in British Columbia, CFB Gander in Newfoundland, and CFS Leitrim south of Ottawa to listen in on the Soviet Union in the north, maritime transmissions on the coasts, and diplomatic traffic out of Ottawa. The CSE's (much larger) American equivalent is the National Security Agency (NSA), a component of the US Department of Defense.

Today, CSE has a threefold mandate: to acquire and distribute foreign signals intelligence; to help protect Canada's electronic information infrastructures; and to assist federal law enforcement and security agencies (the RCMP and CSIS). Much of the mandate centres on satellite communications interception, although its older systems remain in place. The rapid expansion of satellite-based telecommunications in the 1970s prompted the UKUSA network to build satellite-communications interception stations in strategic locations for global coverage, one of which is at CFS Leitrim. Extensive refinements to satellite-interception technologies in the following two decades led to the creation of a tightly networked interception and processing system, known as Echelon. By employing the Echelon "dictionary," CSE and its partner agencies, notably the NSA, scan billions of satellite-intercepted conversations, faxes, and e-mails every day for key words that could indicate a security threat. Previously, for reasons related to civil liberties, CSE was limited to intercepting communications between two foreign countries. Canada's Anti-Terrorism Act of December 2001 expanded CSE's mandate to include communications between Canada and at least one other country.

Intelligence Questions

An ongoing debate within Canada is whether it should create its own foreign human-intelligence service. "With few exceptions," notes CSIS in its 2007–2008 *Public Report*, "the roots of threats to the security of Canada are located outside of our country's borders."[46] Using its electronic eavesdropping techniques, CSE can gather foreign intelligence on individuals, groups, and states. But in the post-9/11 era this has become less salient than human-intelligence efforts because terrorist organizations are far less vulnerable than are states to SIGINT interception. Although SIGINT is still very important, increased human intelligence is necessary to identify, penetrate, monitor, and counter the terrorist threat and to gain accurate information on things like the proliferation of weapons of mass destruction and illegal immigration.

CSIS has about fifty foreign officers in some thirty countries around the world, and these officers are permitted, under section 12 of the CSIS Act, to collect security-intelligence information abroad – that is, information on threats to Canada that originates in a foreign country.[47] In addition, CSIS will sometimes send Canadian-based officers abroad to gather intelligence on security threats to Canada.[48] Nonetheless, experts have argued that Canada's capability to gather foreign intelligence for human intelligence remains insufficient. With only a small number of intelligence officers abroad, Canada relies heavily on allies like Britain and the United States for human intelligence. Although these countries share intelligence with Canada on threats of mutual concern like al-Qaeda, they may or may not have information on groups that are of significant interest to Canada but of low priority for them, such as the Tamil Tigers. Moreover, even where interests overlap, the information Canada receives will inevitably be filtered through the prism of allied perspectives on the threat.[49] The argument, in short, is that Canada needs an increased independent capability to gather information abroad on threats to domestic security so that it can pursue intelligence efforts that are specific to its national interests as well as make its own judgments, interpretations, and threat assessments on intelligence information.

Whether such an increased capability would best be accomplished through the expansion of CSIS or the creation of a separate agency is an open question. Creating a new agency would be expensive, and it may lead to detrimental bureaucratic stovepipes, promoting distinctions between threats at home and threats abroad that are no longer relevant in a globalized world. The lack of interagency cooperation between the CIA and the FBI was, after all, revealed to be a key intelligence shortcoming in the lead up to 9/11. Yet at the same time it could prove to be a delicate balancing act, culturally and legally, for an intelligence agency to conduct both domestic and foreign operations. Back in 1981 the MacDonald Commission on the RCMP security services (which led to the creation of CSIS) argued that responsibility for security intelligence and foreign intelligence should not be shouldered by a single agency. Whereas a security agency must adhere to the rule of law, a foreign-intelligence agency requires a greater degree of flexibility.[50] During the 2005–06 election campaign, the Conservatives promised to create a separate Canadian Foreign Intelligence Agency "to effectively gather intelligence overseas, independently counter threats before they reach Canada, and increase allied intelligence operations,"[51] but once in power they opted instead to do so by giving CSIS increased powers to gather human intelligence abroad.[52]

Beyond CSIS and the RCMP, PSC also includes the Canada Border Services Agency (CBSA). Created in December 2003, CBSA is charged with facilitating and managing the movement of goods and people into Canada by administering and enforcing numerous domestic laws and international agreements related to this movement, most notably the 2001 Canada-US Smart Border Declaration and its follow-on, the 2005 Security and Prosperity Partnership (see below). CBSA integrated the intelligence interdiction and enforcement program from Citizenship and Immigration Canada (CIC), the port of entry program from the Canadian Food Inspection Agency, and the customs program from the former Canada Customs and Revenue Agency (renamed the Canada Revenue Agency). The latter move put customs officers more in line with their American counterparts. In addition to their previous role in collecting cross-border shopping fees, customs officers now perform a public security role. Border guards have been issued bulletproof vests and been given the authority to arrest and detain people for violations of the Criminal Code of Canada, and they are also being trained to carry firearms. CBSA's goal is to have up to 4,800 land and marine guards (not airport border guards) armed by about 2017.[53]

Although PSC can be roughly equated to the Department of Homeland Security, there are some important differences. Most notably, unlike the Department of Homeland Security, PSC has no jurisdiction over citizenship and immigration; the reason for this is that the Canadian government wanted to avoid linking threats to national security to foreign-born residents.[54] Another significant difference between PSC and the Department of Homeland Security is that in Canada CSIS has become part of PSC, whereas in the United States the FBI remains outside DHS. Anecdotal evidence suggests that having CSIS and CBSA in the same organization has facilitated information sharing between Canadian agencies.[55] Finally, in contrast to the US situation, in Canada the Coast Guard has not been transferred to the central homeland department; rather, it remains part of the Department of Fisheries and Oceans. In the period since 9/11 there has been a significant amount of debate within Canada over whether the Coast Guard should be given an armed, coastal policing role similar to that of the US Coast Guard (see chapter 5).

Homeland Security Initiatives

Americans and Canadians, it is often noted, see their common border through different coloured lenses. "Americans see the border as a security issue whereas for Canadians it is an economic issue."[56]

Although this is true, it is perhaps more accurate to say that for both countries the border is a security issue – it's just that for Canada the threat is more of an economically based one. The magnitude of Canada's trade dependence on the United States is such that Canada's access to the American market is not just an economic issue. If one returns to the notion that a threat to national security is something that threatens drastically, and over a relatively brief span of time, to degrade a value Canadians hold essential to their way of life – including a certain level of prosperity – then it is clear that Canada's access to the US market is also a security issue.

The United States is by far Canada's largest trading partner, with more than 80 per cent of Canadian exports, representing about 40 per cent of its gross domestic product, going to the United States. Although roughly 25 per cent of America's exports go to Canada, this represents just 2 per cent of its gross domestic product, and thus a border closure is felt far more acutely in Canada than in the United States. Canada has been aware for decades that its economic dependence on the United States is growing, but this reality became glaring in the hours and days after the 9/11 terrorist attacks, when cross-border traffic came almost to a standstill. Not surprisingly, then CSIS director Ward Elcock stated in the early post-9/11 period that although the prospect of a terrorist bomb going off in a major Canadian centre was one of his biggest worries, an equal if not greater worry was the prospect of a terrorist bomb staged from Canada going off in a major US centre.[57]

THE LAND DIMENSION Canada's earliest post-9/11 homeland security initiatives therefore centred on keeping the Canada-US border open to trade. In December 2001 John Manley and Tom Ridge signed the Canada-US Smart Border Declaration with the specific objective of increasing border security while facilitating the flow of legitimate traffic. This declaration was accompanied by a thirty-point action plan (later thirty-two point) that included a wide range of activities pertaining to the land, air, and maritime environments, all of which have now been implemented.

An important Smart Border initiative at the Canada-US land border is NEXUS, a clearance system that uses high-tech cards to allow frequent travellers between the two countries – especially business travellers – to cross the border more quickly. Under NEXUS, dedicated fast lanes were established at all major border crossings for preapproved low-risk travellers. Another Smart Border initiative was Free and Secure Trade (FAST), a joint Canada-US program for low-risk companies that expedites shipments across the border in either direction by preclearing commercial trucks. Aside from smart cards, Canada and the US are also using a wide range of advanced technologies to promote the secure and efficient passage of vehicles across the land border. The Vehicle and Cargo Inspection System (VACIS) uses gamma rays to search trucks and passenger vehicles for explosives, contraband, and people (being smuggled). Radiation detectors have also been mounted on specially equipped trucks at all land borders to scan trucks and cars for radiation emissions and so-called dirty bombs. Plans to equip US border patrol officers who monitor the open land between border crossings with portable radiation detectors have moved more slowly, but the United States is developing a network of infrared video cameras atop eighty-foot towers at strategic locations along the Canada-US border.

Part of the Smart Border Declaration was a plan to expand existing Integrated Border Enforcement Teams (IBETs), established as a pilot project in 1996. IBETs are joint Canada-US multi-agency law enforcement teams that target cross-border terrorism and criminal activity. They are made up of members of Canadian and American agencies involved in law enforcement, including the RCMP, CBSA, US Customs and Border Protection, US Bureau of Immigration and Customs Enforcement, and US Coast Guard. IBETs work with local, state, and provincial law enforcement agencies to identify, investigate, and interdict organizations and people who pose a threat to national security, such as terrorists or those engaged in organized crime. Under the Smart Border plan, more than twenty IBET teams have been established in fifteen regions along the Canada-US border, including "on-water" IBETs in the Great Lakes-St Lawrence region, an initiative of the Security and Prosperity Partnership's security agenda.[58] Under a pilot project called Shiprider, which became permanent in 2009, RCMP officers travel on US Coast Guard boats in the Great Lakes to interdict transnational threats. In Canada IBETs are supplemented by Integrated National Security Enforcement Teams (INSETs) located in Vancouver, Toronto, Montreal, and Ottawa. Operationally led by the RCMP, they are made up of representatives from CBSA, CSIS, CIC, and provincial and municipal police forces. INSETs focus exclusively on investigating and exposing terrorist threats.

A significant cross-cutting border issue for Canada has been the Western Hemisphere Travel Initiative (WHTI). Legislated in the Intelligence Reform and Terrorism Prevention Act of 2004, the initiative required that by January 2007 all people arriving in the US by air, including US and Canadian citizens, had to have a valid passport to enter. Most significant for Canada, however, is that as of June 2009 this requirement was extended to land (and sea) border arrivals, meaning that all Americans and Canadians have to carry a passport or an enhanced driver's licence to cross the 49th parallel. The concern for Canada (and to a lesser extent for the US states bordering Canada) is the impact on trade and tourism. Although more than 50 per cent of Canadians have a current passport, the figure is much smaller for Americans.[59]

THE AIR DIMENSION With respect to the air dimension, soon after 9/11 the Chrétien government acted to expand Canada's network of immigration-control officers at airports around the world in order to identify and stop terrorists before they could board a plane to Canada. It also created the Canadian Air Transport Security Authority (CATSA) to improve airport screening and to place armed undercover police officers on Canadian aircraft and in airports. Moreover, the Smart Border Declaration was designed to eventually extend beyond land ports of entry to include airports and marine ports. As a result, a NEXUS air program has been put in place at selected airports like those in Ottawa and Vancouver. Beyond this, Canada and the United States have co-located customs and immigration officers in joint passenger-analysis units at major international airports to identify high-risk travellers. The government also piloted "dirty bomb" detectors that would warn of radioactive materials in passenger, baggage, or cargo systems.

These moves are likely to go some way toward allaying concerns about security in Canadian airports, but there is also a need both to increase scrutiny of those who work at airports and to improve communications among the various agencies. A 2004 auditor general's report estimated that as many as 4,500 individuals with access to restricted areas of Canada's airports could have criminal associations that warrant further investigation and possibly the withdrawal of their security clearances.[60] Critics have argued that Canadian airports (and seaports) are "riddled" with organized crime, security responsibilities are fragmented, and overall responsibility for policing at Canadian airports (and seaports) should be assigned to the RCMP.[61] A follow-up report by the auditor general in 2009 was highly critical of Canadian airport security, pointing out that the central concern was the lack of information sharing and communication between Transport Canada and the RCMP.

THE MARITIME DIMENSION The Canadian government has argued that the greatest threat facing North America is international terrorists smuggling a weapon of mass destruction onto the continent through a sea container.[62] To address this concern, it has undertaken a number of steps. In 2005 it joined America's Container Security Initiative, with the result that CBSA receives cargo information on ships destined for Canada ninety-six hours prior to their arrival. CBSA then uses a "state of the art, intelligence-based automated risk scoring tool" to identify high-risk containers. Those with a very high score are not permitted to be loaded on a Canada-bound ship.[63] Meanwhile, in North America, Canadian and American customs agencies have established joint teams of officials at five ports – Vancouver, Montreal, Halifax, Newark, and Seattle-Tacoma – to examine cargo containers that have been identified electronically in transit as potentially posing a risk. VACIS gamma ray scanners are then used to inspect the containers for dirty bombs. Critics have argued that this risk-management, targeted approach is insufficient and that every shipping container entering Canada should be scanned by a VACIS machine.[64] That said, "virtually all" containers arriving in Canada are scanned for radiation.[65] As is the case with respect to Canada's airports, part of the marine security concern arises from activities at the ports themselves; there is evidence of organized crime and a general lack of policing.[66]

Border Perceptions

One of the key reasons the border was all but closed on 12 September 2001 was the perception that Canada has leaky borders and therefore poses a security threat to the United States. None of the nineteen hijackers involved in the 11 September 2001 attacks entered the United States through Canada, but well before the attacks Canada had gained a reputation in the United States as a terrorist haven. This was largely because of the case of Ahmed Ressam, an Algerian who was arrested in December 1999 by an alert US customs agent as he tried to enter the United States, apparently on his way to blow up the Los Angeles airport during New Year's celebrations. Ressam had twice been refused refugee status, yet he continued to live in Montreal, and he carried a (phoney) Canadian passport. In 2003 the auditor general revealed that the Canadian Immigration and Refugee Board had lost track of some 36,000 failed refugee claimants who, like Ressam, had been ordered deported.[67]

The Ressam incident clearly highlighted the necessity for Canada to tighten its immigration, customs, and security laws. The Immigration and Refugee Protection Act has allowed the government to enhance the scrutiny of immigrant and refugee claimants. Canada now, for example, detains suspicious refugee applicants, no longer allowing them to go free until their hearings, and their detention period could last for up to two years. The United States, too, has strengthened its laws concerning immigrants and refugees, and, through its US-VISIT program, it has tightened up the screening and monitoring of visitors and other temporary entrants. This is a step that Canada has so far declined to take. As a result, Canada has no means of knowing whether its visitors, be they tourists, students, or temporary workers, comply with the terms of their visas, attend the schools in which they are enrolled, work with their designated employers, or leave when their visas expire.[68]

It is difficult to know how much of the perception surrounding Canada's lax borders is just perception and how much is based on concrete evidence. In 2008 the then US secretary of homeland security, Michael Chertoff, stated that "more than a dozen" people with links to terrorist groups had been caught trying to enter the US from Canada in the period since 9/11.[69] Outside critics have noted that "Despite government denials, all kinds of undesirables are getting into Canada under the country's dysfunctional 'refugee' system," with the implication that some of these criminals and terrorists may be making their way to the United States.[70] Yet beyond the Ressam case, such statements and critiques have not been accompanied by specific examples of terrorists entering the United States from Canada. That is to say, the only reported instance in the open literature of a terrorist going across the Canadian border into the United States remains the Ressam case – although Secretary of Homeland Security Janet Napolitano has strongly hinted there are others, whose names have not been released "due to security reasons."[71]

A further complicating factor is that, in the past, more than 50 per cent of people seeking refugee status in Canada each year were coming from the United States,[72] and about 80 per cent of the refugees entering Canada from "high-risk" countries (as defined by the United States) were coming through the United States.[73] This phenomenon was the result of Canada's more lenient refugee system – Canada is the easiest country in the developed world in which to obtain refugee status[74] – and the fact that there was no Safe Third Country Agreement in place that would ensure refugees make their claim in the United States, rather than trying to do so in Canada. CBSA defines a safe third country as "a country, other than Canada and the country of alleged persecution, where an individual may make a claim for refugee protection."[75] The Canada-US Safe Third Country Agreement, negotiated and signed as part of the Smart Border Declaration, went into effect at the end of 2004. According to the terms of the agreement, refugees have to make their claims in the first of the two countries they enter. Refugee claimants arriving from the United States at the Canada-US land border are allowed to pursue a refugee claim in Canada only if they qualify for an exemption, such as family reunification.[76]

The implementation of the Safe Third Country Agreement has no doubt reduced the number of claimants arriving at Canadian borders. But Canada should also consider examining why it is that so many asylum shoppers choose to shop in Canada. Although the Canadian and US refugee systems are similar in many ways, they also have some important differences, including the way they define "refugee." As a result, some refugees who would be accepted by Canada would be refused by the United States. As long as there are significant distinctions between the two systems, those seeking to enter Canada will employ increasingly desperate methods. Without a greater harmonization of definitions, the Safe Third Country Agreement could merely serve to increase claimants' vulnerability to smugglers. Not surprisingly, a high-level taskforce on the future of North America recommended the harmonization of asylum regulations.[77]

National Security Policy

Under Prime Minister Paul Martin, the federal government sought to put Canada's approach to national security on a more formal footing by writing Canada's first-ever national security policy. Hastily produced in the weeks before Martin was to meet with US president Bush, *Securing an Open Society: Canada's National Security Policy* was released in April 2004. Although the Harper government indicated in the 2007 speech from the throne that it would release a new statement on national security, to date this has not happened. As a result, the 2004 policy remains Canada's overall guidance for homeland security.[78]

Securing an Open Society highlights three core national security interests: protecting Canada and Canadians at home and abroad, ensuring that Canada is not a base for threats to our allies, and contributing to international security. Although the policy's purported scope was comprehensive, the vast majority of its initiatives in fact pertained to the first two interests, leaving the third to be filled by *Canada's International Policy Statement* of April 2005. Moreover, much of *Securing an Open Society* was a restatement of steps that had been taken by the Chrétien government in the years immediately after 9/11. Nonetheless, the policy has arguably enhanced Canada's homeland security because it put existing activities into an overall framework and in doing so identified important gaps in Canada's security measures.

One of the gaps was the fact Canada had no central organization charged with fusing intelligence from all members of Canada's security and intelligence community. This includes all or parts of some thirty departments and agencies,[79] notably CSIS, the RCMP, CSE, the Department of National Defence, the Department of Foreign Affairs, the Privy Council Office, Transport Canada, and CBSA. Coordination of the various agencies and departments had historically been the responsibility of the Privy Council Office, a task that was made relatively simple by the predictable adversarial dynamics of Cold War intelligence. But the traditional coordinating mechanism of periodic consultative meetings, which remained in place throughout the 1990s, proved unsuited to the increased intelligence demands of the post-9/11 era. Therefore, *Securing an Open Society* announced the creation of the Integrated Threat Assessment Centre (ITAC), which brings together, on an ongoing basis, intelligence from all members of the intelligence community and provides this information to those who require it. The centre is housed in CSIS, but it includes representatives from all parts of the security and intelligence community. ITAC can be roughly equated to America's

National Counterterrorism Center in the White House. It works closely with the national security adviser – a position in the Privy Council Office that the Martin government created when it came to power in 2003 – which in turn can be roughly equated to America's director of national intelligence.[80]

Securing an Open Society also established a more integrated approach to emergency preparedness, whether a particular crisis involved a health pandemic like SARS, the terrorist use of weapons of mass destruction, or a natural disaster. An important outcome was creation of the government operations centre, noted earlier, to provide around-the-clock coordination of key players at the federal, provincial, and municipal levels in the event of a national emergency. One key player in many types of emergencies would likely be the Canadian Forces, which under most circumstances would provide a supporting role to civilian agencies (see chapter 5). Another could be the new Public Health Agency of Canada, created in response to the SARS crisis in order to develop national strategies for managing infectious diseases. The overall objective of *Securing an Open Society* is to create an integrated security system that includes threat assessment, protection against (and prevention of) threats, emergency response, and oversight.[81]

More than anything, the national security policy set out to assure America that Canada's 1938 security pledge (see chapter 1) still holds: Canada will not allow threats to reach the United States via Canadian territory, including its land, sea, or air space. Continued fulfilment of this decades-old commitment is the intent behind the explicit statement that one of Canada's core national security objectives is to ensure that Canada is not a base for threats to its allies. "We refuse to be a weak link or a haven from which terrorists can attack others," argued Minister McLellan when the policy was released. "We have a choice in Canada – to be in denial or be prepared."[82] Being prepared involves numerous civilian measures, but it also requires some military-led initiatives. Chapter 5 examines the second quadrant of security policy responses: military activities at home that are necessary for guaranteeing North American security.

5

Homeland Defence

"Homeland defence" is part of the broader concept of homeland security and refers to military-led activities aimed at guaranteeing the security of a nation's people or property. Traditionally, these activities have been directed against external threats, and such threats continue to be a major and even growing area of focus. But in the post-9/11 era there is also a need for military responses to internal threats, like the hijacking of airplanes in domestic airspace, as well as a greater degree of military support to civilian agencies than there has been historically. This chapter traces significant developments in homeland defence south and north of the Canada-US border since 11 September 2001, and also looks at shared initiatives between the two nations.

HOMELAND DEFENCE IN THE UNITED STATES

NORTHCOM

A key institutional development in response to the post-9/11 security environment has been the creation of US Northern Command. Since shortly after World War II, the US military has divided the world into several areas of responsibility, each of which is overseen by a joint,[1] or unified, command that brings together elements of the army, navy, air force, and Marine Corps. The number of commands, as well as their names and specific regional scope, has changed over the years, and the US Unified Command Plan updates the situation on a biennial basis. Today, the plan includes ten commands, four of which are functional and six geographic.[2]

The geographic command of Northern Command, or NORTHCOM, was established in October 2002 and is headquartered at Peterson Air Force Base in Colorado Springs. Its mission is to anticipate and conduct homeland defence and civil-support operations in order to defend, protect, and secure the United States – with the notion of "anticipating" (rather than simply reacting) considered to be of particular importance.[3] Assigned a region that encompasses the continental United States, Canada, Mexico, and portions of the Caribbean, NORTHCOM thus has overall responsibility for the homeland defence of the United States. It is specifically responsible for the defence of America's land approaches and sea approaches extending out 500 miles, and its mandate also includes collaborating with the Department of Homeland Security on civil-support missions and overseeing military coordination with Canada and Mexico. The commander of Northern Command doubles as commander of the North American Aerospace Defence Command, or NORAD, which is the joint Canada-US command responsible for the aerospace defence of North America. In this capacity, the commander of Northern Command is also in charge of all the combat air patrols conducted over American cities. The arrangement ensures that overall responsibility for the air, land, and sea components of defending the United States resides in one agency. In addition, the commander of Northern Command has been assigned responsibility for America's ballistic missile defence system for North America.

NORTHCOM has a number of subordinate commands, some geographic and some functional. The geographic commands are found in areas of high interest or activity and include Joint Task Force Alaska, Joint Task Force National Capital Region, and Joint Task Force North. Despite its name, the latter is located in Texas near the Mexican border and focuses on combating transnational threats like international terrorism, narcotics trafficking, alien smuggling, and weapons of mass destruction. Its entire mission is to employ military capabilities in order to support law enforcement agencies along the US-Mexico border. Other NORTHCOM subordinate commands are functional in that they are designed to assist the command, if necessary, anywhere in NORTHCOM's area of responsibility. There is an army, navy, and air force subordinate command, a command designed specifically to respond to a WMD crisis called Joint Task Force Civil Support, and a separate standing joint-force headquarters command for planned or crisis operations.

Having a military command dedicated to the defence of North America was an entirely new element in US defence planning.

Previously, US Atlantic Command was responsible for all the forces assigned to defending the continental United States, but its commander was also commander of NATO's Atlantic Command. In the late 1990s Atlantic Command was renamed Joint Forces Command and given the further responsibility of spearheading the US military's force transformation efforts. Yet defending the United States was never the exclusive mission of either Atlantic Command or Joint Forces Command. Moreover, neither command had geographic responsibility for Canada (or Mexico); defence relations with Canada were conducted on a bilateral basis by the Pentagon and through NORAD and on a multilateral basis through NATO. (The only other country never assigned to a command – and with which relations were conducted directly by the Pentagon – was Russia, now part of European Command.)

Although US Northern Command plans, organizes, and executes homeland defence and civil-support missions, it has not historically had very many permanently assigned forces. Originally NORTHCOM's only permanent forces were those that were part of the Joint Task Force Civil Support command, noted above. These units were created in the late 1990s to provide command and control of military forces in support of civil authorities in the event of a WMD attack on US soil. But in 2008 the Pentagon decided to assign a new 4,700-person unit to Northern Command. Known as the CBRNE (Chemical, Biological, Radiological, Nuclear, and High-Yield Explosives) Consequence Management Response Force, or CCMRF, the unit is prepared to respond almost immediately to disasters ranging from chemical spills to terrorist attacks using WMD.[4] Moreover, plans are in place to create two more such units by fall 2011. When smaller National Guard units are added in, this will bring the total number of US military personnel dedicated to domestic response to a level of 20,000 troops.[5] In addition, the commander in chief (CINC) of NORTHCOM can seek "preapproval" from the president on other forces he anticipates needing in any given year. In 2008, for example, the president made available to CINC NORTHCOM about 11,000 active and reserve military forces.[6]

The Role of the US Military in Homeland Security

US military officials have stressed that in all cases in which NORTHCOM's forces operate inside the United States, they will support federal, state, or local civilian agencies. The Posse Comitatus Act[7] of 1878 and amplifying Department of Defense regulations dating to 1982 generally bar the use of military personnel in civilian law enforcement activities in the United States, including investigating and arresting individuals.[8] Northern Command's official Internet site states explicitly that as "per the *Posse Comitatus Act*, military forces can provide civil support, but cannot become directly involved in law enforcement."[9] The military is strongly opposed to assuming a law enforcement role; its view is that military personnel are trained to fight wars, not conduct police operations. Moreover, large segments of the civilian population would likely be concerned about the civil-liberties implications.

The 9/11 attacks prompted a debate within the United States over whether these limits on the role of the military in homeland security should be reassessed. Legal experts made a convincing case that the Posse Comitatus Act is not a significant impediment to DoD participation in law enforcement – rather, it is the DoD regulations surrounding the law that have imposed the restrictions.[10] Members of Congress pressed for thousands of National Guard members to be deployed along America's borders to stop illegal immigration.[11] Reflecting this sentiment, the 2002 *National Strategy for Homeland Security* argued, "The threat of catastrophic terrorism requires a thorough review of the laws permitting the military to act within the United States in order to determine whether domestic preparedness and response efforts would benefit from greater involvement of military personnel and, if so, how."[12]

The outcome of this debate was a Pentagon-established framework, first enunciated in the 2005 *Strategy for Homeland Defense and Civil Support* and later reiterated in the 2006 *Quadrennial Defense Review*, under which US military forces would lead, support, or enable missions to defend North America. The US military has always led missions against external threats to America, and it also plays an enabling role – for example, through training and the sharing of expertise with civilian agencies. But in the post-9/11 era it may also be tasked with supporting civil authorities at home as part of a comprehensive national response to a terrorist attack or natural disaster if such disasters "overwhelm civilian capacity."[13] A good example was Hurricane Katrina, where it rapidly became apparent that the only US government organization capable of restoring order was the Marine Corps.[14] The US military can also provide longer-term support to civilian security efforts. After 9/11, for example, National Guard units were deployed along the Canadian and Mexican borders on an interim basis for six months. National Guard units from four states also helped US Customs and Border Protection to conduct surveillance along the US-Mexico border in the period 2006–08 as part of exercise Jump Start. In neither case were the troops armed, and they did not play an enforcement role. Similarly, when it comes to the CCMRF, noted above, the only time the force would become involved in law enforcement would be to protect the force itself.[15]

HOMELAND DEFENCE IN CANADA

Canada's military institutional response to the 9/11 attacks was also to create a new command dedicated to homeland defence, although not for some years after America had done so. The final chapter of *Securing an Open Society: Canada's National Security Policy*, released in April 2004 (see chapter 4), raised the role of the Canadian Forces in defending Canadian territory but left the details to a promised international policy review. *Canada's International Policy Statement*, released one year later, comprised four components: defence, diplomacy, development, and commerce. The defence component, known as the Defence Policy Statement, or DPS, was a landmark document in that it gave the outlines of an entirely new command structure for the Canadian Forces. In accordance with the DPS and subsequent decisions, Canada established four new commands as of February 2006, one of which – Canada Command – is dedicated to the homeland defence of Canada. The other commands include Canadian Expeditionary Forces Command (CEFCOM), Canadian Special Operations Command (CANSOFCOM), and Canadian Operational Support Command (CANOSCOM).

Canada Command

Canada Command's mission is "to deter, prevent, preempt, and defeat threats and aggression aimed at Canada."[16] In addition to Canadian territory, the geographic areas with which the command is concerned include the continental United States, Mexico, the Caribbean (because of hurricanes), and the Arctic approaches to Canada. Canada Command works closely with Public Safety Canada to provide military assistance to civil authorities, much as NORTHCOM supports America's Department of Homeland Security. The subordinate commands reporting to the commander of Canada Command in Ottawa include six regional joint task forces (RJTFS) located in each of Halifax, Montreal, Toronto, Edmonton, Esquimalt, and Yellowknife; a combined-force air-component command based in Winnipeg;[17] and three search and rescue regions across the country. Comprised of land, sea, and air elements, the RJTFS are meant to be integrated or joint. In actual fact, however, each contains a dominant service with only a relatively small representation from the other services.[18] Nonetheless, each is led by a single commander with guaranteed access to navy, army, and air force assets. This is a significant improvement over the previous situation; during the Red River flood of 1997, for example, military operations were hampered by the fact that there were three chains of command – one each for the navy, army, and air force – all leading to Ottawa.

Like the United States, Canada had never had a joint military command dedicated to the defence of the homeland. "In the past, Canada has structured its military primarily for international operations, while the domestic role has been treated as a secondary consideration," noted the government of Paul Martin in *Canada's International Policy Statement* of 2005. "Clearly, this approach will no longer suffice."[19] The idea behind the creation of Canada Command was to have a single locus of authority for responding to an emergency and also to have a command dedicated to addressing the security of Canadian territory that was not also concerned with overseas operations. Previously, all operations had been the responsibility of one (increasingly overworked) deputy chief of defence staff (DCDS). Under the new structure, operations abroad and operations at home are divided between CEFCOM and Canada Command respectively, with CANOSCOM and CANSOFCOM supporting both of the new "geographical" commands.[20]

Canada's new command structure, the most extensive reorganization of the Canadian Forces (CF) since the 1960s, is still a work in progress. A shortcoming is that the immediate effect of creating several new command structures was to take hundreds of personnel out of operational positions and place them into staff positions, thereby straining an already overstretched military, notably Canada's army, during a period of high operational commitment to Afghanistan. But in the longer term the new structure, particularly the creation of Canada Command, is likely to prove a positive step. The command

provides the operational link with NORTHCOM for homeland defence missions and with Public Safety Canada for homeland security
activities. Anecdotal evidence suggests that the creation of Canada
Command as a rough counter to Northern Command has simplified
and clarified Canada-US cooperation for homeland defence.[21] Moreover, its creation has provided an important focal point for civilian
authorities in seeking CF assistance at home.[22] "Canada Command's
priority is its relationship with other government departments,"
notes one high-ranking official, "to the expense of its relationship
with NORTHCOM and NORAD if need be."[23]

An unresolved issue concerns the future relationship among
NORTHCOM, Canada Command, and NORAD. Originally created
as a Canada-US binational command for air defence, and subsequently for aerospace warning and control, NORAD has been responsible for addressing air threats to North America for over half
a century. Both NORAD and NORTHCOM are headquartered at
Peterson Air Force Base in Colorado Springs. As a result, when the
United States created NORTHCOM in 2002, it was able to accommodate the fact that air defence was already the responsibility of a
pre-existing organization by double-hatting the commander of
NORAD as the commander of NORTHCOM. Although the deputy
commander of NORAD is always a Canadian, a similar double-hatting arrangement is not feasible for Canada. Apart from the fact
that Canada Command is located in Ottawa, optically the Canadian
public would not accept the person responsible for defending Canada
reporting to an American general. To clarify command arrangements, a "tricommand study" has been underway for some years to
examine how NORAD may relate to Northern Command and
Canada Command in the future. One possibility is that NORAD
could become a subcommand reporting to the commanders of
Northern and Canada Command.[24]

The Role of the Canadian Forces in Homeland Security

ASSISTANCE TO CIVIL AUTHORITIES The CF's regular force members play a significant role in providing assistance to civil authorities
in countering terrorist and asymmetric threats. For many Cold War
years, they were trained to deal with weapons of mass destruction
in an overseas environment, long before it was ever expected that
such expertise would be needed at home. It only makes sense that

their skills in this area be adapted for use in the event of a WMD terrorist attack on North American soil. After 9/11 the CF established
a Joint Nuclear, Biological and Chemical Defence Company at
Canadian Forces Base Trenton. Now renamed the Canadian Incidence Response Unit, it comprises about 150 regular force personnel drawn from the army, navy, and air force. Joint Task Force 2,
Canada's special operations force (and the core of CANSOFCOM), is
also trained to operate in a WMD-contaminated environment at
home and abroad. In the event of a WMD-related terrorist incident
in Canada, these units could be called upon to assist the RCMP in
responding to the crisis.

Over the past several years, there have been calls for the CF's military reserves to play an expanded role in homeland security and defence. These calls are tied to changes in the international security
environment, but they are better understood in the context of an
ongoing debate over the role and operational tasks of the army reserves, or militia, that well predates the 9/11 attacks. Such questions do not arise as often with the naval and air reserves because
the navy and air force have found specific and valid roles for their
reserves. Naval reserves crew the maritime coastal defence vessels,
while air reserves fly two squadrons of Griffon helicopters and otherwise are integrated into regular air force flights.[25] It has proven
more difficult to assign a specific role to the militia. After World
War II, Canada's army reserve was assigned the task of mobilization, in addition to assisting the regular army in the defence of
Canada. But as the Cold War took hold, mobilization came to be
considered a dead issue; there would not be enough time to mobilize during a nuclear war. Prime Minister John Diefenbaker responded to the threat of thermonuclear war by assigning civil-
defence duties to the militia. The army, despite its bitter resistance,
was compelled to retrain its reserve component for "national survival" duties, like rescuing and feeding survivors of a nuclear war.[26]
Many units lost their heavy weapons and armoured vehicles.

Once NATO adopted a strategy of flexible response in the 1960s,
mobilization for a long war increased in importance and the militia
resumed its previous role. Over the next several decades, the role
remained essentially unchanged, even as personnel and equipment
levels continued to decline. The 1994 *Defence White Paper* identified the primary role of the reserves as the augmentation, sustain-
ment, and support of deployed forces, while a Special Commission

on the Restructuring of the Reserves created by the Government of Canada in 1995 stated the militia should be organized and trained to augment the regular force and be capable of expansion to meet mobilization needs. Similarly, a 2000 government statement on the restructuring of land force reserves identified the raison d'être of the militia as providing the framework for expansion and mobilization of forces, augmenting deployed units and individuals on peace-support operations, and representing a "footprint" in communities across the country.

The 9/11 attacks sparked calls for a greater focus on this "footprint." At the political level, the military reserves were touted as "the first line of defence" in the event of a terrorist attack on Canadian soil. The view was that the reserves had to be prepared to be called out en masse in support of civilian first-responders in times of national emergency.[27] At the military level, those in charge of the Land Force Reserve Restructure Program envisioned an expanded role for Canada's militia that would see highly trained security platoons deployed almost immediately to help civilian authorities.[28] This idea was consistent with the opinion expressed in an early post-9/11 Senate committee report that army reserves should be employed across the country as chemical, biological, radiological, and nuclear defence specialists assisting local first-responders.[29]

The role of the (army) reserves received renewed attention with the election of Prime Minister Stephen Harper in early 2006. During the election campaign, the conservatives had promised the creation of some fourteen "territorial defence battalions" at major centres across the country. Comprised of 100 regular force troops and 400 reservists, these battalions would be designed to respond to domestic emergencies like a natural disaster or a terrorist attack. But this proposal proved unworkable because with the ongoing commitment to Afghanistan, the army simply did not have the regular forces to free up for such a domestic-defence commitment. Moreover, the plan provoked familiar critiques that reservists are needed above all to augment regular forces abroad "rather than manning new battalions that would be waiting for forest fires, floods, or ice storms to strike at home."[30]

The final outcome of all these deliberations is a larger domestic role for the reserves while maintaining their overseas contribution. In accordance with a 2009 national plan, the army reserves are to be "remodelled" over the course of three years. This remodelling will involve the creation of seven all-reserve battalion-size units across the country trained with specialist skills to respond to natural or manmade disasters, including those involving WMD. An entire battalion will be committed to the North. At the same time, reservists will continue to be called up for missions abroad. This is in part because Canada's overstretched regular army could not fully man its overseas units without them. Moreover, since 9/11, decision makers have consistently insisted the overseas role will remain in place – a major distinction between today's renewed homeland emphasis and the civil-defence mandate of the Diefenbaker era. The new framework, in short, is one where the regular force forms the core for expeditionary operations, augmented by reservists, while reservists form the core for domestic operations, augmented by the regular force.[31]

AID OF THE CIVIL POWER Section 275 of the National Defence Act states that the Canadian Forces may "be called out for service in aid of the civil power in any case in which a riot or disturbance of the peace [is] beyond the powers of the civil authorities to suppress, prevent or deal with." The key distinction between the CF assisting civil authorities and acting in the aid of the civil power is that in the latter scenario the CF temporarily becomes the lead agency because civil authorities are unable to do so. In the contemporary security environment, this is quite a plausible circumstance. A WMD terrorist attack against a civilian population would likely create a sense of panic greater than the actual effects of the weapons.[32] Alternatively, it could incapacitate first-responders and render them unable to deal with the situation. In either case, the military would need to take control; that is, soon after a WMD terrorist attack, it is likely the CF would no longer be *assisting* a civilian lead agency but instead would *be* the lead agency.

Maritime Surveillance and Control

CF CAPABILITIES One of the most important roles the CF plays in the homeland defence of Canada is the surveillance and control of Canadian approaches and territory. Part of this involves air surveillance and control, a mission that is carried out in cooperation with the United States through NORAD (see below). But equally crucial is the surveillance and control of Canada's maritime approaches.

Here, CF capabilities are relatively limited, although initiatives are underway to address various shortfalls. Canada has eighteen Aurora long-range patrol aircraft, which travel about once a week up and down the East and West Coasts and semi-annually over the Arctic. Yet the aircraft are quite old, having been purchased by the government of Pierre Elliott Trudeau. They are often under repair and unable to carry out scheduled surveillance missions. In 2007, for example, Arctic flights were cancelled for several months because of long-term maintenance issues. The Department of National Defence had originally planned on upgrading all the Auroras, which have a subsurface surveillance capability dating from the Cold War, with ground moving-target indicators that would have enabled them to track movements on land and on the surface of the sea. But the increasing cost of upgrading an aging fleet prompted a new course of action. In 2008 Defence Minister Peter MacKay announced that only about half of the Auroras would be upgraded, while the others would be phased out by about 2016. This will leave only a handful of aircraft available for maritime surveillance missions until a new Canadian Multimission Aircraft (CMA), perhaps a version of the Poseidon used by the United States, arrives sometime after 2020.

Canada's maritime surveillance and control capability also includes maritime coastal defence vessels (MCDVs) and frigates. Acquired in the mid-1990s, Canada's twelve MCDVs are manned by the naval reserves and conduct surveillance missions along the East and West Coasts. But since they have no ability to operate in ice-infested waters, they are limited in how far north they can go. Moreover, because they were designed for patrolling and mine warfare, they are not very fast and are therefore not well suited for interdiction. And the MCDVs are too small to handle the rough seas off some parts of Vancouver Island and the Grand Banks of Newfoundland; they cannot be used effectively to monitor Canada's Economic Exclusion Zone out to 200 nautical miles. Meanwhile, Canada's eight frigates, which date from the 1990s but are in the process of being upgraded, provide an important Canadian military capability for maritime interdiction missions around North America that are some distance offshore. Maritime helicopters enhance this capability by extending a ship's range of view outward, so the fact that Canada's fleet of aging Sea King maritime helicopters is being replaced with the new Cyclone is an important development. Yet apart from the fact that they, too, have no ability to operate in ice-infested waters, Canada's frigates are not an ideal maritime surveillance and control vessel for Canada close to North American shores because they are too big and are costly to operate.[33] Finally, once fully operational in the early 2010s, Canada's four Victoria-class diesel-electric submarines will be able to conduct surveillance missions off the East and West Coasts and in the summer travel as far as the Northwest Passage.

Canada's existing naval vessels cannot provide the necessary maritime surveillance and control capability off Canada's East and West Coasts, much less in the Arctic. The requirement in the post-9/11 security environment, which also features rapid climate change in the North, is for a mid-sized, ice-capable naval vessel to carry out armed tasks in support of other government departments in Canada's territorial waters. To tackle these capability shortfalls, in 2007 the Harper government announced Canada would acquire between six and eight Arctic offshore patrol vessels by the middle of the 2010s. The size and speed of these ships will be such that, once they arrive, they will be ideal for operations off Canada's East and West Coasts.

To fill some of the gaps in the surveillance of its maritime approaches, Canada is turning to advanced technology. One project under consideration is a network of long-range radars, called High Frequency Surface Wave Radars, at spots along the East and West Coasts. Such radars transmit high-frequency waves that follow the curvature of Earth, allowing them to detect and track ships or low-flying aircraft over the horizon, up to 200 nautical miles (or 350 kilometres) away. Two sites on the East Coast were built and activated in the early post-9/11 period, but in 2006 the government halted the program after receiving a complaint that the frequency the sites used interfered with civilian frequencies. More recently, the government decided to re-evaluate the project, seeking companies that may be able to address the frequency issue.[34] If the program were to be restarted, the radar sites would form a sort of naval version of the North Warning System of NORAD radars. Defence and Research Development Canada is examining the technological feasibility of using high-frequency wave radars in the Arctic; under a revitalized program, earlier plans to extend the network to sites that look at each end of the Northwest Passage[35] would therefore logically be included.

The CF has also experimented with unmanned aerial vehicles (UAVs) to determine how such drones can be used to monitor Canada's approaches. "Today, if I want to have a look at something, I have to sail a ship or have to task an Aurora patrol aircraft," pointed out the then commander of Canadian Forces Pacific in 2004. "With ... UAVs ... you would have the capability to send a vehicle out to localize the area of the contact and even to take a picture."[36] In the summer of 2003 the CF tested unmanned aerial vehicles off Vancouver Island to see how drones could be used to detect smugglers, and the following summer it tested a version of America's Predator unmanned aircraft over Baffin Island to see whether UAVs could be adapted to the extreme conditions of the North. The CF had originally hoped to have an operational UAV capability for Arctic surveillance, sovereignty, and counterterrorism patrols off Canada's coasts by 2008,[37] but plans in this area have proceeded more slowly than expected. Under the Joint UAV Surveillance and Acquisition System (JUSTAS) program, the Department of National Defence is seeking proposals for eighteen UAVs that can be used for both domestic and international operations. Current plans are for a contract to be awarded in 2010, with the drones – which are likely to be weaponized[38] – delivered between about 2012 and 2016.[39]

Strategically, Canada's ability to conduct the surveillance of its maritime approaches, especially in the Arctic region, also includes the space dimension. Under Project Polar Epsilon, the Department of National Defence has purchased a payload on Radarsat II, Canada's newest commercial Earth-imaging satellite, giving the CF regular space-based surveillance information about Canada's vast Arctic region. Polar Epsilon, which became operational a few months after Radarsat II was launched at the end of 2007, allows the military to monitor the waters and coastline of the Arctic for traditional threats to Canada's security, like weapons and military movements, and also to watch for emergencies and environmental disasters. From an altitude of 800 kilometres, Radarsat II can pinpoint any foreign vessel down to the size of a family car. But this surveillance is not continuous; rather, the satellite makes a pass every several hours, so to track movement it is necessary to compare one snapshot with the next. Simple physics dictates that continuous space-based monitoring of the Arctic or any other part of the world requires a constellation of satellites. To this end, Canada plans to launch three radar satellites in the early 2010s under the Radarsat

Constellation project, with the mission of boosting both maritime *and* land security. Once in place, the system will significantly increase the surveillance of Canada's coastlines and Arctic territories because with three satellites in orbit, at least one will likely be flying over an area of interest at any given time.[40]

OTHER AGENCIES The CF is not the only agency involved in securing Canada's coasts – far from it. Indeed, one of the complicating factors in Canadian maritime surveillance and control is that there are a multitude of government organizations involved. In the United States there is one agency in charge of guarding American coasts: the US Coast Guard, an armed enforcement agency. In Canada, by contrast, the lead agency in any given situation may be one of five government agencies, depending on the issue involved and how close it occurs to Canadian shores. They include the Canadian navy (with support from air force assets like the Aurora), Transport Canada, the Canada Border Services Agency (CBSA), the RCMP, and the Canadian Coast Guard, which is part of the Department of Fisheries and Oceans and, unlike its American counterpart, has never been an enforcement or security agency. Transport Canada is the lead department for marine security in Canada, developing, for example, boating regulations, while the RCMP conducts police/enforcement functions along the coasts, assisted, if necessary, by the navy. The CBSA is responsible for things like addressing stowaways arriving by ship and collecting Container Security Initiative information (see chapter 4). The Coast Guard can support enforcement activity by transporting RCMP officers to vessels of interest, but its primary mission lies in the areas of marine navigation and safety, traffic management, and pollution control. Meanwhile, the general coastal protection role remains with the navy.[41] This somewhat confusing framework, with its occasionally overlapping agency mandates, has been discussed in the following terms:

> Looking at the mission of national defence for the country and establishing a boundary around the country, that is the sole responsibility of the navy. Whether you draw that line 200 miles off the coast or whatever, the navy takes responsibility and protects the coasts, conducts regular surveillance, monitors the situation, and basically interdicts and does the high seas missions. As you start getting in closer to the country, other players come to the

table. Domestic industry, container shipping, vessels that move cargo and so on ... [are] the responsibility of Transport Canada. They look at registering vessels, licensing them, and protecting them. The regulatory component is done by the Canadian Coast Guard. Port protection, control of shipping within the St Lawrence Seaway and so forth fall as a mission to the Department of Transport. Drug traffic on the coasts is a police responsibility. The military has the capacity to deliver interdiction teams to vessels of interest. We do not do the boarding, and we do not do the arrest, but we assist the RCMP in conducting that operation at sea. When you go to the United States, you enter a different domain with different players. Their Coast Guard functions as an interdiction agent within 200 miles. There is a standing agreement in the United States where the navy basically looks out 200 miles and beyond and the Coast Guard looks in 200 miles.[42]

Thus, when it comes to operations off Canada's coasts, a whole host of players is involved on the Canadian side. To bring together the intelligence gathered by various government departments about activity off Canada's coasts, Canada has created a Maritime Security Operations Centre (MSOC) in each of Victoria and Halifax. Led by the navy, the MSOCs have representation from the RCMP, CBSA, Transport Canada, and the Canadian Coast Guard. The centres use advanced technologies to combine information that is gathered from all five agencies and present it in a coordinated fashion, thereby giving a comprehensive picture of what is happening along Canada's coasts. The information, in turn, is fed into various national headquarters like Canada Command and the Government Operations Centre.[43] A third MSOC, this one led by the RCMP, is also being established in the Great Lakes region to monitor activity on the Great Lakes and the St Lawrence Seaway.

Like Canada's navy, other government departments involved in Canada's maritime surveillance and control have limited resources for doing so. The RCMP is overstretched and has only a few boats and a relatively small number of personnel to carry out enforcement missions along hundreds of miles of coastline. The Coast Guard's boats are aging; a plan to purchase new Coast Guard midshore patrol vessels was cancelled in 2008 only to be revitalized a year later, thereby setting back any projected delivery date.[44] Moreover, although the Coast Guard has and is being equipped with the appropriate vessels for interdiction missions within two or three miles of the coast, it has neither the security mandate nor the weaponry to intervene in criminal activity. This disjuncture has led many interested parties to argue that the Coast Guard's mandate should be changed such that it more literally guards Canada's coasts. The House of Commons Fisheries Committee has argued the agency should be returned to the Department of Transport, where it was until 1995, and given a new mandate as an armed maritime security agency to help protect the country.[45] Similarly, the Standing Senate Committee on National Security and Defence has argued the Coast Guard should be elevated to a national security agency and be given both an enforcement mandate and the necessary equipment and weapons to carry it out.[46]

Equipping and training the Coast Guard for a security role close to shore – and in the Great Lakes region – would be a sensible move. It would provide clarity among Canada's maritime surveillance and control agencies, and it would go some way toward addressing the increased policing and interdiction requirements of the post-9/11 security environment. The Coast Guard knows Canada's shoreline best; assigning it an enforcement role would allow the RCMP to concentrate its resources on land. Such a mission change would demand a significant cultural shift in the Coast Guard. Nonetheless, it is a necessary transition, one that is consistent with adaptations already made by land-border customs officers, who have made public security – instead of cross-border shopping – their primary area of focus (see chapter 4).

THE ARCTIC

One needs hardly to pick up a newspaper or turn on a newscast to know that the Arctic is an area of growing security concern for Canada. The core of the issue is that the polar icecap is melting at a much faster rate than was expected to be the case only a few years ago. Experts in Canada and the United States now project the Arctic's sea ice could vanish in summer as early as 2013.[47] Surrounded by islands, the fabled Northwest Passage is melting somewhat more slowly, but even here it is expected the channels will be open to unimpeded summer navigation by 2015.[48] "It is no longer a matter of if, but when, the Arctic Ocean will open to regular marine transportation and exploration of its lucrative natural-resource deposits,"[49] notes former US Coast Guard officer Scott Borgerson of the Council of Foreign Relations.

That the Arctic region is getting warmer is of concern for Canada for three distinct yet overlapping reasons. In the first instance, as the Arctic territory – roughly defined as anything above the 66th parallel – gets more hospitable, there will be growing resource exploitation, and with this could come criminal and terrorist elements. Warmer weather is allowing for increased mining in the North, like diamond mining, and this in turn is bringing population growth and increased air traffic. Already there is significant evidence of organized crime.[50] Moreover, as security holes are closed in southern borders, terrorists could see the Arctic as the "soft underbelly of the continent."[51] Northern ports could be used for illegal immigration, while terrorist elements could seek to board aircraft for southern destinations. "It is unsettling to know," Arctic expert Rob Huebert has noted, "that there is still no security screening of passengers boarding aircraft in many of the Canadian northern airports."[52] The 2005 Defence Policy Statement reflected many of these concerns. In an ironic echo of Canada's Cold War concern about the Soviets using the North as a staging ground for strikes southward, the document stated explicitly the requirement that Canada must prepare for "asymmetric threats that are staged through the North."[53]

Further north, a second area of concern centres on the potential for increased traffic in the Northwest Passage. Here, there are differing views on the extent to which the passage could be used commercially in the future. Some experts argue that although the Northwest Passage will become navigable over the coming years, it will remain ice-infested and therefore hold little attraction for international shipping lines.[54] Because of the unpredictable nature of Arctic ice, lack of Arctic infrastructure, narrow channels, and increased insurance costs, argues one shipping executive, "No one in the industry is really talking about the Northwest Passage being a serious alternative to the Panama Canal."[55] A counterview centres on the reality that shipping routes through the Arctic would cut off thousands of miles of transit distance between various spots on the globe. Although future ice conditions are not precisely known, notes Canada's foremost Arctic security expert, even if the waters are ice-infested the economic incentives will be such that at least some ships will transport goods between Europe and North America's eastern seaboard, and between Europe and Asia, by sailing through the passage.[56] Moreover, the risks of ice must be balanced against the risks of sailing through pirate-infested waters in other areas of the world. "As soon as marine insurers recalculate the risks involved in [Arctic] voyages," argues Borgerson, "trans-Arctic shipping will become commercially viable."[57]

For Canada, the possibility and even likelihood of increased maritime traffic through the Canadian Arctic in the not too distant future brings with it environmental concerns like the possibility of an oil spill and possible search and rescue issues like responding to a cruise ship in distress. Not surprisingly, Canada wants to control who and what travels through the Northwest Passage. Canada has historically maintained that the Northwest Passage is an internal waterway to be regulated by Canadian national law. But the United States, along with all other major countries in the world, maintains that this is an international strait connecting two large international bodies of water, much as the Strait of Malacca connects the South China Sea with the Andaman Sea and the Indian Ocean. For America, the fundamental issue is one of precedence: recognizing the Northwest Passage as an internal waterway would result in demands, for example, from Iran that the Straits of Hormuz be treated as an internal waterway.[58] Back in 1986, in the wake of the transit of the *Polar Sea*, a US Coast Guard ship (see chapter 1), the United States and Canada came up with an informal compromise that amounted to the US agreeing to ask permission for the transit of vessels and Canada agreeing that it would always say "yes." This "agreement to disagree" is no doubt still in place. Nonetheless, in one of his final acts as president, George W. Bush signed a new directive on the Arctic that states explicitly the intention of the United States to preserve its right to navigation through strategic straits, including the Northwest Passage.[59]

More northerly still, a third area of concern centres on the exact extent of Canadian territory as it extends beyond the Arctic archipelago and on the related issue of control over resources on the ocean bed. The US Geological Survey estimates that the extensive Arctic continental shelves hold 13 per cent of the world's undiscovered oil reserves and over 30 per cent of the world's untapped gas reserves.[60] Under the 1982 UN Convention on the Law of the Sea (UNCLOS), countries have exclusive rights over an economic zone extending 200 miles offshore, but this can be increased if the seabed is shown to be an extension of the continental shelf. Canada and Denmark are working together to prove that a vast underwater ridge reaching as far as the North Pole, known as the Lomonosov Ridge, is an extension of Ellesmere Island and Greenland. Russia, meanwhile, is taking measures to demonstrate the ridge is geologically linked to Siberia, including by sending a remote-controlled submarine to the North Pole's ocean floor in 2007 to collect soil samples. Beyond this, Canada has longstanding and unresolved disputes with the United States over the boundary delineation between the Yukon and Alaska in the Beaufort Sea and with Denmark over the ownership of Hans Island between Greenland and Ellesmere Island. And the United States has begun to map areas north of the Bering Strait to determine the extent of the Alaskan continental shelf along the boundary with Siberia.[61]

All this activity is raising the potential of the Arctic as an international flashpoint in the future. In a 2007 report released by the Center for Naval Analysis, a group of retired American admirals argued that a warming Arctic holds great implications for military operations as a result of competition for resources.[62] The following year, Borgerson stated in stronger terms that without diplomatic leadership competing claims in the Arctic could lead to "an armed mad dash for its resources."[63] Meanwhile, in 2008 European Union leaders published a report on climate change that found the changing geostrategic dynamics of the Arctic region brought on by climate change could have consequences for international stability.[64] NATO military leaders have met to examine the prospect of standoffs among nations laying claims to the Arctic's energy reserves, while NATO's secretary general has cautioned the alliance's Arctic nations to stay united despite growing potential for conflict.[65] In 2009 Russia released a government security report that predicts possible military conflict over energy resources in the Arctic.[66]

Clearly, a key component of Canada's future policy response must be increased diplomacy. Of the five nations laying claim to the Arctic, four are longstanding allies – the United States, Canada, Denmark, and Norway – while the fifth is Russia. It is in the interest of Canada and the United States to resolve boundary disputes and find a new compromise over the status of the Northwest Passage. This is partly because when it comes to the Northwest Passage the two countries have shared concerns about the impact of increased shipping. It is notable that even as they raise the possibility of a confrontation with Canada over the Northwest Passage, US officials lament that Canada does not have the military capability to handle threats to North America originating in an ice-free North-west Passage.[67] Without an armed Coast Guard, Canada's Senate Committee on Fisheries and Oceans, has argued, "We're not in control in the Arctic. If we showed that we were ... a lot of that dispute [with the United States] would fade away."[68] This is doubly the case considering that any Canada-US disagreement "pales into insignificance compared with the storm brewing with Russia" over its plans for the Arctic.[69] Russia has already announced plans to create a dedicated military force to help protect its interests in disputed areas of the Arctic.[70] The potential might exist here for some sort of a joint initiative between Canada and the United States, perhaps building on the NORAD framework. Already, Norway is seeking a cooperative route with allies, suggesting that NATO needs a comprehensive approach to the Arctic, just as it has in Afghanistan.[71]

Another component of Canada's response must necessarily lie in ensuring it has the ability to exercise control over its Arctic regions. Canada's frigates, submarines, and MCDVs have already begun to carry out exercises in the Northwest Passage in the summer months, such as during Op Nanook in the summer of 2008. The melting ice-cap will increase the stretch of northern waters in which Canada's ships and submarines can operate and the annual number of weeks during which they will be able to do so. But none of Canada's current naval vessels can operate in ice-infested waters. Unlike their nuclear-propelled counterparts, diesel-electric submarines are restricted in ice-covered areas because they must surface periodically to regenerate their power. And unlike countries such as Denmark, Canada has not chosen to design its navy's frigates or other vessels with ice-strengthened hulls. The Canadian Coast Guard does have icebreakers, but the largest and most capable of these, the massive *Louis St Laurent*, is old and nearing the end of its operational life.

The Harper government has sought to rectify some of these short-falls. Once they arrive in the mid-2010s, Canada's Arctic offshore patrol vessels, with their ice-strengthened hulls, will significantly increase Canada's ability to conduct maritime patrols of the Arctic regions. But these armed vessels will be far different from the three "armed ice-breakers" the Conservatives had originally promoted during the 2005–06 election. Rather than providing an icebreaking capability, they will be able to go through only fresh ice of about one metre thick and therefore will not be able to operate in the North on a year-round basis. Their acquisition makes better sense if made in conjunction with the building of a new Coast Guard icebreaker, and for this reason it is significant that the 2008–09 federal budget included plans for the construction of a new Polar-class icebreaker by the late-2010s.[72]

In 2007 the government also announced Canada would construct a deepwater port and refuelling station in Nanisivik, Nunavut, as a staging area for vessels operating in the High Arctic; establish a CF Arctic Training Centre for the army in Resolute Bay, Nunavut, from which the CF can conduct year-round patrols; and increase the size of the Canadian Rangers – part-time reservists who are native to the Arctic region – by some 900 members to a total of 5,000 by about 2012.[73] As a means of demonstrating sovereignty in the North, teams made up of Rangers along with a few members of the Canadian army have already conducted armed sovereignty patrols on snowmobile across the Arctic, such as in the early spring of 2006 and 2007. More recently, Canada's army has designated four reserve units to form the backbone of a new Arctic force, with about 500 personnel in total, to be created by the middle of the 2010s.[74]

HOMELAND DEFENCE – THE UNITED STATES AND CANADA

Air Surveillance

The primary means through which Canada conducts the surveillance and control of its air approaches is through the binational NORAD command. Over the years, NORAD's mission has evolved with the changing threat environment. It first assumed air defence against Soviet bombers, then took on aerospace warning of Soviet (and Chinese) ballistic missiles, and finally, in the late 1980s, added the surveillance and monitoring of smaller aircraft, often from Latin America, suspected of illegal drug trafficking. In both its 1996 and May 2001 renewal agreements, NORAD's mandate was stated to be twofold: "Aerospace warning for North America," meaning detecting and providing warning of attack against North America by aircraft, missiles, or space vehicles; and "Aerospace control for North America," meaning directing, coordinating, and controlling the operational activities of forces assigned to NORAD. Throughout the pre-9/11 period, and even with the addition of new responsibilities toward the end of the Cold War, one feature of NORAD remained consistent: it always looked outward to address threats approaching the continent.

The most dramatic change in NORAD's mission after 9/11 is that it broadened its focus from looking exclusively outward to looking both outward *and* inward at potential airborne threats. NORAD is still responsible for detecting, identifying, and, if necessary, intercepting potentially threatening air traffic entering North American airspace, but it has also adjusted to a new mission of handling threats arising from within the continent. A good example of resulting changes in NORAD's operating procedures is that today the NORAD operations centre listens to conversations on the Federal Aviation Administration network twenty-four hours a day, seven days a week, and would know instantly of a suspected hijacking.[75] As part of Operation Noble Eagle, a joint US-Canadian operation launched after 11 September 2001, Canadian and US forces are monitoring and intercepting all flights of interest within continental North America. In the years since 9/11, fighter aircraft have been sent out hundreds of times to determine whether aircraft that did not immediately identify themselves had been hijacked.

Ironically, in recent years NORAD has increasingly had to look outward again. Beginning in August 2007, Russia restarted its Cold War practice of sending Bear bombers through neutral skies close to North American airspace. In 2007–08 alone, there were about seventy-five such flights.[76] In almost every case Moscow did not file a flight plan for the patrol, forcing NORAD to scramble fighter jets to intercept and escort the bombers. The concern here is not that Russian bombers are entering North American air space – they are not – but that they are flying into areas that during the Cold War the two sides implicitly agreed would be a buffer zone.[77]

Apart from aircraft approaching or flying over North America, cruise missiles, small aircraft, and UAVs represent a potential danger. For terrorist groups operating without the support of a nation-state, such platforms are more easily attainable than ballistic missiles. Moreover, given America's decision to deploy a limited ballistic missile defence system (see chapter 6), those who want to strike North America may seek alternative means of attack, including cruise missiles or aerial drones. Of particular concern is that missiles or drones could be armed with a nuclear, biological, chemical, or radiological warhead and launched from ships off the North American coast. Indeed, high-ranking NORAD officials have stated that the command is worried more about cruise missiles and UAVs than about ballistic missiles and bombers.[78]

Addressing the Airborne Threat

In the evolving security environment, Canada and the United States have to be able to track and intercept aircraft approaching North America, or already over North America, and to detect and intercept cruise missiles and unmanned aerial vehicles launched by terrorists or rogue states from international waters close to North America. NORAD gets surveillance and early-warning information about aircraft approaching North America from the North Warning System (NWS) of radars, as well as from coastal radars on the East and West Coasts of Canada. Constructed in the late 1980s and early 1990s, the NWS is comprised of fifteen long-range radars (eleven in Canada, four in Alaska) and thirty-nine short-range radars (thirty-six in Canada, three in Alaska) along the 70th parallel. Apart from this, however, Canada has only intermittent surveillance coverage of much of its vast airspace. America's Airborne Early Warning and Control System (AWACS) aircraft can be used to fill in the "void of radar cover" in central and northern Canada during a crisis, but it is not practical to fly these aircraft on a continual basis.[79]

Currently, civilian air traffic controllers rely on the signals emitted by aircrafts' transponders to locate them. Nav Canada, a private corporation that operates Canada's civil air navigation system, has also launched new technology in Canada's North that uses satellite links and onboard equipment to give air traffic controllers the same kind of information as radar.[80] But threatening aircraft will turn off their transponders, as well as any other kind of equipment designed to give their location – and *The 9/11 Commission Report* revealed the difficulty of finding aircraft that do not want to identify themselves.[81] Moreover, Nav Canada radars are optimized for managing air traffic flow, not addressing security threats.[82] Therefore, defence experts have argued that NORAD's existing capabilities for the detection of aircraft that do not comply with the rules for identification need to be extended to cover most of North America's land mass.[83] Already, the CF has two mobile military radars, normally stationed in each of Cold Lake and Bagotville, and they were deployed to Vancouver during the 2010 Olympics to "look for threats coming from behind the mountains."[84] In addition, in 2005 the government tasked Canada's air force with examining the acquisition of additional radars to provide better coverage of population centres and vital areas of infrastructure.[85] But the subsequently planned Ground-Based Urban Radar Detection (GUARD) project was put on hold in 2008 due to other CF priorities.[86]

Apart from aircraft, no system yet exists to continuously monitor the cruise missile threat to North America. The United States uses a patchwork of surveillance systems, including AWACS and navy E-2C aircraft, ship-based Aegis scanners, and land-based radar.[87] Since 9/11 the United States has been attempting to overcome the challenge of detecting cruise missiles, which travel close to the surface of Earth, but progress has been limited.[88] The cruise missile threat is a prime motivation for the real-time sharing, between Canada and the United States, of information on vessels approaching North America – the warning time for a sea-launched cruise missile could be as little as ten minutes.[89]

For several years the United States pursued a Space-Based Radar (SBR) system to fill in many of the surveillance gaps. In fact, the idea dated back to the mid-1980s with the decision of Ronald Reagan's administration to pursue a space-based follow-on to the North Warning System. Comprising a constellation of satellites, the system would use a combination of phased-array radars (for tracking) and synthetic-aperture radars (to distinguish objects from their backgrounds) to enable ground moving-target indication.[90] In this way, SBR – which was renamed Space Radar in the mid-2000s – would be able to watch thousands of square miles, tracking ships, low-flying aircraft, drones, and cruise missiles approaching North America. But ongoing funding issues forced the Pentagon to cancel the program in 2008. The United States is now seeking alternate solutions, one of which may be to buy some clones of Canada's Radarsat satellites.[91]

For the "control" component of aerospace surveillance and control, NORAD relies on tactical fighter aircraft to intercept threatening aircraft. In the post-9/11 era, fighter aircraft are arguably more relevant to homeland defence than they have been since bombers were displaced by ballistic missiles as the primary threat to North America in the early 1960s. In the years since 9/11, as noted earlier, Canadian and US military aircraft have been called out to intercept suspicious aircraft (and now Russian bombers) hundreds of times – a steep rise in the handful of intercepts NORAD undertook each year before the terrorist attacks. Canada's current contribution to the air interception mission is four squadrons of CF-18 Hornets.

In the future, Canada must ensure that it has an appropriate land-based fighter for its renewed air defence role at home and that it has enough aircraft on ready alert in the right locations to quickly shadow, and if necessary intercept, threatening aircraft approaching or already over Canada's major cities. Here, there are a number of potential shortfalls. The auditor general has questioned whether, in light of new threats to North America, Canada has enough fighters to properly defend Canada and contribute to North American defence.[92] Under the *Canada First Defence Strategy* of June 2008, beginning around 2017 Canada's eighty CF-18s are to be replaced with about sixty-five next-generation fighter aircraft, probably the Joint Strike Fighter. In addition, the locations of Canada's fighter bases – Cold Lake, Alberta, and Bagotville, Quebec – are appropriate to yesterday's circumpolar threat but may be too far from the large civilian population centres that are the focus of contemporary threats.[93] A hijacked airliner heading for Toronto, for example, might have to be engaged by US fighters because Canadian fighters are based too far away. To mitigate risks, fighters are sent on an ad hoc rotating basis to deployed operating bases close to specific high-profile events, such as G-8 or other leaders' summits.[94]

Meanwhile, Canada and the United States have only a limited ability not only to detect but also to defend against cruise missiles. The US Army has made improvements to its Patriot missile, which has capabilities against cruise missiles and short-range ballistic missiles, while the US Navy has extended the capability of its Standard Missile (SM-3) so that it can intercept ballistic and cruise missiles and aircraft. It is also possible that the Canadian army's Air Defence Anti-Tank System (ADATS) could be used to destroy cruise missiles, coastal vessels, and aircraft approaching the continent.[95] But although the ADATS played an air defence role around venues associated with the 2010 Olympics and G-8 Summit, there are as yet no plans to maintain these decades-old systems beyond 2011.[96] Clearly, increased research and investment in the area of defending against cruise missiles will be necessary.

Land and Maritime Threats

In contrast to the air dimension, Canada and the United States have historically carried out most of their maritime and land-based surveillance and control activities on a national basis. But the nature of the contemporary security environment is such that it is driving increased binational cooperation in these areas. Specific scenarios might include a WMD terrorist attack somewhere along the Canada-US land border or on a border-spanning bridge as well as terrorists planting a nuclear device on a container ship headed for a major North American port.

Such concerns have already led to at least two concrete developments. In the May 2006 NORAD renewal, the agreement included, for the first time, the provision that the command's mandate would include not only the longstanding missions of "Aerospace warning for North America" and "Aerospace control for North America" but also "Maritime warning for North America."[97] This consists of integrating and assessing information about North America's ocean approaches as well as internal waterways like the Great Lakes. NORAD does not have its own maritime surveillance capability; rather, intelligence on shipping data and threats to sea lanes is sent from other agencies directly into NORAD headquarters. After integration and assessment, NORAD disseminates the information to agencies that are responsible for maritime defence and security, like the US Coast Guard, so that they may respond to the threat. In the lead-up to the NORAD renewal, there had been concerns that US warships would be patrolling Canadian waters, but this is not the case. Under the NORAD agreement, command arrangements have been established such that US fighters may respond to an air threat in Canadian airspace and vice versa. But the maritime dimension is qualitatively different in sovereignty terms; unless otherwise agreed, only American or Canadian vessels would respond to threats in US or Canadian waters respectively.

There is no mention of land forces in the NORAD renewal document. Nonetheless, a second concrete development in recent years is a Canada-US agreement involving land-based cooperation. In February 2008 the commanders of NORTHCOM and Canada Command signed the Civil Assistance Plan (CAP), establishing a framework for allowing the militaries from each nation to cross the other's border in the event of an emergency. Primarily a facilitating mechanism, the CAP was first instituted on Labour Day weekend 2008 when the Canadian Forces provided assistance in responding to Hurricane Hanna and Tropical Storm Gustav. A significant feature of the CAP is that it does not allow for the use of force or weapons. A joint Canada-US team at NORTHCOM headquarters in Colorado Springs has spent some time working on a follow-on agreement, called the Combined Defence Plan, which would establish a similar framework to the CAP but would allow for the use of force in responding to a disaster, such as the terrorist use of WMD. Even more so than the maritime dimension, this has proven complicated in sovereignty terms – so much so that NORTHCOM officials now doubt the plan will go forward.[98]

Land threats to North America are unique in that, apart from natural disasters, they are likely to be generated by terrorists who are difficult to detect. They could involve rapidly spreading and highly lethal weapons of mass destruction, and there may be very little time to assess the nature of the threat and decide on an appropriate response. Because most of Canada's population live close to the Canada-US border, any threat to it is likely to materialize within a few hundred miles of the frontier. This, combined with the fact that the threat knows no borders, means that US interests would likely be directly involved in the event of a crisis. It only makes sense that the United States would respond if Canada were militarily unable to do so. Clearly, the old adage "If we don't secure our own territory, then the Americans will do it for us" would be highly relevant in such situations. Therefore, it is imperative – both in terms of sovereignty and security – that Canada maintain sufficient military forces to take control of these sorts of operations.

CONCLUSION

The post-9/11 security environment is arguably driving the Canada-US defence relationship to be more closely integrated than it has been at any other point in history. No longer confined to the aerospace dimension, Canada-US cooperation for the defence of North America is expanding to the land and maritime dimensions. This is largely because potential direct threats to the continent have increased as a result of both international terrorism and the melting polar icecap. At play is the notion of "defence against help" – the view, first expressed during the Cold War, that if threats to Canada have the potential to impact the United States, America will "help" to address them when Canada is unable to do so.[99] This is an underlying theme that emerges both in the context of the Arctic and along our common southern border, for differing reasons. "When stripped to its bare essentials," points out one scholar, "sovereignty is the ability of an identifiable group of people to control what happens within a specific geographic region."[100] Canada must ensure it has the forces and capabilities to address threats on its territory and in its maritime and aerospace approaches, both for its own security and for that of its giant neighbour. The next chapter turns to a particular aspect of homeland defence: space and ballistic missile defence.

6

Space and Ballistic Missile Defence

It is not too much of a stretch to date the issue of Canada's possible involvement in an American-led ballistic missile defence (BMD) system back to the Soviet launch of *Sputnik* in October 1957. Because it was a satellite propelled into orbit atop a multistage missile, *Sputnik* not only marked the beginning of the space age but was also a vivid indication that the Soviet Union was on the verge of developing long-range ballistic missiles. The United States immediately set about getting its own satellite, *Explorer I*, into orbit, but it turned its attention to ballistic missiles as well. By early 1958, offensive and defensive long-range missile development had become a priority in the United States.[1]

Space and ballistic missile defence are two separate issues, but they have so many linkages that it is difficult to discuss them in isolation. Long-range ballistic missiles pass through space (but do not go into orbit). Some sensors designed to detect ballistic missiles can also track satellites, while others can detect terrestrial projectiles, like Scud missiles. Conversely, systems designed to track satellites and space objects can also be used to detect incoming ballistic missiles. These linkages have been reflected in the mission and responsibilities of the North American Aerospace Defense Command (NORAD) almost from the outset. Since the early 1960s NORAD has been mandated with detecting and warning of aircraft and ballistic missiles, intercepting aircraft, and tracking space objects. The mandate is officially captured as Integrated Tactical Warning and Attack Assessment, or ITWAA, with the "integrated" referring to the fact that the assessment involves both air-breathing (e.g., aircraft and cruise missiles) and ballistic missile threats.

NORAD's role in the surveillance and control of North American airspace was discussed in chapter 5. This chapter examines the other two elements of NORAD's mission: ballistic missile early warning and space surveillance; and developments surrounding Canada's decision not to participate in America's ballistic missile defence system. It begins by outlining technological progress in ballistic missile early warning systems and space surveillance systems over the past half-century. It then gives a brief overview of the various US initiatives to create a missile defence capability, including the most recent undertaking, before looking more closely at command and control arrangements. It concludes that ballistic missile early warning, space surveillance, and ballistic missile defence are difficult to separate. In practical terms, Canada's decision to allow ballistic missile early warning information to flow from NORAD to the US ballistic missile defence system, but not to participate in the system itself, is likely to prove unsustainable. Indeed, in some ways, this has already been shown: the NORTHCOM and NORAD operations centres have been amalgamated. Contrarily for some, the result is an increase – not a decrease – in Canadian sovereignty and security.

BALLISTIC MISSILE EARLY WARNING SYSTEMS

The United States responded to the launch of *Sputnik* by constructing the Ballistic Missile Early Warning System (BMEWS), beginning in 1958. Giant radars built at sites in Alaska, Greenland, and England became operational in the early 1960s, providing the capability to detect ballistic missiles coming over the polar icecap and giving the United States a fifteen-minute attack warning. They also provided tracking data on most orbiting satellites. None of the sites for this system were on Canadian territory, nor did Canada contribute financially to the enterprise. Nonetheless, the decision was made to channel all the ballistic missile surveillance information to the commander of NORAD, and the elaborate BMEWS computer and display facilities were installed at NORAD headquarters.[2] Beginning in the 1970s, the mechanical BMEWS radars, which required several people to operate and could track only one object at a time, were replaced with phased-array radar systems that could maintain tracks on multiple objects simultaneously. Also at this time, the United States established two phased-array warning system sites further south – one on Cape Cod and the other on the coast of California – to monitor the growing threat of missiles fired from Soviet submarines.

Ground-based radars are one means by which NORAD and the US Air Force have monitored the ballistic missile threat over the years. But even by the early 1960s, technology had progressed to the point that a space-based infrared system could reliably detect missile launches. The Missile Defense Alarm System (MIDAS) was a successful program that explored the use of long-wave infrared sensors to detect missile launches and meet what was perceived to be a growing Soviet intercontinental ballistic missile threat. In 1962 MIDAS was reorganized as a long-term research and development effort that eventually yielded the Defence Support Program (DSP) system of satellites. Over the years, the DSP satellite system has consisted of between eight and ten satellites at any one time, the first launched in 1971 and the most recent in 2007. Operating some 37,000 kilometres above Earth's surface in geosynchronous, or high-Earth, orbit,[3] the system provides strategic and tactical missile-launch warnings by detecting the infrared radiation in a missile's exhaust trail.[4] Although the DSP system was designed to pick up intercontinental ballistic missile launches, it has also proven useful for other applications, such as detecting Iraqi Scud missile launches during the 1991 Gulf War.

Since the mid-1990s the US Air Force has been pursuing a new generation of space-based sensors to detect ballistic missiles. The Space-Based Infrared System (SBIRS) of satellites involves a mix of satellites in geosynchronous and highly elliptical orbit, the first of which is scheduled to be launched by 2010. Once the (much delayed) system is in place, SBIRS will significantly increase the US military's ability to detect ballistic missiles at all ranges, from the tactical (battlefield) to strategic (intercontinental) level. In an effort to build in redundancy and reduce the risk surrounding ballistic missile detection, the United States is also pursuing a constellation of satellites in low-Earth orbit designed to detect and track ballistic missiles throughout their trajectories. The first two satellites in this Space Tracking and Surveillance System (STSS) were launched in 2009.

Beyond this, the US Navy is playing an important role in ballistic missile early warning. It has installed a giant X Band radar – weighing 50,000 tons – on a self-propelled oil-rig platform based off the Aleutian Islands. The radar's role is to pick up tracking information on long-range ballistic missiles and provide this information to land-based interceptors. The resolution of the X Band is such that it can distinguish between warheads and decoys, while the fact that the radar is mobile means that it can move to areas of greatest threat. The US Navy has also modified some of its Aegis cruisers to operate in the Sea of Japan and the North Pacific to provide ballistic missile early warning information to the ground-based system being established in Alaska (discussed later).

SPACE SURVEILLANCE SYSTEMS

Space surveillance systems can also contribute to ballistic missile early warning and detection. Such systems, like America's Space Surveillance Network and the emerging Canadian Space Surveillance System, have as their primary mission monitoring objects in orbit around Earth, including thousands of pieces of space junk and hundreds of actual satellites. But by determining whether or not a space object is a ballistic missile in midcourse phase, space surveillance systems also provide an indirect contribution to ballistic missile defence systems.

Soon after the United States began deploying its BMEWS radars, it grew concerned that because they could detect only ballistic missiles coming at North America from over the polar icecap, the radars might end up being some sort of a Maginot Line that the Soviet Union could go around by launching a ballistic missile from southern regions or from space.[5] The individual US military services moved quickly to develop sensor systems that could track space objects coming from all directions. In 1958 the US Navy established the Space Surveillance System, or SPASUR, an electronic fence stretching across the southern United States. Meanwhile, the US Air Force set up a worldwide network of radars and space-probing cameras called Spacetrack. In 1960 the Space Detection and Tracking System, or SPADATS, was formed to bring these systems together under a single military management. Like BMEWS, SPADATS was placed under the operational control of NORAD.

In subsequent years the network expanded to include two Canadian sites (now disbanded) at St Margarets, New Brunswick, and Cold Lake, Alberta, each equipped with a Baker-Nunn satellite-tracking camera. In the early 1980s a number of space-tracking radars, notably the Pacific Barrier System of sites in Southeast Asia, were added to SPADATS, which was renamed the Space Surveillance Network (SSN). Later that decade the US Air Force replaced the old Baker-Nunn cameras with the Electro-optical Deep Space Surveillance System, based at sites in New Mexico, Hawaii, and a British island in the Indian Ocean and featuring ground-based telescope sensors linked to a video camera. Finally, in 1996 the United States launched an experimental space-based space sensor, the Space-Based Visible Sensor aboard the Missile Defense Agency's Midcourse Space Experiment satellite, which was operational until mid-2008. Today, the SSN includes army-, navy-, and air-force-operated ground-based radars and optical sensors located at about thirty sites around the world (including the BMEWS sites). Using a combination of phased-array radars, conventional radars, and deep space surveillance telescopes, the network is mandated with detecting and tracking space objects and with predicting when and where a decaying space object will re-enter Earth's atmosphere.

In contrast to ballistic missile detection systems, historically, almost all space surveillance systems have been physically based on Earth. But this is changing as more nations launch satellites, and possible threats from space-based antisatellite (ASAT) capabilities, such as microsatellites, have emerged. "A growing number of nations have access to satellites which could be used against Canada [and the United States]," notes a member of Canada's surveillance of space project, "to ensure the integrity of space-based assets ... it is essential to be aware of foreign satellite activities."[6] To this end, the United States and Canada are increasingly turning to space-based space surveillance systems. These have an advantage over their ground-based counterparts because they are not inhibited by atmospheric effects, lighting conditions, or the curvature of Earth. Since 2002 the United States has been pursuing a Space-Based Space Surveillance (SBSS) constellation of four satellites, the first of which, the Pathfinder, is slated to be launched by 2010. Meanwhile, Canada's ability to contribute to America's SSN ended when the Baker-Nunn sites were decommissioned in 1992, but for several years it has been seeking to revitalize its contribution with a space-based space surveillance capability. Under Project Sapphire, the Department of National Defence is building a satellite with an optical sensor that will be able to look at objects in deep space, approximately 6,000 to 40,000 kilometres from Earth. Scheduled for deployment in mid-2011, Sapphire will gather information on foreign satellites, track space debris, and feed this data into America's SSN. The satellite, along with associated ground segments, is collectively known as the Canadian Space Surveillance System.

BALLISTIC MISSILE DEFENCE SYSTEMS

Early Systems

America's interest in ballistic missile defences predates even the first intercontinental ballistic missile. The United States began exploring the idea of ballistic missile defence in the late 1940s, but it was not until the launch of *Sputnik* that its efforts became more focused. The earliest American anti-ballistic missile (ABM) was the Nike Zeus, developed in the late 1950s for the point defence of army units. Despite being a US Army system, the Nike Zeus was strongly supported at the time by the commander of NORAD, who, even in those early days, believed that it was fruitless to have air defences (through NORAD) without being able to defend against ballistic missiles. By 1960, only two years after NORAD had been established as an integrated binational air defence organization, the US commander of NORAD had declared the organization's first priority to be ballistic missile defence.[7] Concerned that the Soviet Union could deploy nuclear warheads on satellites over US territory, the US Air Force pressed for a satellite interception system, and in 1964 a rudimentary ground-based antisatellite capability was established on a remote Pacific island. Other experimental anti-ballistic missile systems included the US Army's Sprint-Spartan ABM, developed in the late 1960s as a defence against accidental Soviet launch and the threat from China, and its Safeguard ABM system, which used a nuclear-armed missile as its interceptor and was actually deployed operationally for a brief period in 1975–76 at a site in North Dakota.

The Canadian Response to Early BMD Efforts

US statements and activities with respect to ballistic missile defence in the early 1960s did not receive much attention in Canada, whose public and politicians were much more caught up in the issue of arming the US Air Force's Bomarc missile – designed to target Soviet bombers, not ballistic missiles – with nuclear warheads. But in the latter part of the decade, Canadian officials became concerned that the United States might want to build ABM sites in Canada and/or pursue nuclear warheads for its ABMs. At the time of the 1968 NORAD renewal agreement, Canada insisted on, and succeeded in getting, a clause stating that Canada would not be obliged to participate in any future BMD system. Regardless of the clause, in the following years the issue of BMD declined in importance on the Canada-US defence relations agenda. In 1972 the United States and the Soviet Union signed the Anti-ballistic Missile Treaty, which precluded nationwide missile defences by stating that each side could deploy only two (amended to one in 1974) ABM sites. The treaty was intended to ensure mutual vulnerability to nuclear weapons, to remove incentives to build more weapons as a means to overcome adversary defences, and therefore to contribute to deterrence and strategic stability. The United States built its treaty-compliant ABM site in North Dakota in the mid-1970s but abandoned it almost immediately because of the cost and lack of military effectiveness. Russia's ABM system, which surrounds Moscow and employs technology similar to that of Safeguard, remains nominally in operation. The existence of the ABM Treaty, combined with the absence of an American BMD system, persuaded Canada to drop the BMD clause in 1981.[8] That year, Canada also accepted a change in the NORAD agreement such that the organization became the North American Aerospace Defense Command – a formal recognition of the fact that NORAD had been involved in aerospace activities almost since its inception.

Strategic Defense Initiative

Ironically, less than two years after Canada agreed to the removal of the BMD clause in the NORAD treaty, US president Ronald Reagan made his dramatic speech announcing the Strategic Defense Initiative (SDI). In his March 1983 address, Reagan asked, "What if free people could live secure in the knowledge that their security did not rest upon the threat of instant US retaliation to deter a Soviet attack, that we could intercept and destroy ballistic missiles before they reached our own soil or that of our allies?"[9] The president was, in effect, turning the offence-defence debate on its head, arguing that the best way to guarantee North American security was not offensively, through mutual assured destruction, but defensively, through ballistic missile defences. His answer – an elaborate system of futuristic weapons like orbital particle-beam stations and space-based kinetic kill vehicles to fend off a massive Soviet ballistic missile attack – soon became known as "Star Wars."

The SDI announcement took America and its allies by surprise; Reagan had not even consulted most of his own officials. It triggered a few years of furious activity, as US officials tried to implement Reagan's vision. Research programs were established, and allies were asked to participate. In Canada it sparked a fierce debate that was finally quelled in 1985 when the Conservative government of Brian Mulroney decided that it would sign no government-to-government cooperative agreement but that Canadian firms could participate and compete for contracts under existing bilateral defence-development and production-sharing agreements. This decision met immediate political requirements, but it did nothing to resolve long-term questions about Canadian participation in any American BMD system. Nonetheless, it was not long before BMD once again declined in importance as a Canada-US issue. Technological challenges and the end of the Cold War led to Congressional funding cuts and a dramatic scaling-back of the original SDI vision.

Global Protection against Limited Strikes

The 1991 Gulf War and the performance of the Patriot missile led to a refocusing of BMD research toward defences against shorter-range missiles and the protection of American and allied forces deployed abroad. The administration of George H.W. Bush announced its intention to focus on a system called Global Protection against Limited Strikes (GPALS), which would be less than half the size of even the Phase I component of the old SDI. Rather than protect the United States against an all-out Soviet missile attack, GPALS would protect US and allied deployed forces, as well as US and allied territory, against limited ballistic missile strikes, accidental or otherwise. Sensors would be based on land and in space (as had been the case for decades), while interceptors could be ground-, sea-, or space-based.[10]

National Missile Defense

Under the administration of Bill Clinton, SDI continued to be refocused. Congress scaled back the funds allocated to ballistic missile defence but at the same time supported continuing research into a limited National Missile Defence (NMD) system for the United States. The plan envisaged under Clinton centred on protecting all of the US states (including Alaska and Hawaii) against a small number of missiles from rogue states or an accidental launch by Russia or China using land-based interceptors against missiles in their mid-course phase. In 1996 the US formally adopted the "three plus three" approach to developing a ballistic missile defence capability – within three years the country would attain the technological capability to field an NMD system and then be in a position to put the system in place within three years of any decision, based on the threat, to go ahead with deployment.

Throughout much of the 1990s, US authorities believed that no new intercontinental ballistic missile threat to North America would emerge for many years. But in 1998 the Commission to Assess the Ballistic Missile Threat to the United States, chaired by Donald Rumsfeld, stated in a report to Congress that North Korea and Iran could possess intercontinental ballistic missiles within as little as five years and Iraq within ten years. Moreover, it argued that during several of those years the United States might not be aware that these countries were pursuing a ballistic missile capability. The ability of intelligence agencies to monitor the emerging threat was eroding as nations became increasingly sophisticated at concealing evidence of ballistic missile activity and gained greater access to technical assistance from outside sources. The conclusions of the Rumsfeld report, which was released in July 1998, were reinforced the following month, when North Korea test-fired a new longer-range missile over Japanese territory. Within six months the Clinton administration had announced that the rate of proliferation had reached the point at which the threat criterion had been met and that deployment should go ahead once the technology criterion was also fulfilled.[11] The 1999 National Missile Defense Act, signed by President Clinton and strongly supported by Congressional Democrats and Republicans alike, *required* the United States to implement a system to protect against limited attacks "as soon as technologically possible." But the president did not decide, as required by the three-plus-three formula, to go ahead with NMD deployment. This was primarily due to ongoing concerns about the technological feasibility of such a system. In the fall of 2000 Clinton deferred for the next administration the decision of whether to pass beyond research and development to the deployment stage of ballistic missile defence.

The administration of George W. Bush entered office strongly in favour of ballistic missile defences. In its view the US-Russian strategic framework, as embodied in the 1972 ABM Treaty, was no longer appropriate to contemporary realities. The treaty served to reinforce Cold War threat perceptions that were no longer relevant in the post–Cold War era, and it limited America's ability to respond to the new threat environment. Depending on one's perspective, the terrorist attacks of 11 September 2001 either reinforced the perceived need for or demonstrated the irrelevance of ballistic missile defences. Whereas some pointed out that an effective missile defence system over the United States would have done little to stop planes from flying into buildings, others argued that the attacks served only to highlight that anything is possible, including rogue-state ballistic missile attacks. Concurring with the latter view, three months after the attacks President Bush announced that the United States would withdraw from the ABM Treaty (effective six months later).

Throughout 2002 the Missile Defense Agency built and tested mobile and sea-based sensors that detect and track missiles, and it conducted tests with short-range missile defence systems that had been prohibited by the ABM Treaty. Although one test failed, four were successful. Meanwhile, late in 2002 North Korea revealed that it had been secretly developing uranium-based nuclear weapons and would restart nuclear reactors that had been shut down under a 1994 agreement negotiated by the Clinton administration. The potential for technical feasibility and new developments in the international security environment prompted Bush to make the decision, in December 2002, to begin deploying a limited ballistic missile defence system.

Global Ballistic Missile Defense

The BMD system envisaged by the Bush administration, called Global Ballistic Missile Defense (GBMD), is far broader in scope than the Clinton administration's National Missile Defense. The plan, which has not been formally replaced with one specific to Barack Obama's administration, is designed to protect the continental United States as well as allied territory and American and allied deployed forces, much like the GPALS system of the early 1990s. It features a multilayered missile defence system to engage missiles in all three phases of flight (rather than just the midcourse phase) using sea-, land-, and air-based interceptors (rather than just land-based interceptors). More specifically, the Missile Defense Agency is seeking to develop a system to shoot down missiles during the following phases: the boost phase, from launch to the completion of propulsion fuel burn, using sea-based and airborne interceptors; the midcourse phase, outside the atmosphere, using sea- and land-based interceptors; and the terminal phase, when the missile re-enters the atmosphere, using land-based interceptors. Already about twenty ground-based interceptors have been installed at Fort Greely, Alaska, and three at Vandenberg Air Force Base in California; Aegis cruisers with their anti-ballistic missile capability are on station in the North Pacific and the Sea of Japan; and the airborne laser is approaching its final test phase.[12] Under the Bush administration, the Missile Defense Agency also sought funding to pursue space-based interceptors.

Early indications are that the Obama administration supports most major elements of GBMD, notably a focus on protecting allies and deployed forces, as well as the United States itself. The new administration plans fewer long-range ground-based interceptors in Alaska than under the original Bush plan (thirty instead of forty), while at the same time stressing short- and medium-range capabilities on Aegis ships and perhaps new types of ground-based interceptors. It is also strongly supportive of missile detection using the Space Surveillance and Tracking System.[13]

America's BMD system was declared "up and running" as far back as 2007.[14] That said, there remains much debate over whether a defence against ballistic missiles is truly achievable. The United States pursued BMD in the 1960s but abandoned it in the 1970s because of technological unfeasibility. In the 1980s President Reagan announced a grand design for ballistic missile defence, but within a few years the plan was set aside because it was beyond technological reach. President Clinton signed the National Missile Defense Act, which required the US to implement a BMD system as soon as technologically possible, but technology did not make it possible, and Clinton deferred a deployment decision to the next administration. President Bush decided to proceed with a BMD system, but it remains very difficult to "hit a bullet with a bullet." Even if a BMD system "demonstrated a 90 percent rate of technical effectiveness," former secretary of defense William Perry noted in the months after 9/11, "it is reasonable to question whether it could ever come close to that under operational conditions."[15] In the past, the US General Accounting Office has criticized BMD testing as being "repetitive and scripted" because the tests have failed to fully simulate the speed and altitude of a real-life enemy missile.[16] The Obama administration has called for a revamping of the testing program and an aggressive schedule of intercept tests in the coming years.[17]

The Canadian Response to Recent BMD Efforts

Notwithstanding the technological difficulties surrounding BMD, Bush's 2002 decision to deploy a system presented a qualitatively new situation. "The general idea of getting [a BMD] capability has always been there," noted a senior Missile Defense Agency official, "but it has never been approved with long-term program planning and budgets behind it."[18] At a minimum it was apparent that a ballistic missile defence system comprised of sea-, land-, and space-based sensors, as well as sea- and land-based based interceptors, was set to become a permanent feature of North American homeland defence. This reality meant that the Canadian government, after years of fence-sitting, would finally have to make a decision on Canada's participation in America's ballistic missile defence system. The Mulroney government's "nondecision" (noted above) had been followed by the Chrétien government's position, expressed in the 1994 *Defence White Paper*, that Canada was "interested in gaining a better understanding of missile defence through research and in consultation with like-minded nations."[19] Ten years later this remained the official, and increasingly untenable, official government position. In August 2004 Canada agreed to an amendment to the NORAD agreement such that ITWAA information would be transmitted to NORTHCOM for its ballistic missile defence mission. Critics and supporters alike saw this as a first step in Canada joining the BMD system. But in February 2005 the Martin government made the surprising decision to formally state Canada would not participate in America's BMD system.

Historically, Canada has resisted invitations to participate in America's ballistic missile defence programs partly out of concern that a BMD system might set off a new arms race. It believed that Russia and possibly China would respond to a missile defence shield by building more missiles in the hope that at least some would get through. This concern was originally dismissed when

America's withdrawal from the ABM Treaty in 2002 elicited only muted criticism from Russia and China. In the intervening years, however, both Russia and China have focused on increasing their nuclear arsenals, giving greater weight to the arms race argument. Both countries are developing mobile intercontinental ballistic missiles (ICBMs), while Russia is also focusing on submarine-launched ballistic missiles and on developing missiles with several warheads.[20]

Canada has also resisted participation in ballistic missile defence because it is against the weaponization of space. The crux of the issue is the differing US and Canadian interpretations of the 1967 Outer Space Treaty, of which both Canada and the United States are signatories. The only activity the Outer Space Treaty explicitly forbids is the orbiting of nuclear weapons or other weapons of mass destruction, their installation on celestial bodies, or the stationing of such weapons in outer space in any other manner.[21] Beyond this, the treaty permits the "peaceful use" of outer space in accordance with "international law, including the Charter of the United Nations."[22] Canada has focused on the "peaceful use" component and interpreted it to mean that outer space can be used only for non-aggressive purposes, such as surveillance and communications. The United States, by contrast, has focused on the reference to the UN Charter. Because article 51 of the charter recognizes the inherent right of self-defence, the Outer Space Treaty is interpreted as permitting those outer space missions necessary for national security, including not only surveillance and communications but also the application of military force from space-based weapons.

Command Arrangements

In the almost five decades since NORAD was created, the command arrangements pertaining to NORAD's ballistic missile warning and space surveillance mission have essentially remained the same, although the names and mandates of organizations on the American side have changed. Ballistic missile detection and space surveillance information is gathered by a US-only command, but this information is then channelled into NORAD for assessment and early warning. From 1954 to 1975, the US-only command was Continental Air Defense Command (CONAD). The provision of information to NORAD was facilitated by the fact that the commander of CONAD was also the commander of NORAD. When CONAD was disestablished, one of its subordinate commands, Aerospace Defense Command, was reorganized to incorporate the functions formerly carried out by CONAD.

In 1979 administrative control of the missile warning and space surveillance sites was transferred to Strategic Air Command, which controlled America's long-range bombers. But it was not long before this situation, which left most other air force space systems scattered among different agencies, was found to be unsatisfactory. In 1982 the Pentagon created US Air Force Space Command, a major command on a par with Strategic Air Command that brought together all air force space assets. Yet this decision, too, was insufficient because it did not incorporate the space assets of the US Army and the US Navy. Finally, in 1985 the Pentagon created US Space Command (SPACECOM), a unified command encompassing all US military space assets, including the missile warning and space surveillance systems of US Air Force Space Command that supported NORAD. SPACECOM headquarters was co-located with that of NORAD at Peterson Air Force Base in Colorado Springs. Also at this time, the Pentagon clarified US Space Command's relationship with NORAD: Space Command would provide missile warning and space surveillance data to NORAD as necessary to fulfil America's commitment to the NORAD agreement. This arrangement, once again, was facilitated by the fact that the commander of Space Command was double-hatted as the commander of NORAD.

Strategic Air Command was disestablished in 1992, and on the same day Strategic Command (STRATCOM) came into being. It brought together command and control of all three arms of America's nuclear triad – intercontinental ballistic missiles, submarine-launched ballistic missiles, and the long-range bomber force. The creation of this new command was not directly relevant to Canada and NORAD until 2002, when SPACECOM ceased to exist and its functions were transferred to STRATCOM, which is headquartered at Offutt Air Force Base in Nebraska. NORTHCOM was also created at this time, and is headquartered at Peterson Air Force Base; the commander of NORTHCOM is double-hatted as the commander of NORAD (see chapter 5). These new command arrangements mean that NORAD no longer enjoys as direct a relationship as it once did – with CONAD from 1957 to 1975 and with SPACECOM from 1985 to 2002 – with the US-only command that controls American space assets. NORAD continues to receive information from STRATCOM that is necessary for its ITWAA mandate. But when the new command arrangements came into place, experts predicted they could have the effect of cutting Canada out of its previously privileged access to other space-related information.[23] These predictions have proven prescient: today, between 600 and 800 members of STRATCOM and US Air Force Space Command go to work every day in the bottom of Cheyenne Mountain, gathering information to which Canada is not necessarily privy.[24]

The Bush administration's decision to deploy a ballistic missile defence system necessitated further changes in the command system as it relates to NORAD. Continuing the practice that was established in the early years of NORAD, sensor information is gathered by a US-only command (in this case STRATCOM) and channelled to NORAD for its ITWAA function. The added feature now (as noted above) is that NORAD then transmits the integrated information to NORTHCOM for its BMD mandate. When the Canadian government agreed to this arrangement, it took pains to stress that this did not make Canada a party to America's ballistic missile defence system.[25] But others made the case that it would be difficult, if not impossible, to divide the warning of and response to ballistic missiles. "Battle management of the missile-defence system will be closely linked to providing warning and assessment. Physically, it will all take place in the same room."[26]

These words, too, have proven prescient. Within a few years of NORTHCOM's creation, it became clear that the collaborative nature of the NORAD and NORTHCOM missions was such that the two operations centres would have to be co-located. Since there was insufficient space in the mountain for the NORTHCOM personnel, the decision was taken to consolidate the NORTHCOM and NORAD operations centres in the basement of a building on Peterson Air Force Base. In 2008 NORAD's primary operations centre completed its move out of Cheyenne Mountain; an alternate command centre manned by a few people remains on "warm standby" in the mountain. In the consolidated operations centre – known as the NORAD-NORTHCOM Command and Control centre, or N2C2 – the American commander of NORAD/NORTHCOM and the Canadian deputy commander of NORAD sit right beside one another. This physical arrangement makes its inconceivable that Canada would not be involved in a response to a ballistic missile attack. "I can tell you that the Canadian deputy commander sits at my side and has full access to information," the NORTHCOM commander has stated.[27] This information includes what is provided by new sensors like the X Band radar on the oil rig near the Aleutians and the Aegis cruisers in the Pacific.[28] "He would not be frozen out. In fact he plays a very key role."[29] If there were a missile strike, the NORTHCOM commander would be on the phone to the president, while the Canadian deputy would be on the phone to the chief of defence staff.[30]

The evolution of command arrangements between NORTHCOM and NORAD in the last half of the 2000s was such that, for all practical purposes, Canada has become a participant in America's ballistic missile defence system for North America. This is a positive development. The alternative, with separate operations centres, would have been a situation where Canada would likely have been progressively cut out of information on missile strikes on North America. To fulfil the requirement of having assessment and response take place in "the same room," the United States would likely have set up a separate ITWAA capability within NORTHCOM, using information directly from STRATCOM, and "gradually eased" Canada out of access to information from America's ballistic missile early warning and space surveillance systems.[31] Since Canada has no such systems of its own (its first will be Sapphire in 2011), this would have represented a significant blow to Canada's knowledge about its aerospace approaches. In addition, Canada would have had no role in a US response to a missile strike, including whether a decision were taken to attempt an intercept over Canadian territory. Thus recent command changes provide an increase in Canada's sovereignty and security. "Our sovereignty is stronger when we are closely tied to the US," the Canadian deputy commander of NORAD has pointed out, "[because] we are in the room."[32]

Logical drivers of the future, both technological and political, are such that Canada could potentially formally join America's BMD system in the coming decade. Previously, ballistic missiles were detected from space, aircraft/bombers were detected from ground-based radar, and nothing detected cruise missiles and UAVs. In the not too distant future, space-based systems will be used to detect everything from ballistic missiles to cruise missiles and UAVs, to low flying aircraft and ships. Technologically, the lines between systems used to detect air-breathing threats (against which Canada has always found it acceptable to defend) and non-air-breathing threats are becoming increasingly blurred. At the same time, as a member of NATO, Canada has endorsed the alliance's view that a ballistic missile defence to cover all of Europe is a necessary response to the increasing threat of ballistic missile development.[33] Politically, it may become increasingly difficult for the Canadian government to explain why it supports a missile shield for Europe but not for its own territory.

CONCLUSION

Almost since its inception, NORAD has been closely involved in the two interrelated missions of ballistic missile early warning and space surveillance. These tasks are arguably inseparable: systems dedicated to ballistic missile warning are also relevant to NORAD's space surveillance and tracking mission; conversely, those systems dedicated to space surveillance and tracking have important applications to ballistic missile early warning. Throughout the Cold War these missions were important to the homeland defence of North America in that they were to warn of a ballistic missile attack, allowing the US to launch a retaliatory strike. Today, time may be even more of the essence because the intention is to intercept an incoming missile rather than to absorb an attack and respond in kind. Canada's decision to allow NORAD's ITWAA information to flow to NORTHCOM for its BMD mission formed part of the required response, but it soon proved necessary to consolidate the ballistic missile warning and response locations. Consolidating the NORTHCOM and NORAD operations centres is a positive step for Canadian sovereignty. It guarantees that Canada will know about potential missile strikes on North America, and with the Canadian and American commanders sitting side by side, it makes it highly likely Canada would have a role in any response. In the coming decade, further logical drivers, both technological and political, could result in Canada more formally reversing its 2005 decision not to participate in a ballistic missile defence system for North America.

Chapter 7 turns to the third quadrant of requirements for Canadian security and defence: military forces for combating the threat to Canada far from its shores in overseas theatres of operation.

7

Canadian Military Capabilities
and Missions Abroad

Canada's commitment of military personnel abroad is often framed in terms of "restoring influence," "making a difference," or making a "meaningful contribution." In the past, for example, the Standing Committee on National Defence and Veterans Affairs has spoken of making a meaningful Canadian Forces (CF) contribution to United Nations, NATO, or coalition operations;[1] editorials on the subject have argued Canada should spend more on defence because Canadians want to make a difference and because such spending would rehabilitate Canada's standing as a leading international citizen;[2] the Liberal government has stated it wants to see Canada's "place of pride and influence in the world restored";[3] while the Conservative government sees the CF as integral to ensuring Canada is "a credible and influential country, ready to do its part."[4]

Quite apart from Canada's role in the world and its desire to promote a particular set of values, however, there is a Canadian security argument to be made with respect to the ability of the Canadian Forces to participate in military missions far from home. The nature of the threat to North America today is such that its origins are most often found overseas. Since 9/11 CSIS public reports have consistently noted the link between the terrorist threat to Canada and circumstances abroad. In the early 2000s it pointed out "religious, political, ideological, and territorial agendas continue to drive terrorist activities, and remain largely associated with the extension of foreign conflict";[5] by the end of the decade it continued to assess that the activities of individuals within Canada who support the use of violence to achieve their political goals are "often linked to conflicts around the globe."[6]

Addressing threats to North America abroad may or may not involve a military response. Officials in Canada and the United States have stressed that tackling international terrorism requires action on a number of fronts, including diplomatic, humanitarian, and financial. Nonetheless, there will be circumstances in which the use of military force will be assessed as necessary. When it comes to military responses overseas, Canadian security will require the CF to be able to participate in warfighting or "find-and-strike" operations, stabilization missions, and counterinsurgency activities. Warfighting and stabilization each demand a military force with a particular set of characteristics, some of which overlap. Counterinsurgency missions arguably require attributes of both. This chapter examines the military requirements for warfighting operations and then does the same with respect to stabilization missions. It integrates current Canadian military capabilities in each of these areas[7] and closes with a discussion of warfighting and stabilization in the context of counterinsurgency missions.

MILITARY REQUIREMENTS
FOR WARFIGHTING OPERATIONS

Precision Force

The historical progression from the vast armies of the Napoleonic Revolution to the more technologically sophisticated yet still large armies of the Cold War era and finally to smaller forces targeting smaller units (for example, missile batteries around Sarajevo) in the peace enforcement operations of the 1990s reached its logical conclusion in the fist decade of the twenty-first century. Today, military forces may be involved in targeting not a corps, a division, a battalion, or even a small military unit but in many cases a specific individual. Just as the perpetrator of threats to North America has become more precise, the eradication of these threats has demanded ever greater precision in warfare.

Since the end of the Cold War there has been a trend toward using more standoff precision air power in military campaigns. This development was first made evident with the 1991 Gulf War, but it became even more apparent during the 1999 war in and around Kosovo. The potential utility of precision force was further highlighted in the 2001–02 war in Afghanistan when special operations forces on the ground and unmanned aerial vehicles (UAVs) flying overhead pinpointed coordinates for precision naval and air strikes against Taliban and al-Qaeda positions. Similarly, in the 2003 war in Iraq precision firepower from a variety of air and naval platforms targeted and destroyed Iraqi command and control sites, communications lines, and air defence installations. The number of close air support missions in both Iraq and Afghanistan increased significantly in subsequent years,[8] and manned standoff air power continues to play a significant role in Afghanistan as coalition ground forces without the necessary precision artillery call in supporting fire.

Canada's CF-18 Hornets, which were originally Cold War air-to-air fighters, have progressively moved into a ground attack role. They played a major precision air power role in the Kosovo crisis and could do so again in a similar crisis now that command and control upgrades to the aircraft – including Link16 data links and an onboard global positioning system device – have been completed. Since 1996 the CF-18s have been equipped with the capability to conduct precision bombing with laser-guided munitions. More recently, Canada's air force has begun upgrading its fighter munitions with Enhanced Paveway 2 kits that will transform the CF-18s' Mk82 "dumb" bombs into satellite-guided precision weapons.

Yet no amount of upgrades can reverse the fact that the CF-18s' airframes will come to the end of their operational life around 2020. Canada has participated in, and contributed financially to, the US Joint Strike Fighter program for some years, and it is likely that this will be its future strike aircraft.[9] In its 2008 *Canada First Defence Strategy* (CFDS), the government of Stephen Harper announced Canada would buy sixty-five next-generation fighter planes, but it did not specify which aircraft this would be. A firm decision does not have to be made until 2012; until then Canada's office for next-generation fighter capability will be determining exact requirements, including a possible mix of manned and unmanned strike aircraft.

It follows that Canada has also begun to think about acquiring an unmanned combat capability in the form of unmanned combat aerial vehicles (UCAVs). Unmanned combat is a relatively new type of warfare, having made its debut in Afghanistan in the fall of 2001 when America's Predator UAVs were fitted with Hellfire precision-guided munitions. In 2007 the United States deployed the first UCAV that had been developed from the beginning as a combat platform, the Predator B, or Reaper.[10] In 2009 Canada's air force confirmed that the UAV Canada eventually acquires under its Joint UAV Surveillance and Target Acquisition (JUSTAS) project (see chapter 5), in the 2012–16 timeframe, will carry precision-guided weapons.[11]

Support to Forces Ashore

Standoff precision force also includes maritime forces. Since the end of the Cold War, Western air forces and navies have not confronted an enemy with technologically sophisticated forces at sea or in the air. As a result, the primary function of air forces and navies has been to protect and deliver ground forces to a particular area and to support those forces with precision firepower.[12] These trends are behind the move to upgrade existing fighters for a ground attack role. But it also follows that navies are expected to operate in the littoral regions in support of ground forces ashore.

Since the mid-1990s, when precision strike from sea onto land was proven useful in the Balkan wars, Canada's naval leadership has made the case for acquiring a land strike capability. The 2005 Defence Policy Statement was the first to indicate government support for a precision sea-to-land attack capability, stating that the CF would acquire weapons systems that would enable surface ships to support and protect forces ashore. Current plans are for Canada's frigates to be armed with upgraded Harpoon antiship missiles that will include a limited land or coastal target suppression capability.[13] But it is possible – perhaps even likely – that by the end of the 2010s Canada's navy will have a land attack capability with cruise missiles. Already, Raytheon Canada has presented information to Department of National Defence officials about outfitting the future Canadian Surface Combat (see below) with Tomahawk cruise missiles.[14]

Advanced ISR and Command and Control

Striking hard with a high degree of precision depends on precise targeting information and the ability to disseminate it in near-real time. As the British Ministry of Defence has pointed out in the past, "Terrorist organizations are very difficult to identify, locate, quantify, monitor and target ... There is no magic solution to this problem. But it does reinforce the importance of maximizing our ability to acquire, process, and disseminate information."[15] Acquiring information demands advanced intelligence-gathering, surveillance, and reconnaissance (ISR) capabilities, while processing and disseminating information requires advanced command, control, communications, computing, and intelligence-processing (C4I) methods. The two are often combined as C4ISR.

Advanced ISR can be achieved with a variety of platforms, including satellites and manned aircraft like America's Joint Surveillance Target Attack Radar System (JSTARS) aircraft and Britain's Airborne Stand-Off Radar aircraft, both of which are deployed in Afghanistan. But the surveillance platform that has received the greatest attention in the post-9/11 era is the unmanned aerial vehicle. First used in the 1991 Gulf War, UAVs have become crucial to the ability of militaries to "see over the next hill." The long-range Predator UAV and the strategic Global Hawk UAV figured prominently in the 2001–02 war in Afghanistan. The medium-altitude Predator tracked individuals on the ground, while the high-altitude Global Hawk conducted strategic surveillance and reconnaissance. Both continue to be used extensively in the Afghan theatre of operations, as well as in other areas of the world.

Canada's advanced ISR capabilities include a satellite payload, Polar Epsilon, and Aurora long-range patrol aircraft with a ground moving-target indicator capability (see chapter 5). In addition, its CF-18s are being upgraded with new targeting pods that will allow these fighter jets to track enemy formations on the ground. Yet when it comes to activities abroad, Canada's primary ISR focus of the future is on unmanned aerial vehicles. Not only can UAVs like the Predator pinpoint targets – whether in Afghanistan or Yemen or ungoverned areas of Sub-Saharan Africa – but they can also provide the "persistent ISR" necessary to watch for terrorists planting roadside bombs, commonly known as improvised explosive devices (IEDs). In the 2000s Canada's army acquired two battlefield UAV systems for the Afghanistan mission, Sperwer tactical UAVs and Skylark mini-UAVs. The Sperwer UAVs, in particular, were valuable for transmitting information about enemy movements back to commanders on the ground. But they had their shortcomings, most notably their limited endurance and range.[16] A key recommendation of an independent panel convened in 2007–08 to look at the future of Canada's mission in Afghanistan was that Canada must secure, within a year, high-performance UAVs for its troops.[17] Heron UAVs were subsequently leased and sent to Afghanistan to provide surveillance coverage, and also to help detect insurgents planting IEDs. This is an interim arrangement until such time as Canada's air force acquires medium-altitude, long-endurance UAVs (such as the Predator) under its JUSTAS program.

Intelligence, surveillance, and reconnaissance information is of little use unless accompanied by technologies that can rapidly transmit and also interpret all the information that is gathered. The rapid transmission of information increasingly depends on access to communications satellites. Canada will receive its first dedicated military satellite capability in the early 2010s by virtue of having bought some dedicated channels on America's Advanced Extremely High Frequency (AEHF) satellite system. At the same time, its three military services are pursuing their own advanced command and control capabilities. All naval vessels are equipped with the Link16 data link, allowing for the transfer of a significant amount of data and also secure communications. As noted earlier, Canada's CF-18s have also been upgraded with Link16. The Canadian army is pursuing an advanced command and control capability through its Intelligence, Surveillance, Target Acquisition and Reconnaissance (ISTAR) program. Approved in the early 2000s, the project is well underway and is seeking to develop a capability to link all land force battlefield platforms (like tanks and armoured personnel carriers), as well as airborne platforms like UAVs. The army is also pursuing a capability to integrate information from the navy and air force into its own systems, with the goal of creating a picture of the battle space that includes maritime, land, and air assets.

Special Operations Forces

In the post-9/11 era, precision warfare has gone beyond air and sea power to include increasing precision in land warfare through the extensive use of special operations forces (SOFs). SOFs can be defined as "specially organized, trained and equipped military and paramilitary forces that conduct ... operations to achieve military, political, economic or informational objectives by generally unconventional means in hostile, denied or politically sensitive areas."[18] In the 2001–02 war in Afghanistan, SOFs called in air strikes from air and naval platforms, conducted operations to eradicate al-Qaeda and Taliban forces in caves, and provided support to indigenous land forces. All told, some 6,000 special operations forces were deployed to Afghanistan in 2001–02, and even this large (by historical standards) figure was surpassed in Iraq in 2003, when 10,000 special operations forces were deployed in the war's first week.[19] SOFs continue to operate extensively in both theatres of operations.

Once used sparingly, since 2001 SOFs have become important components of military missions. Their growing role not only reflects the requirement for greater precision in warfare but is also a response to the unconventional nature of the threats Western militaries are facing in the contemporary security environment. Simply put, unconventional threats require unconventional responses. These trends have meant that Western defence establishments have placed a greater emphasis on special operations forces than was previously the case. After the 2001–02 war in Afghanistan, the United States significantly increased the budget and forces assigned to its Special Operations Command and elevated its status. Australia created a new Special Operations Command and doubled the number of its SOF troops to some 2,500 personnel, while Britain created a new Special Forces regiment for covert reconnaissance and intelligence gathering.

Canada has also focused on SOFs. In its "security budget" of December 2001, the Canadian government allocated a significant portion of the funds to Joint Task Force 2 (JTF 2), Canada's longstanding special operations force, enabling the force to double in size (from about 300 to 600 personnel) within a few years. Later, the CF created a new Canadian Special Operations Command (CANSOFCOM) as one of four new CF command structures (see chapter 5). CANSOFCOM integrates four special forces formations: JTF 2, the Joint Incidence Response Unit (see chapter 5), an aviation squadron of Griffon helicopters that provides dedicated special operations aviation support to JTF 2 and that will eventually be equipped with Canada's new battlefield troop lift helicopters, and a newly created "tier-2" Canadian Special Operations Regiment (CSOR) being formed and trained to support the "tier-1" JTF 2. This latter move will make Canada's Special Forces more interoperable with those of its allies, most of which already have tier-2 and even tier-3 SOFs.

Announced in the mid-2000s, original plans called for CSOR to number some 750 troops and for Special Operations Command to comprise about 2,300 troops overall by about 2010. But JTF 2 and CSOR draw their forces primarily from the ranks of the army, and the army itself is severely stretched as a result of the Afghanistan mission. As a result, the complete Special Operations expansion is unlikely to be achieved until well into the 2010s.

Deployability and Mobility

An overarching theme in the transformation of military forces to meet future threats is the need to make the shift from the massive, heavy armies of the Cold War to lighter, more deployable "expeditionary" armies that can quickly move to operational theatres around the world. Moreover, once in theatre, military forces need to be mobile and agile because in most cases they face no front line of "enemy" combatants. Soldiers have to be able to move quickly to respond to rapidly changing situations.[20]

The Canadian Forces is taking measures to make its units both rapidly deployable to theatre and highly mobile in theatre. Canada moved into a new league of expeditionary capability with the purchase, under the first Harper government, of four of America's giant C-17 Globemaster strategic transporters. For decades prior to this, Canada – and indeed all countries except the Cold War superpowers – was dependent on US or Russian/Ukrainian strategic airlift (the Antonov) if it wanted to get its troops quickly to problem spots around the world. Canada's new C-17s – which have already been used extensively – can transport even Canada's heaviest military equipment, the Leopard II tanks, to overseas crises. The CF is also replacing its aging fleet of C130 Hercules tactical lift planes with 17 C-130J Hercules, with delivery set for between 2010 and 2012. Considered the workhorse of the Canadian air force, such aircraft are critical for Canada's air mobility requirements – not only abroad but also at home. The air mobility focus lately tends to be on Afghanistan, Chief of Defence Staff Walt Natynczyk has noted, but given it can take up to eight hours to fly between two points in Canada, "we need those aircraft in a domestic situation as much as in an international situation."[21]

At one time the deployability of Canada's forces was to be enhanced with the acquisition of three multirole joint support ships (JSS), which, among other things, would have had sealift capacity for vehicles and troops and would therefore have reduced Canada's reliance on commercial chartered sealift. But the JSS program, which was announced with great fanfare by the governments of both Paul Martin and Stephen Harper, was abruptly halted in 2008 for cost reasons; its future configuration may or may not include a sealift component (see below).

Force deployability abroad also depends to a certain degree on having lighter equipment and on needing less ammunition through the adoption of precision technology. In 2002 Canada's army began a process of reconfiguring its three brigade groups to create a medium-weight land force. The service began replacing its heavy main battle tanks with lighter, wheeled platforms like the Light Armoured Vehicle (LAV) III and the Coyote reconnaissance vehicle. Later, it deployed new battlefield artillery, the air-portable M777 Howitzer, armed with Excalibur GPS-guided artillery rounds.

This trend toward lighter, wheeled vehicles was expected to continue. In 2003 the Martin government announced that Canada would acquire the Mobile Gun System, a wheeled platform that would give troops more protection than a LAV but less than a tank. However, the NATO mission in Afghanistan, where Canada was heavily engaged throughout the latter half of the 2000s, revealed the limitations of wheeled systems; the LAVs repeatedly became bogged down in the rough terrain. Moreover, in the fall of 2006 Canadians carrying out combat operations against the Taliban were surprised to encounter a "semi-conventional" enemy with dug-in lines of defences,[22] demonstrating the need for heavy armour to protect troops. In a significant reversal of previous decisions, in 2006 the government signalled it would not proceed with the Mobile Gun System purchase and instead would revitalize the tank. The CF deployed its Cold War–era main battle tanks to Afghanistan, leased Leopard II tanks from Germany, and announced the purchase of up to 100 Leopard IIs from the Dutch.

More recently, the army is seeking to square the circle of mobility and force protection with the purchase of about twenty light (34 tons as compared to the Leopard's 64 tons) tanks that can operate in areas along riverbanks where the Taliban often seeks to stage its ambushes.[23] The army's future plans may also include buying the next generation of LAV, the LAV-H for high capacity, which would be better armoured against IEDs and have increased mobility.[24] Finally, Canada is pursuing a longer-term plan to acquire a series of land combat vehicles and systems that will likely centre on platforms that are comparatively light but still approximate the survivability of a tank.

Meanwhile, for increased battlefield mobility, the CF is buying sixteen medium-to-heavy lift Chinook helicopters from Boeing, with delivery set to begin in 2012 for an initial operating capability by 2014. Helicopter transport on the battlefield is a critical capability shortfall for Canada, which for more than fifteen years in the 1990s and 2000s had no troop lift helicopters at all and therefore was completely dependent on its allies for battlefield mobility in places like Afghanistan. In 2008 the independent panel on Canada's future role in Afghanistan recommended Canada secure a medium helicopter-lift capacity within a year.[25] To this end, the CF purchased six used Chinook helicopters from the United States and has retrofitted them with heavy machines guns to counter Taliban attacks. Moreover, it has deployed Griffon helicopters, upgraded with infrared sensors and a door-mounted gun system, to Afghanistan to escort and protect the Chinooks. Much like the acquisition of the C17, this move marks a significantly new military capability for Canada. Unlike many of its allies, including the United States, Britain, France, Australia, and the Netherlands, Canada has never had an armed combat helicopter like the Apache or Eurocopter Tiger; the deployment of modified Griffons represents a step in this direction.

Maritime Interdiction Operations

In the contemporary security environment, naval forces may need to interdict ships potentially carrying terrorists and their weapons, as well as address the growing issue of piracy in key maritime corridors. Maritime interdiction operations like those carried out by the Canadian navy in the Arabian Sea from 2001 to 2003 (Operation Apollo) make a tangible contribution to international security. Future operations of this nature are likely to be carried out under the Proliferation Security Initiative, launched by the United States in 2003. Prompted by the case of the *Sosan*, a North Korean ship that was discovered carrying Scud missiles to Yemen in December 2002, the initiative aims to create a multilateral setting for stemming the proliferation of weapons of mass destruction and their delivery systems by allowing the United States and its allies to interdict ships suspected of carrying such weapons and systems. Canada joined the initiative in 2004. Although some countries have questioned its legality, Canada has argued that the legal basis can be found in the Nuclear Non-proliferation Treaty and other international agreements.[26]

Since 2008 Canada's navy has also been increasingly engaged in missions to combat piracy, particularly in the waters off Somalia and the Horn of Africa. "Canadian and international law is clear," the legal advisor to a Canadian task force operating in the Gulf of Aden has pointed out, "Canadian sailors have the right to arrest anyone caught in an act of piracy in international waters."[27] To this end, Canadian sailors are being schooled in the Law of the Sea, hand-to-hand combat, and how to scale the sides of suspected vessels.[28]

The US Navy is in the process of building a Littoral Combat Ship (LCS) specifically designed, in terms of speed and size, for terrorist interdiction, anti-mining operations, and antisubmarine warfare in so-called "green" waters (as opposed to blue ocean) about 100 miles off the world's coasts. This vessel, one of which has already been commissioned, will also be ideally suited to antipiracy operations. But the LCS is currently beyond the CF's financial reach. Rather, whether stopping terrorists, pirates, or illegal shipments of weapons, Canada's toolbox for these missions is essentially the same: a naval task force comprised of a command and control destroyer, a supply vessel, and at least one frigate, which apart from the LCS is considered the naval platform best suited to the "global coast guard role" of interdiction operations.[29]

Canada's eight Halifax-class multirole patrol frigates are among the navy's most modern, having been commissioned in the early to mid-1990s. Between 2011 and 2017 they will undergo a modernization program that will include equipment applicable to littoral operations, like the Harpoon antiship missiles noted above. But the navy's three aging Iroquois-class destroyers, which date to 1970 and were upgraded in the early 1990s, will reach the end of their operational life by 2016 or 2017. Under the Canadian Surface Combatant program, Canada will build fifteen ships in the latter half of the 2010s that combine the capabilities of a frigate and a destroyer. Nonetheless, there will almost certainly be a gap in its naval command and control capabilities. As the chief of the maritime staff has noted, "Even an aggressive procurement strategy won't be capable of delivering replacements for the ... destroyers before the Navy is forced to retire the last of the three warships."[30]

Equally critical, if not more so, is that Canada's two remaining supply vessels – called auxiliary oil replenishers, or AORs, because they provide fuel as well as other supplies – are also very close to the end of their operational life. Navy officials note that many of the AORs' systems, such as boilers to generate steam, are all but obsolete.[31] Without a supply ship, Canada's naval task groups cannot operate independently; they become dependent on allies or on the existence of shore facilities wherever in the world they are operating for refuelling and resupply.

In 2010–11 one of Canada's AORs will be in refit, allowing it to operate beyond 2015 yet leaving Canada in the unprecedented position of being able to deploy a task group off only one of its coasts. The navy anticipated this state of affairs years ago, launching the Afloat Logistics Sealift Capability program in the early 1990s. The follow-on Joint Support Ship (JSS) program was to have produced three ships, each of which would have combined three capabilities: refuelling and resupply for frigates and destroyers, a certain amount of sealift for the army (noted above), and a command and control capability for directing operations ashore, the result of a doctrinal shift among Western navies from open ocean warfare to projecting power from the sea onto land in support of ground forces. But integrating so many capabilities into one vessel proved unachievable given the cost envelope provided. Early indications are that the reworked JSS program, which is unlikely to produce a ship until near the end of the 2010s, will go back to basics, focusing on the resupply and refuelling aspects that are central to naval operations.

Even before the JSS was sent back to the drawing board experts had questioned the advisability of putting so many capabilities on one ship. Although joint support ships would be useful for inserting troops and equipment into benign environments, a vessel carrying lots of people and lots of fuel would make an attractive enemy target.[32] Moreover, one could easily have envisaged a scenario in which the navy needed refuelling capabilities in one part of the world, while the army needed sealift and offshore command and control in an entirely different region.[33]

A final component of Canada's naval task groups is the maritime helicopters that operate from surface vessels. These helicopters play a key operational role because they increase the flexibility of the vessel by allowing for the transport of troops and equipment between ship and shore and because they dramatically increase a ship's situational awareness by enabling it to see well beyond the horizon. The history of the CF's attempt to acquire a replacement for its aging Sea King maritime helicopters includes the announcement of a new maritime helicopter program near the end of Brian Mulroney's tenure, the abrupt cancellation of the program by the first government of Jean Chrétien, and years of postponed replacement decisions, even as the 1960s-era aircraft became increasingly difficult to maintain in an operational state. The Martin government finally signed a contract in 2004 for twenty-eight new Sikorsky H92 Cyclone maritime helicopters, but various delays have meant the first is unlikely to be delivered before 2011.

MILITARY REQUIREMENTS
FOR STABILIZATION OPERATIONS

Warfighting is only one role of military forces abroad in the post-9/11 security environment – and not the most likely. Stabilization and reconstruction missions to rebuild a country in the wake of a combat operation, prevent a slide into warfare, or stabilize and restore order to a failed or failing state will likely be more commonplace in the future. Failed states create an environment in which terrorists can establish a base of operations to inflict harm on North America. Countries such as Afghanistan, where terrorists have been routed out, pose a security threat to the Western world until they have been reconstructed and stabilized. Peace building in the 1990s was primarily seen as a humanitarian undertaking that, although worthy, was not directly related to the security of North America. The events of 11 September 2001 profoundly altered this view, demonstrating that North America is not immune to troubles impacting other parts of the world and indicating that stabilization and reconstruction missions, no less than those of warfighting, can be central to North American security and defence.

As is the case with "find-and-strike" operations, stabilization operations demand a military force with a particular set of characteristics. Many of these characteristics are consistent with those identified as essential to effective warfighting in the future. Advanced intelligence, surveillance, and reconnaissance capabilities are crucial for gaining a complete picture of circumstances throughout the area that military forces are attempting to stabilize. This means that the acquisition of unmanned aerial vehicles, for example, is equally an investment in stabilization capability and in combat strength. UAVs are seen to be particularly useful in overcoming the challenges of concealment associated with the urban environment.[34] Similarly, advanced command and control capabilities are required to link the many military and civilian forces engaged in a stabilization task. Therefore, systems that are designed to enable the rapid transmission of information between platforms and forces in wartime also contribute to stabilization capability. Indeed, the challenges here may be even greater than in warfighting: networked communications among services and allied militaries are crucial for combat operations, but in stabilization missions it is necessary to go a step further and couple the military network with civilian communications systems. Special operations forces, too, are well suited to carrying out important aspects of a stabilization and reconstruction mission, such as ensuring the security of critical infrastructures. Force mobility in theatre through the use of helicopters is central to any mission, whether warfighting or stabilization; many humanitarian missions, for example, will take place where there is little or no viable road system. Finally, force deployability and access to strategic airlift and sealift capabilities are just as relevant to stabilization as they are to warfighting missions since, ultimately, both tasks take place far from North American shores.

Larger Force

That said, certain attributes of a warfighting force have limited application to stabilization operations. Air- and sea-launched precision munitions, for example, and all their associated platforms, may be of little value in this phase of a conflict. In addition, some characteristics of a stabilization mission are significantly different from those of warfighting. Perhaps the greatest distinction in requirements is the overall size of the force. Warfighting calls for smaller units to move rapidly over the battlefield using advanced technology to ensure that they are just as lethal as yesterday's larger forces. In comparing the Cold War and post-9/11 eras, we see that new technologies have already brought about a roughly two-thirds reduction in the number of forces required for warfighting: a contemporary brigade can command as much ground as a Cold War division.[35]

The principle of substituting technology for troops is of less relevance in a stabilization mission. Nation building demands a certain critical mass of people – not larger units but more units and thus a larger overall force size. In Iraq in 2003 the United States needed nine brigades to fight the war, but in the years since then it has needed a far larger force, including a "surge" of troops in 2007–09 to secure the peace. Similarly, although a small coalition force routed the Taliban in 2001–02, a much bigger NATO force has operated there since that time, and many would argue the force needs to be many times larger if the country is to be stabilized.

In recognition of the growing role of manpower-intensive stabilization and reconstruction missions, beginning in 2005 the Canadian government committed to increasing the size of the Canadian Forces for the first time since the post–Cold War cuts of the 1990s. The Martin government sought to increase the CF by 5,000 troops, whereas the Harper government, when it entered office, raised this figure to 12,000, for a total force level goal of 75,000 CF personnel. But the costs of Canada's ongoing commitment to Afghanistan, as well as the purchase of new equipment, forced the government to scale back this vision.[36] In its 2008 *Canada First Defence Strategy* the Harper government committed to providing the resources to increase the size of Canada's regular force to 70,000 troops and its reserve force to 30,000 troops but gave no specific time frame for when this goal would be achieved.

Specialized Units?

Another distinction between warfighting and stabilization missions is in the balance of units required. Generally speaking, stabilization missions call for more combat support (signals, combat engineers, military police) personnel and for more combat service support (transport, supply, administration, psychological operations, civil-military affairs, medical, water purification) personnel than do warfighting operations. Traditionally, brigades have been designed with three battalions of combat soldiers and roughly one battalion of combat support and combat service support units. At the division level, this 3:1 ratio translates into roughly nine battalions of combat forces and three of support elements. The combat support and combat service support units are deployed over and over again in response to stabilization mission requirements, with the result that some – but not all – of the army experiences a very high degree of operational tempo.

To rectify this problem and, in effect, to spread the workload around, the Pentagon has in the past looked at creating military forces specifically for stabilization operations. In 2003, for example, the Pentagon's Office of Force Transformation recommended the US field one or two "stabilization and reconstruction" divisions of about 15,000 soldiers, designed for preventative or postconflict measures to build or rebuild a society.[37] Each division would have included a mix of combat and combat support/service support personnel better suited to the stabilization and reconstruction mission than are traditional combat divisions. In essence, the traditional 3:1 ratio of combat to combat support units would have been reversed. But this proposal did not go any further, primarily because it was felt within the Pentagon that it is best to give all troops new skills in conducting stabilization missions rather than designating only specific military units.[38]

Historically, Canada's position has been that the best peacekeeper is a well-trained soldier. This was the view put forward throughout the Cold War. But as traditional peacekeeping gave way to the more complex and in some cases dangerous missions of the first post–Cold War decade, and with the still more complex and dangerous counterinsurgency and reconstruction and stabilization missions of the post-9/11 era, it was not unreasonable to question this long-standing dictum. Soldiers must have certain skill sets to effectively carry out tasks that do not fit into the traditional warfighting mould. Nonetheless, creating specialized, non-warfighting units has never been seriously considered in Canada. The army has attempted to meet shortfalls in combat support and combat service support through additional recruiting in these areas, but it has not had the resources or manpower to develop separate units designed specifically for stabilization. Nor would it necessarily want to: combat veterans have indicated it is easier for troops trained in high-intensity combat to switch to peacekeeping than the other way around, and since the nature of missions can change rapidly, it is best to err on the side of warfighting capability.[39]

Technologies Unique to Stabilization Missions

A final key distinction between warfighting and stabilization operations concerns necessary technologies and weapons for stabilization operations. In some cases, the military role in a stabilization operation may be similar to the role required in a domestic military operation in aid of the civil power. Whereas nonlethal weapons do not figure in warfighting calculations, they would be very useful in stabilization missions. Forces need technologies designed to counter guerrilla and sniper fire, engage in crowd control, conduct border and perimeter security, and ensure the safe transportation of passengers. More traditional postconflict activities may also be necessary, such as mine detection and removal, while increased intelligence from local sources to detect, track, and ultimately neutralize hostile individuals such as suicide bombers will be imperative.

COUNTERINSURGENCY

Since the mid-2000s Western military forces have been heavily engaged in counterinsurgency missions, most notably in Iraq and, in Canada's case, in Afghanistan. An insurgency can be defined as "an organized movement aimed at the overthrow of a constituted government through the use of subversion and armed conflict," while counterinsurgency can be understood as "those political, economic, military, paramilitary, psychological, and civic actions taken by a government to defeat an insurgency."[40] This definition indicates that counterinsurgency missions are difficult to categorize as warfighting or stabilization; in some ways, they are both. Indeed, debates about how best to conduct counterinsurgency missions largely boil down to whether one leans toward the stabilization or warfighting viewpoint. Some focus on the importance of winning "hearts and minds" – the political, economic, and social/civic aspects of addressing an insurgency; others make the case that "An insurgency is still war, and the key is finding or capturing or killing terrorist and militia leaders."[41]

A Mix of Requirements

Canada places counterinsurgency on the spectrum of conflict in between peace support missions and major combat operations.[42] According to Canadian counterinsurgency doctrine, "The military's role is one of supporting other agencies by creating manoeuvre space for them through the provision of security and protection and the neutralization of the insurgent threat."[43] In other words, the Canadian approach to counterinsurgency operations, approved by the chief of the land staff in 2008, is for the military to clear a particular area of terrorists and insurgents and then to hold it secure while civilian agencies move in to rebuild and boost economic development.[44]

In practical terms, this means that counterinsurgency encompasses a mixture of warfighting and stabilization requirements. Activities of a warfighting nature may be necessary in the process of clearing an area or neutralizing a threat. The army doctrine speaks, for example, of the employment of precision artillery against pinpoint targets.[45] And army leaders see tanks, normally central to a conventional war, as critical to Canada's counterinsurgency campaign in the south of Afghanistan.[46] But following combat, things like quickly getting aid and reconstruction to people whose homes have been flattened in battles are considered absolutely imperative for stabilization.[47] Finding the appropriate mix of warfighting and stabilization can be framed as the degree to which a force uses "fires," or physical activities, versus "influence," or psychological activities, to affect the understanding and perceptions of the civilian population. Ultimately, "The campaign theme, together with the situation at hand, will dictate the balance that is struck between fires and influence."[48] Generally speaking, however, Canadian doctrine emphasizes the latter over the former. "Offensive operations – fires and their effects – will only go so far ... attempts [at attrition] will likely drive more individuals to the insurgency and provide additional support for the insurgent's narrative."[49]

3D, Whole of Government, Comprehensive Approach

Canada's engagement in efforts to rebuild failed states in the post–Cold War and post-9/11 eras, followed by its involvement in the counterinsurgency mission in Afghanistan from the mid-2000s, has led to a range of concepts to capture the necessary policy response. The first was "3D" – defence, diplomacy, and development – an approach that emerged in the early 2000s to signal that rebuilding failed states required activity on the part of the Canadian Forces, the Department of Foreign Affairs, and the Canadian International Development Agency, all working together within a particular theatre of operations. After Canada committed forces to Kabul in 2003 and it became clear that additional government agencies would need to be involved to address many issues – entities like CSIS and the RCMP immediately come to mind – the phraseology shifted to "whole of government." Finally, once Canada moved southward in 2005 and counterinsurgency became a central focus, the required response broadened further to the comprehensive approach. From this perspective, a counterinsurgency mission demands a full range of military, paramilitary, political, economic, psychological, and civic actions on the part of national government agencies, and also international organizations and nongovernmental organizations, to effectively address an insurgency.

CONCLUSION

In the terrorist era, Canadian security will require the CF to be able to undertake warfighting and stabilization missions as well as, potentially, counterinsurgency missions. A number of attributes of a military force stand out as relevant to warfighting and stabilization, including unmanned aerial vehicles, advanced command and control systems, mobile and deployable forces, and strategic airlift and sealift. At the same time, a mixture of both warfighting and stabilization military attributes are relevant to a counterinsurgency mission. If one takes into account military requirements of homeland defence missions, then equipment and personnel priorities become even clearer. UAVs will need to keep watch along Canada's vast shorelines, strategic and tactical airlift will be required to get disaster response forces and their equipment across the country, and Canada's navy will have to carry out interdiction operations off North American shores as well as foreign shores. A small warfighting force can form the nucleus of a larger stabilization force, but that larger size also responds to homeland requirements for aid of the civil power. At one time it was possible to argue that Canada's best response to the post–Cold War security environment was to focus on those force attributes cross-suited to warfighting and stabilization. In the contemporary security environment, it is imperative to add counterinsurgency and homeland defence considerations into the equation.

8

Canadian Security and Defence
in the Terrorist Era

"Getting the right balance between domestic and international security concerns," argues Canada's first national security policy, "will be an important consideration in determining the roles and force structure of the Canadian Forces."[1] Although this is true, the real issue is much broader in scope. Finding the right balance between measures at home and those abroad is central to whether the Canadian government can carry out its ultimate responsibility for national security, including, among other things, the physical security of Canada, the safety of citizens, the protection of critical infrastructures, national sovereignty, control over our territory, and a certain measure of economic well-being or prosperity.

ADDRESSING TERRORISM

Successive CSIS public reports indicate that the most immediate direct threat to the physical security of Canada, its citizens, and its critical infrastructure is al-Qaeda-inspired terrorism originating abroad and increasingly homegrown. The salient question here is whether it is more effective to defend North America against terrorism through homeland security and defence measures or by seeking out and destroying international terrorism overseas. The answer will not be absolute; inevitably, a mix of both approaches will be required. Rather, the task is to find the most appropriate balance.

The Nature of the Threat

Part of the answer will come in looking at the nature of the threat. The threat comes from individuals and networks of individuals operating in dispersed terror cells around the world, including in North America. To secure the safety of citizens, governments are on the lookout not for military formations, as they would have been in the past, "but for a lone, unknown person in a visa line."[2] This is an exceedingly difficult threat to detect. "For a state to seek out individuals and networks," points out one scholar, "is like seeking the needle of criminal activity in the haystack of an increasingly complex society."[3] That said, it might be possible to narrow the field by focusing on detecting behaviour in which only members of terrorist groups are likely to engage.

Today's equivalent of looking for armies massing is picking up increased "chatter" pertaining to a planned terrorist attack, particularly specific threat information from electronic eavesdropping/communications intercepts.[4] Chatter from intercepted phone calls and e-mails has in the past been very useful from an intelligence-gathering perspective, but now that terrorists have become wise to the pitfalls of using cell phones, a larger proportion of intelligence on possible attacks must come from interrogating captured terrorists.[5] The goal is to develop a robust intelligence network that can warn the government of an attack so that it can be stopped before it is launched.[6] But achieving this is far from assured. The ambiguity of partial warnings and the ability of terrorists to overcome obstacles and manipulate information mean that no system can be foolproof. "The awful truth," says one intelligence expert, "is that even the best intelligence systems will have big failures."[7]

In some ways, the difficulty-of-detection issue is less pronounced abroad. US intelligence agencies appear quite adept at identifying the failed states most likely to harbour terrorists and therefore to pose a security threat to North America. Since 9/11 the United States has focused on places like Somalia, Sudan, Eritrea, Ethiopia, and Djibouti, providing military training, humanitarian aid, and intelligence operations to ensure that these countries do not become the next Afghanistan. Given scarce resources, time, and energy, it is necessary to identify a clear set of high-priority countries.[8] Decisions about which states to focus on should be based on the need to avert terrorists from establishing a base of operations.[9] But even though it is useful to focus on failed states, the fact is that an international terrorist organization like al-Qaeda has numerous small cells in dozens of countries, only a handful of which are failed states (and some of which are Western countries). Moreover, as noted in chapter 2, scholarly research in the late 2000s has indicated terrorists prefer to operate in moderately functioning states, not those considered entirely failed.

Geography

Geography is one factor that has traditionally formed part of a state's calculation of whether to focus on "offensive" measures abroad or on "defensive" measures at home. In the past, analysis in this area centred on the fact that barriers to movement and distance generally favoured defenders[10] and that national borders coinciding with natural barriers hindered conquest.[11] With oceans on the east and west and friendly continental neighbours, Canada and the United States have historically enjoyed a geography that largely protects them from the outside world. But globalization has chipped away the geographic advantage of living in North America. Every year millions of passengers, airplanes, and ships arrive at North American airports and seaports. Individuals around the world can reach North America within several hours. Globalization has opened North America to the benefits of a global trading environment, but it has also made the continent vulnerable to international terrorism.

In addition, advances in technology have made it possible to target North America without setting foot on, or indeed coming anywhere near, North American soil. The overwhelming dependence of modern societies on the smooth functioning of computer systems, combined with the interconnectedness of such systems around the world, makes computer systems an attractive target for computer-savvy terrorists. Historically, to attack a state an adversary had to physically make its way to that state – or at least develop accurate long-range weapons. But geography is no barrier to terrorists choosing to target a nation's critical information infrastructure. Today, it is possible for an enemy to wreak havoc on North America without ever leaving home. Thus although "the oceans continue to act as a buffer against attack for many countries, the greater interconnectedness of the world and the more diffuse nature of today's threats has diminished this traditional role."[12]

Another change in the role of geography is that today the greatest threat to a state may not be at its borders but within its borders. The terrorist attacks of 11 September 2001 were a tragic demonstration that the enemy at the gate may already be inside the gate. Prior to the

1990s, terrorism was considered an evil that resided far from North America.[13] The 1993 attack on the World Trade Center and the 1995 Oklahoma City bombing shook this perception, but not until 9/11 was it clear that geographic locations traditionally defined as "rear area," such as the US homeland, could no longer be so categorized.[14] The threat and incidence of domestic, or homegrown, terrorism since that time has only reinforced a marked shift from previous historical periods, in which states always looked to their borders and beyond to identify potential threats to their citizens.

Military Technologies

Another factor that has historically been used to calculate whether to act abroad or to defend at home has been the prevailing types of military technologies. Fortifications are the most obvious example of a primarily "defensive" military technology, while mobility and striking power have been identified as the essential characteristics of an "offensive" weapon.[15] In this regard, the increased precision, mobility, and long-range striking power of modern military forces can be seen as increasing the ability of Western countries to address threats "over there," before they reach North American shores. This may be particularly the case when it comes to deterring rogue states like Iran and North Korea that are intent on developing nuclear weapons. America's ability to destroy a hostile nation's launch sites, storage sites, and production facilities with conventionally armed precision weapons, it is argued, makes a direct nuclear attack on the United States or an American ally unlikely.[16] If deterrence broke down, the same military attribute upon which deterrence policies are based – rapid force projection overseas – would be effective in conducting the warfighting effort.

New military technologies and the accompanying doctrinal changes in Western forces are also relevant to some degree to directly targeting the international terrorist threat to North America in overseas settings. To take the offensive, the United States and its allies need to exploit intelligence on the existence and location of terrorist cells, supplementing general ideas about locations with specific intelligence – especially from tactical unmanned aircraft – on the precise coordinates of terrorist camps or clandestine units in hiding. Special operations forces are especially suited to the counterterrorist mission, as are the mobile and lethal ground force units being developed by many Western armies.

That said, many new military technologies are far less relevant to addressing terrorism abroad than they are to responding to threatening state actors. Quite apart from the fact that military force forms only one tool in a comprehensive approach to addressing terrorism, finding targets to attack militarily can be extremely difficult. Amorphous in nature, terrorist groups operate in small cells, sometime mixed in with civilians. "Targeting terrorism at its source is an appealing notion," notes one homeland security expert. "Unfortunately the enemy is not cooperating. There is no central front on which al Qaeda can be cornered and destroyed."[17] Meanwhile, there have been some advances in homeland defence technologies, with promises of more to come. Most notably, satellites and unmanned aerial vehicles (UAVs) are being used to monitor ocean approaches; increased capability and investment in these areas can be expected in the future. But challenges remain, particularly in the area of defences against cruise missiles and UAVs launched from offshore ships.

Civilian Technologies

A final factor to consider is advances in civilian technologies. Such technologies have played an important role in military affairs for centuries. A good example is the railway – its introduction transformed the ability of militaries to move large forces over great distances. But what is notable in the information age, which first took hold in the 1970s, is that civilian technologies have become ever more central both to the conduct of military operations abroad and to a state's ability to combat threats at home.

Since 9/11 the United States and Canada have implemented an enormous array of technologies to detect the terrorist threat and increase the security of the continent. Just a few examples include a sensor network in major cities designed to detect a biological weapons attack; technology to track visitors entering and leaving the United States; the NEXUS system of high-tech border clearance cards; the Vehicle and Cargo Inspection System (VACIS), which uses gamma rays to search trucks, passenger vehicles, and shipping containers for illegal items; radiation detectors to scan vehicles and shipping containers for radiation emissions; high-tech video surveillance systems along the border; an automatic identification system to analyze ship manifests and identify high-risk cargo containers before ships reach North American waters; and well-established but ever-advancing technologies for intercepting and processing billions of satellite-transmitted e-mails, faxes, and telephone conversations every day.

Clearly, progress in homeland security technologies has been significant. Although the magnitude of the task of monitoring goods and people entering the United States and Canada is mammoth, technological advances may, in the medium term, be largely up to the challenge. Indeed, it is probable that "technology – biometrics, data-mining, superfast data-processing, and ubiquitous video-surveillance – will move [the] needle-in-the-haystack problem into the just-possible category."[18] Experts have cited better security everywhere, "from airports to ballparks to nuclear plants," as well as dramatically improved intelligence-gathering at home and abroad, to explain why no repeat terrorist attacks were launched in the years immediately following 9/11.[19]

ASSESSING THE BALANCE

As assessment of whether the terrorist threat to North America can best be addressed by focusing on the home game or the away game reveals a mixed picture. The nature of the threat is such that it is an exceedingly difficult one to detect, in North America and elsewhere. Detection is dependent on picking up chatter – now possible due to technological advances – as well as on increased human intelligence, but no intelligence network can ever be foolproof. The advantages and pitfalls of intelligence figure equally in terms of measures abroad and those at home since enhanced intelligence capabilities are necessary for both.[20] One area where the nature of the threat points to an overseas posture is in the rebuilding of failed states that clearly pose a security risk to North America.

Globalization, modern technologies, and the existence of internal threats have largely erased North America's historical defensive geographic advantage. But advances in civilian technologies are beginning to cancel out this loss, moving the enormous task of defending North America into the realm of the just possible. Advances in military technology make it possible to target terrorists abroad with military force, yet this is still an extraordinarily difficult task. At the same time, important strides have been made in homeland defence technologies, or are on the horizon, but challenges remain in areas like cruise missile defence. Taken together, the nature of the threat, geography, and developments in military and civilian technologies indicate Canada should give roughly equal weight to measures at home and those abroad in responding to international terrorism. Such a path would represent a departure in Canada's historical approach to guaranteeing its security, which since World War II has been predominantly overseas in nature (see chapter 1).

REINFORCING A NEW BALANCE

Moreover, beyond terrorism, there are other important national security considerations for Canada that have grown in relevancy since the mid-2000s and that reinforce a greater home game focus. The melting Arctic and the associated challenges of increased criminal activity, commercial and military maritime traffic, and competition for resources point to a set of issues of rising importance that are quintessentially homeland defence in nature. Meanwhile, the decision of Barack Obama's administration to bring the same rigour to monitoring the US-Canada border as the US-Mexico border has highlighted the importance of homeland security measures.[21] "The free movement of goods and people across our shared border is Canada's centre of gravity," notes an internal Canadian defence document, "Should this border be closed ... Canada's economy will suffer"[22] – and with it a key element of Canadian national security.

Prime Minister Pierre Elliott Trudeau focused his security and defence policy on increased Canadian sovereignty but ultimately allocated the bulk of defence commitments to the away game. The promises of Brian Mulroney's government for increased military capability in and around Canada were defeated by the end of the Cold War, while the White Paper vision of Jean Chrétien's government proved incompatible with defence budget cuts. Prime Minister Paul Martin's *Canada's International Policy Statement* argued for a greater homeland focus, but since 2005 the Canadian Forces, and its resources, have been manifestly "over there." This has remained the case under the government of Stephen Harper, despite years of promoting a defence strategy with "Canada First" in its title. An assessment of how to appropriately respond to international terrorism, combined with the heightened issues at the dawn of the 2010s of climate change in the North and US perceptions of the Canadian border, suggests the imperative of breaking this historical cycle. Certain aspects of the away game remain critical. But the overall requirement is to adjust the balance in measures at home and those abroad to best address the many dimensions of Canadian national security.

Notes

INTRODUCTION

1 Quoted in Buzan, *People, States and Fear,* 17.
2 This definition is adapted from Ullman, "Redefining Security," 133.
3 Dewitt and Leyton-Brown, eds, *Canada's International Security Policy,* 4.
4 R.B. Byers, quoted in ibid., 2.

CHAPTER ONE

1 Bland, ed., *Canada's National Defence,* vol. 1, 2.
2 Government of Canada, *Securing an Open Society.*
3 Dewitt and Leyton-Brown, "Canada's International Security Policy," 6.
4 Foreign Affairs and International Trade Canada, "Canada and the World."
5 Bland, ed., *Canada's National Defence,* 20.
6 Ibid., 3.
7 Lindsey, "Canada-U.S. Defence Relations in the Cold War," 62.
8 Bland, ed., *Canada's National Defence,* 4.
9 Ibid., 11.
10 Hampson, Hillmer, and Molot, "The Return to Continentalism in Canadian Foreign Policy," 5.
11 The North American Air Defence Agreement was approved by Parliament in 1958. In 1981 NORAD would be renamed the North American Aerospace Defense Command (see chapter 6).
12 Eayrs, *In Defence of Canada,* 183.
13 Lindsey, "Canada-U.S. Defence Relations," 69–70.

14 Government of Canada, *White Paper on Defence*, 5–6.
15 Ibid., 11.
16 Ibid., 15.
17 Ibid., 21.
18 Ibid., 22.
19 Ibid., 17.
20 Ibid., 19.
21 Gosselin, "Hellyer's Ghosts," 11.
22 What the 1964 *White Paper on Defence* called "combined operations" is what is referred to today as "joint operations" – the services of a single country working together. The contemporary meaning of "combined operations" is the ability of services from different countries to work together.
23 Government of Canada, *Defence in the 70s*, 25.
24 Ibid., 3.
25 Ibid., 8.
26 Ibid., 16.
27 Government of Canada, *Challenge and Commitment*, 47.
28 Ibid., 6.
29 Ibid., 52.
30 Government of Canada, *Defence Update 1988–89*, 2.
31 Government of Canada, *Canadian Defence Policy*, 1.
32 For a discussion of cooperative security, see Dewitt and Leyton-Brown, "Canada's International Security Policy," 14; and Dewitt, "Directions in Canada's International Security Policy."
33 Government of Canada, *1994 Defence White Paper*, 2.
34 Ibid., 41.
35 Cohen, *While Canada Slept*, 160–1.
36 Government of Canada, *Canada's International Policy Statement: Overview*, 17.
37 Ibid., 8.
38 Government of Canada, *Canada's International Policy Statement: Defence*, 2.
39 Government of Canada, *Canada's International Policy Statement: Overview*, 6–10.
40 Ibid., 26.
41 Government of Canada, *Canada's International Policy Statement: Defence*, 4.
42 Government of Canada, *Canada First Defence Strategy*, 3.
43 See Blanchfield, "MacKay Touts $60B for New Military Equipment."

CHAPTER TWO

1 Negroponte, *Annual Threat Assessment of the Director of National Intelligence*, 18 January 2007, 3.

2 Eggen, "Air Plot Said to Target Cities," A07.

3 Bruce Hoffman, as referenced in ibid.

4 National Intelligence Council, *National Intelligence Estimate*.

5 McConnell, *Annual Threat Assessment of the Director of National Intelligence*, 5.

6 Blair, *Annual Threat Assessment of the Intelligence Community*, 6.

7 National Intelligence Council, *National Intelligence Estimate*, http://www.dni.gov/press_releases/20070717_release.pdf (accessed August 2009).

8 As paraphrased in Carter, "U.S. Strikes More Precise on Al Qaeda."

9 Blair, *Annual Threat Assessment*, 4.

10 See "On the March, Not on the Run"; Hoffman, "Remember Al Qaeda? They're Baaack"; MacLeod, "Next Wave of 'Thrill Seeking' Terrorists"; Warrick, "U.S. Cites Big Gains against Al-Qaeda"; Bergen, "Al-Qaeda at 20 ... Dead or Alive?"; and "The Growing, and Mysterious, Irrelevance of al-Qaeda."

11 National Intelligence Council, *Global Trends 2025*, 69.

12 Ibid., 70.

13 Ibid., 69; Shane, "U.S. Report Predicts Decline for Al Qaeda."

14 National Intelligence Council, *National Intelligence Estimate*, http://www.dni.gov/press_releases/20070717_release.pdf (accessed August 2009).

15 McConnell, *Annual Threat Assessment*, 4.

16 Blair, *Annual Threat Assessment*, 4.

17 Ibid., 6.

18 Carter, "U.S. Strikes More Precise."

19 As quoted in Sullivan, "Homeland Security's 5–Year Threat Picture."

20 Falkenrath, "Confronting Nuclear, Biological and Chemical Terrorism," 44–5.

21 "The New Terrorism," 17.

22 Falkenrath, "Confronting Nuclear, Biological and Chemical Terrorism," 56.

23 Cronin, "Rethinking Sovereignty," 123.

24 Perry, "Preparing for the Next Attack," 32.

25 Negroponte, *Annual Threat Assessment of the Director of National Intelligence*, 2 February 2006, 4.

26 McConnell, *Annual Threat Assessment*, 7.

27 National Intelligence Council, *Global Trends 2025*, ix.

28 Commission on the Prevention of WMD Proliferation and Terrorism, *World at Risk*, xv.

29 Blair, *Annual Threat Assessment*, 21.

30 "U.S.-Born Militants Seen as Growing Terror Threat."

31 Malone and Deans, "Homegrown Terrorists Flying 'Under Radar' Says FBI Chief."

32 Bell, "Terrorists Made Plan in Toronto."

33 Phares, "Future Terrorism Mutant *Jihads*," 101.

34 Grier, "Al Qaeda Still a Threat to U.S., Intelligence Chiefs Say."

35 Skerry, "The American Exception"; "British Exceptionalism."

36 Blair, *Annual Threat Assessment*, 7.

37 Johnson, "FBI Director Warns of Terror Attacks on U.S. Cities."

38 National Security Council, *The National Security Strategy of the United States* (2002), 14.

39 Tenet, *The Worldwide Threat in 2003*.

40 Blair, *Annual Threat Assessment*, 25.

41 Gellman, "Qaeda Cyberterror Called Real Peril."

42 Blair, *Annual Threat Assessment*, 39.

43 Sullivan, "Homeland Security's 5-Year Threat Picture."

44 Blair, *Annual Threat Assessment*, 39.

45 Ibid., 38.

46 Office of the Secretary of Defense, *Annual Report to Congress*, 3–4. See also "A Chinese Ghost in the Machine?" 62.

47 Canadian Security Intelligence Service (CSIS), *2001 Public Report*.

48 Ken Calder, assistant deputy minister of policy, Department of National Defence, testimony before the Standing Senate Committee on National Security and Defence, 25 October 2004.

49 The other countries named were Britain, France, Italy, Germany, and Australia.

50 Sallot, "Canada Could Escape Attack, CSIS Says."

51 Jim Judd, director of CSIS, comments to students in a class on North American security and defence policy at Carleton University, Ottawa, 15 March 2006.

52 CSIS, *2007–2008 Public Report*, 11.

53 Goodspeed, "Canada Seen as Having 'Soft Belly,' Terror Expert Says."

54 Blair, *Annual Threat Assessment*, 5.

55 Chase, "US Terrorist Advisory Targets Canadian Flights."

56 Stephen Flynn, comments made at the conference "The Canada-US Partnership: Enhancing Our Common Security," Washington, DC, 14 March 2005.

57 Rudner, *Protecting Canada's Energy Infrastructure against Terrorism*, 6.

58 CSIS, *2006–2007 Public Report*, 4, 11.

59 An internal CSIS document, as quoted in Gordon, "Avoiding Iraq Has 'Mitigated' Terror Threat."

60 MacLeod, "Latest Terror Threats 'Scare Us.'"

61 CSIS, *2006–2007 Public Report*, 17.

62 Rennie Marcoux, assistant secretary to the Cabinet on security and intelligence, Privy Council Office, comments to students in a class on North American security and defence policy at Carleton University, Ottawa, 28 October 2008.

63 MacLeod, "Homegrown Terror Rising, RCMP Security Boss Warns."

64 CSIS, *2002 Public Report*.

65 Tenet, *Worldwide Threat in 2003*, https://www.cia.gov/news-information/speeches-testimony/2003/dci_speech_02112003.html (accessed August 2009).

66 Office of the Secretary of Defense, *Annual Report to Congress*, 20.

67 Tenet, *Worldwide Threat in 2003*, https://www.cia.gov/news-information/speeches-testimony/2003/dci_speech_02112003.html (accessed August 2009).

68 US Commission on Weak States and National Security, *On the Brink*, as discussed in Eizenstat and Porter, "Weak States Are a US Security Threat."

69 Rice and Patrick, *Index of State Weakness in the Developing World*.

70 "Failed States: Fixing a Broken World," 66.

71 Ibid., 67.

72 Stewart Patrick of the Council on Foreign Relations, as quoted in ibid.

73 Lewis, "The Roots of Muslim Rage," 49.

74 Doran, "Somebody Else's Civil War," 30.

75 "The Next War, They Say."

76 Hashim, "The World According to Usama Bin Laden."

77 Lewis, "License to Kill."

78 Posen, "The Struggle against Terrorism," 39.

79 Pape, "The Strategic Logic of Suicide Terrorism," 343.

80 Walt, "Beyond Bin Laden," 70.

81 Stern, "The Protean Enemy," 29.

82 Lewis, "Roots of Muslim Rage," 52.

83 Purdy, "Countering Terrorism," 23.

84 "Survey of Islam and the West."

85 Huntington, "The Clash of Civilizations?"

86 "Next War, They Say."

87 Rubin, "The Real Roots of Arab Anti-Americanism," 74.

88 "Survey of Islam and the West," 6.

89 National Commission on Terrorist Attacks upon the United States, *The 9/11 Commission Report*, 53.

90 Mousseau, "Market Civilization and Its Clash with Terror."

91 National Commission on Terrorist Attacks upon the United States, *9/11 Commission Report*, 48, 51.

92 Cronin, "Rethinking Sovereignty," 34, 38.

93 Mazarr, "Extremism, Terror, and the Future of Conflict."

94 Barnett, *The Pentagon's New Map*, 123.

95 Blair, *Annual Threat Assessment*, 20.

96 de Luce, "Iran Can Build Nuclear Bomb, Top US Military Officer Says."

97 Lederer, "US Sees Nuclear Network Threat."

98 Reid, "Forty States 'Have Nuclear Capability.'"

99 Garrett, "The Nightmare of Bioterrorism," 76.

100 Tenet, *Worldwide Threat in 2003*.

101 Falkenrath, "Confronting Nuclear, Biological and Chemical Terrorism," 54.

102 Barrett, "US Study."

103 Dareini, "Iran Launches Missile Threat."

104 Blair, *Annual Threat Assessment*, 19.

105 Hildreth, *North Korean Ballistic Missile Threat to the United States*, 2–3.

106 US national intelligence director, as quoted in Glionna, "Neighbors Angry about North Korea's Satellite Launch Plans."

107 Perry, "Preparing for the Next Attack," 33.

108 Harden, "North Korean Nuclear Blast Draws Global Condemnation."

109 Tenet, *Worldwide Threat – Converging Dangers in a Post 9/11 World*.

110 Gutkin, "Terrorists Pursuing WMD Capability."

111 Stern, "The Protean Enemy."

112 Linzer, "Nuclear Capabilities May Elude Terrorists, Experts Say," A01.

113 Gertz, "'Eroded' Al Qaeda Still a Threat."

114 Smith, "Seizures of Radioactive Materials Fuel 'Dirty Bomb' Fears."

115 Gardham, "Muslim Was Planning Dirty Bomb Attack in UK."

116 Carter, "Al Qaeda Eyes Bio Attack from Mexico."

117 "Al Qaeda Claims to Have Bought Nuclear Weapons"; Bronskill, "Spy Agency Sure Bin Laden Intent on Going Nuclear."

118 Mintz, "US Officials Warn of New Tactics by Al Qaeda."

119 Bronskill, "Spy Agency Sure."

120 Innes, "Terrorists 'Would Use WMD If They Could.'"

121 Quoted in "Warning about WMD."

122 Seper, "FBI Director Predicts Terrorists Will Acquire Nukes."

123 Sokolski, "Rethinking Bio-chemical Dangers."

124 Parformak and Frittelli, *Maritime Security*, 15–16.

125 Betts, "The New Threat of Mass Destruction," 32.

126 CSIS, *2007–2008 Public Report*, 16.

127 Simon, "The New Terrorism," 21.

CHAPTER THREE

1 Government of the United States, *Quadrennial Defense Review* (1997), http://www.fas.org/man/docs/qdr/sec2.html (accessed August 2009).

2 Ibid.

3 Ibid., http://www.fas.org/man/docs/qdr/sec3.html (accessed August 2009).

4 National Defense Panel, *Transforming Defense*, i, ii.

5 Ibid., ii.

6 National Security Council, *National Security Strategy for a New Century*, iv.

7 U.S. Commission on National Security/21st Century, *New World Coming*, 4, emphasis added.

8 U.S. Commission on National Security/21st Century, *Seeking a National Strategy*, 5.

9 U.S. Commission on National Security/21st Century, *Road Map for National Security*, viii, emphasis in original.

10 Government of the United States, *Quadrennial Defense Review* (2001), 11.

11 Ibid., 17.

12 Ibid., 18.

13 National Security Council, *The National Security Strategy of the United States* (2002), cover letter.

14 Ibid., 15. Against this argument, the case has been made that there is no evidence that rogue states cannot be deterred from employing WMD through credible threats of unacceptable retaliation. See Record, *Bounding the Global War on Terrorism*, 42.

15 National Security Council, *National Security Strategy of the United States* (2002), cover letter.

16 High-Level Panel on Threats, Challenges and Change, *A More Secure World*, 54.

17 International law on the pre-emptive use of military force is often traced to the *Caroline* case of 1837, in which it was established that permissible pre-emptive self-defence requires the state to demonstrate that the "necessity of self-defence is instant [and] overwhelming, leaving no choice of means, and no moment of deliberation"; see Secretary of State Daniel Webster, quoted in Arend, "International Law and the Preemptive Use of Military Force," 91.

18 High-Level Panel on Threats, Challenges and Change, *More Secure World*, 57–8.

19 Evans, "When Is It Right to Fight?" 76–7.

20 United Nations General Assembly, *World Summit Outcome*, para. 79.

21 National Security Council, *National Security Strategy of the United States* (2006), 23, emphasis added.

22 Ibid., 44.

23 Most of this paragraph is taken from Sloan, *Military Transformation and Modern Warfare*, 42.

24 This section is adapted from ibid., 42–4.

25 Government of the United States, *Quadrennial Defense Review* (2006), 22.

26 Ibid., 24.

27 Ibid., 25.

28 Ibid., 34.

29 Posen, "The Struggle against Terrorism," 45.

CHAPTER FOUR

1 Office of Homeland Security, *National Strategy for Homeland Security* (2002), 3.

2 Babington, "Congress Votes to Renew Patriot Act, with Changes."

3 Krim, "Cyber-Security to Get Higher Profile Leader."

4 Nakashima, "Obama Set to Create a Cybersecurity Czar with Broad Mandate."

5 Segal, "After So Much Spent on Security, Are We Secure Yet?"

6 Marks, "Hard Work Still ahead for Homeland."

7 As quoted in "Imagining Something Much Worse than London," 27.

8 Betts, "Fixing Intelligence," 54.

9 International Institute for Strategic Studies, "US Intelligence Reform."

10 The US intelligence community comprises five agencies in their entirety, as well as the intelligence components of eleven other departments or agencies, for a total of sixteen US government agencies involved in intelligence-gathering. The former include the CIA, Defense Intelligence Agency, National Geospatial-Intelligence Agency, National Reconnaissance Office, and National Security Agency – all of which are part of the DOD, with the exception of the CIA. The latter include army, navy, air force, Marine Corps, and Coast Guard intelligence; parts of the Departments of Energy, Homeland Security, State, Treasury, and Justice (the FBI); and the (relatively) newly created National Counterterrorism Office in the White House. The director of central intelligence had a coordinating role over all intelligence agencies and was also director of one of the agencies, the CIA.

11 Matthews, "Momentum Builds for Single US Intel Chief."

12 National Commission on Terrorist Attacks upon the United States, *The 9/11 Commission Report*, 403, 411–12.

13 Executive Order 13354 of 27 August 2004.

14 This statement, as well as the next two sentences, are taken from Elinor Sloan, "Continental and Homeland Security," 194–5.

15 Author discussion with NSA board member during the 2008 NORTHCOM Civic Leader Tour, 9–13 June 2008.

16 Shane, "In New Job, Spymaster Draws Bipartisan Criticism," 1.

17 Risen, "Ex-government Officials Recommend Intelligence Overhaul."

18 "Cutting through the Red Tape."

19 Chicago Law Professor Richard Posner, as quoted in Boswell, "CSIS a Model for US Spies, Expert Argues."

20 National Commission on Terrorist Attacks upon the United States, *9/11 Commission Report*, 423–4.

21 "US Intelligence Community in Poll Position."

22 Eggen, "FBI Applies New Rules to Surveillance."

23 Seper, "FBI 'Reprioritized' after '01 Terror Attacks, Report Says."

24 Office of Homeland Security, *National Strategy for Homeland Security* (2002), ix.

25 Homeland Security Council, *National Strategy for Homeland Security* (2007), 5.

26 Shenon, "US to Put Inspectors at Muslim Ports."

27 Fife, "Terrorism Draws Us Closer to US."

28 Bailey et al., "Sticky Issues for Coast Guard."

29 "Imagining Something Much Worse than London," 28.

30 Hsu and Branigin, "Congress Passes Bill to Bolster Homeland Security."

31 Nickerson, "US-Canada Security Brings Frustration to Both Sides of Border."

32 White, "Unmanned Drone Prowls over the Lonely Prairie."

33 Matthews, "US Lawmakers Push 'Prompt Global Strike.'"

34 Mintz, "Bioterrorism Procedures Are Outlined."

35 Taylor and Ramstack, "Ridge Adds 5,000 Air Marshals to Help Get 'Surge Capacity.'"

36 Hall, "Passenger Jets Get Anti-Missile Devices."

37 http://www.ocipep.gc.ca (accessed December 2004; website no longer available).

38 http://www.publicsafety.gc.ca (accessed April 2009).

39 Ibid.

40 Ibid.

41 Duffy, "Canada Developing Strategy to Protect against Foreign Hackers."

42 This refers to "measures that eliminate or reduce the impacts or risks of hazards through proactive measures taken before an emergency or disaster occurs"; see http://www.publicsafety.gc.ca (accessed April 2009).

43 http://www.publicsafety.gc.ca (accessed April 2009).

44 Rudner, "Contemporary Threats, Future Tasks," 141–2.

45 Hurst, "Canada Listens to World as Partner in Spy System."

46 Canadian Security Intelligence Service, *2007–2008 Public Report*, 24. The report was tabled in Parliament in March 2009.

47 Ibid.

48 Ibid., 25.

49 Cooper, *A Foreign Intelligence Service for Canada*, 55.

50 Standing Committee on National Defence and Veterans Affairs, *Facing Our Responsibilities*, 21.

51 Conservative Party of Canada, *Stand Up for Canada*, 26.

52 Mayeda, "Tories Drop Plan to Build Foreign Spy Agency"; Galloway, "No New Agency for Foreign Intelligence, Top Spy Says."

53 Williamson, "1 in 5 Border Guards Fails Shooting Lessons."

54 Margaret Bloodworth, then deputy minister of PSEPC, comments to students in a class on North American security and defence policy at Carleton University, Ottawa, 8 March 2005.

55 Jon Allen, Embassy of Canada in the United States, comments made at the conference "The Canada-US Partnership: Enhancing Our Common Security," Washington, DC, 14 March 2005.

56 "A Fence in the North, Too," 40.

57 Ward Elcock, comments to students in a class on North American security and defence policy at Carleton University, Ottawa, 24 February 2004.

58 Security and Prosperity Partnership of North America, *Report to Leaders*.

59 Passport Canada, *A Year to Remember*, 16.

60 Auditor General of Canada, *National Security*, para. 3.149.

61 Standing Senate Committee on National Security and Defence, *Canadian Security Guide Book: Airports*, 9; Standing Senate Committee on National Security and Defence, *Canadian Security Guide Book: Seaports*, 18.

62 Defence Minister Peter MacKay, as paraphrased in "Ports at Risk for Smuggled 'Dirty Bombs.'"

63 Denis Lefebvre, vice president, Canada Border Services Agency, testimony before the Standing Senate Committee on National Security and Defence, 7 February 2005.

64 Standing Senate Committee on National Security and Defence, *Canadian Security Guide Book: Seaports*, 29–32. See also Bronskill, "Ports Deemed Soft Touch for Terrorists."

65 Canada Border Services Agency, *Departmental Performance Report to the Treasury Board Secretariat, 2007–2008*.

66 See Standing Senate Committee on National Security and Defence, *Canadian Security Guide Book: Seaports*.

67 Tibbetts, "Our Border 'Not a Conduit for Terrorists.'"

68 See Rekai, *United States and Canadian Immigration Policies*.

69 MacLeod, "US Revives Cross-Border Talk."

70 "A Haven for Villains," 48.

71 As quoted in Alberts, "Napolitano Chided for Linking Canada to 9/11."

72 Ronald Bilodeau, security and intelligence coordinator, Privy Council Office, testimony before the Standing Senate Committee on National Security and Defence, 24 February 2003.

73 Robert Wright, national security advisor, testimony before the Standing Senate Committee on National Security and Defence, 23 February 2004.

74 "Haven for Villians," 48.

75 http://www.cbsa.gc.ca (accessed April 2009).

76 Ibid.

77 Manley, Aspe, and Weld, *Creating a North American Community*, 10.

78 Rennie Marcoux, assistant secretary to the Cabinet on security and intelligence, Privy Council Office, comments to students in a class on North American security and defence policy at Carleton University, Ottawa, 28 October 2008.

79 Marcoux, comments to students in a class on North American security and defence policy at Carleton University, Ottawa, 13 March 2008.

80 Marcoux, comments to students in a class on North American security and defence policy at Carleton University, Ottawa, 28 October 2008.

81 Robert Wright, national security adviser, comments to students in a class on North American security and defence policy at Carleton University, Ottawa, 5 April 2005.

82 Ljunggren, "Ottawa Vows to Do More to Prevent Attacks on US."

CHAPTER FIVE

1 "Joint" in military terminology means comprising the navy, army, and air force of a single country; "combined" means comprising the navy, army, and/or air force of two or more countries.

2 The functional commands are Joint Forces Command, Special Operations Command, Transportation Command, and Strategic Command. The geographic commands are Northern Command, Southern Command, European Command, Africa Command, Pacific Command, and Central Command.

3 General Gene Renuart, CINC NORTHCOM, comments to participants on the 2008 NORTHCOM Civic Leader Tour, 10 June 2008.

4 Harrington, "US Pledges More Troops to Northcom."

5 Hsu and Tyson, "Pentagon to Detail Troops to Bolster Domestic Security."

6 General Gene Renuart, CINC NORTHCOM, comments to participants on the 2008 NORTHCOM Civic Leader Tour, 10 June 2008.

7 Literally, "the power or authority of the county." See Felicetti and Luce, "The *Posse Comitatus Act*," 95.

8 Carafano, *Citizen-Soldiers and Homeland Security*, 8.

9 http://www.northcom.mil (accessed April 2009).

10 Felicetti and Luce, "*Posse Comitatus Act*," 94.

11 Boyer, "Troops for Border Sought."

12 Office of Homeland Security, *National Strategy for Homeland Security* (2002), 48.

13 Government of the United States, *Quadrennial Defense Review* (2006), 26.

14 Sappenfield, "Disaster Relief? Call in the Marines."

15 Hsu and Tyson, "Pentagon to Detail Troops."

16 http://www.canadacom.forces.gc.ca (accessed April 2009).

17 This command is also part of the NORAD structure and therefore is "combined" in the sense that it involves the militaries of both the United States and Canada.

18 Combined Force Air Component Command, briefing to members of the NORAD Familiarization Visit, Winnipeg, Manitoba, 7 October 2008.

19 Government of Canada, *Canada's International Policy Statement: Defence*, 18.

20 This paragraph is taken from Sloan, "Defence and Security."

21 Author impression of various presentations and comments by General Gene Renuart, CINC NORTHCOM, during the 2008 NORTHCOM Civic Leader Tour, 9–13 June 2008.

22 Author interview with J. Scott Broughton, assistant deputy minister of emergency management and national security, Public Safety Canada, Ottawa, 5 May 2008.

23 Navy captain Kevin Greenwood, deputy chief of staff, Canada Command, presentation to a class on North American security and defence policy, Carleton University, Ottawa, 4 November 2008.

24 Much of this paragraph is taken from Sloan, "Defence and Security."

25 Standing Senate Committee on National Security and Defence, *Canadian Security and Military Preparedness*, 27, 30.

26 Morton, "'No More Disagreeable or Onerous Duty,'" 139–40.

27 David Price, parliamentary secretary to then defence minster David Pratt, as paraphrased in Wattie, "Reservists Touted as Terrorism Fighters."

28 Major General Edward Fitch, as paraphrased in Slobodian, "General Sees Reserve Force as Vital for Terror Response."

29 Standing Senate Committee on National Security and Defence, *Canadian Security and Military Preparedness*, 97.

30 Freeman, "Hillier Cool to Ottawa's Reserve Plan."

31 Brigadier General Jean Collin, commander of the army in Ontario, as quoted in Humphreys, "Military Revamps Domestic Defence."

32 See Falkenrath, "Confronting Nuclear, Biological and Chemical Terrorism."

33 Pugliese, "Navy Shops around for New Midsized Patrol Vessels."

34 "Ottawa to Revive Scrapped High-Tech Coastal Radar."

35 Humphreys, "Canada's Troops to Reclaim Arctic."

36 Forcier, "Interview."

37 Pugliese, "Canada to Try uavs in Arctic."

38 McLean, "Canada's Next Drones Will Carry Bombs."

39 Pugliese, "Canada Plans Long-Range uav Fleet."

40 Pugliese, "Canada to Launch Design Work on Radarsat," 10.

41 Tim Meisner, director of policy, Canadian Coast Guard, testimony before the Standing Senate Committee on National Security and Defence, 17 February 2003.

42 Colonel Rick Williams, director, Western Hemisphere Policy, Department of National Defence, testimony before the Standing Senate Committee on National Security and Defence, 17 March 2003.

43 Pugliese, "Canada to Establish Marine Security Centres," 18.

44 Lambie, "Midshore Coast Guard Patrol Vessels Back on Ottawa Radar."

45 Paraskevas, "Make Coast Guard an Armed Military Force, Committee Urges."

46 See Standing Senate Committee on National Security and Defence, *The Longest Under-Defended Borders in the World.*

47 Ljunggren, "Arctic Summer Ice Could Vanish by 2013, Expert Says"; Revkin, "The Arctic's Alarming Sea Change."

48 Brewster, "Flying Flag in the Arctic Could Cost Forces $843 Million a Year."

49 Borgerson, "Arctic Meltdown," 63.

50 VanderKlippe, "Arctic a Potential Terror Target."

51 Ibid.

52 Huebert, "Renaissance in Canadian Arctic Security?" 28.

53 Government of Canada, *Canada's International Policy Statement: Defence,* 7.

54 See Griffiths, "The Shipping News."

55 Ljunggren, "Ships to Shun Northwest Passage."

56 See Huebert, "The Shipping News Part II."

57 Borgerson, "Arctic Meltdown," 70.

58 Ivison, "Arctic Hot in More Ways Than One."

59 President of the United States, *National Security Presidential Directive 66,* section iii, para. B5.

60 McCarthy, "Arctic Contains 13% of Remaining Oil."

61 Spotts, "US Coast Guard Joins in Arctic Oil Rush."

62 Center for Naval Analysis, *National Security and the Threat of Climate Change,* 38.

63 Borgeron, "Arctic Meltdown," 65.

64 Boswell, "eu Report Warns of Trouble over Arctic Resources."

65 Boswell, "NATO Cautions against Division over Arctic."
66 Boswell, "Arctic Conflict Possible, Russian Report Says."
67 Alberts, "US Report Raises Alarm over Arctic Defence as Ice Melts."
68 Senator William Rompkey, chairman, Standing Senate Committee on Fisheries and Oceans, as quoted in Weber, "Arm Icebreakers, Beef Up Rangers to Assert Canadian Control of Arctic."
69 Ivison, "Arctic Hot."
70 "Russia Dedicates Force to Arctic."
71 O'Dwyer, "NATO's High North Ambitions May Have Russian Input."
72 Maher, "Little News Not Good News for Region."
73 Government of Canada, "Backgrounder – Expanding Canadian Forces Operations in the Arctic."
74 Pugliese, "Reserve Units to Form Core of New Arctic Force."
75 By contrast, on 11 September 2001, Federal Aviation Administration flight controllers took fifteen minutes to notify NORAD that they thought a flight out of Boston had been hijacked, leaving NORAD only six minutes to respond before the plane hit the World Trade Center.
76 Harrold, "Canada to Respond Tit for Tat to Russian Jet Fighter."
77 Lieutenant General Charles Bouchard, deputy commander, NORAD, presentation to students in a class on North American security and defence policy, Carleton University, Ottawa, 25 November 2008.
78 Ibid.
79 Lindsey, "Potential Contributions by the Canadian Armed Forces to the Defence of North America against Terrorism," 326–7.
80 "Breakthrough Technology Brings Air Traffic Surveillance to Hudson Bay."
81 National Commission on Terrorist Attacks upon the United States, *The 9/11 Commission Report*, 16, 22.
82 Major General Marcel Duval, commander, 1 Canadian Air Division, presentation to participants on the NORAD Familiarization Visit, Winnipeg, Manitoba, 7 October 2008.
83 Lindsey, "Canada, North American Security, and NORAD," 3.
84 Major General Marcel Duval, commander, 1 Canadian Air Division, presentation to participants on the NORAD Familiarization Visit, Winnipeg, Manitoba, 7 October 2008.
85 Government of Canada, *Canada's International Policy Statement: Defence*, 19.
86 Pugliese, "Canada Buys Radars, Puts Portable Surveillance on Hold," 22.
87 Graham, "U.S. Urged to Broaden Defense against Terrorist Missiles."

88 Briefing to members of the 2008 NORTHCOM Civic Leader Tour by officials at the Space and Naval Warfare Systems Center, Charleston, South Carolina, 12 June 2008.

89 Mason, *Canadian Defense Priorities*, 4.

90 Tirpak, "The Space Based Radar Plan."

91 Pugliese, "Pentagon Looks to Buy Canadian Spy Satellite Technology."

92 Auditor General of Canada, "National Defence – Upgrading the CF-18 Fighter Aircraft," 7.

93 Lieutenant General Ken Pennie, chief of the air staff, comments made at the Centre for Security and Defence Studies, Carleton University, Ottawa, 29 November 2004.

94 Major General Marcel Duval, commander, 1 Canadian Air Division, presentation to participants on the NORAD Familiarization Visit, Winnipeg, Manitoba, 7 October 2008.

95 Lindsey, "Potential Contributions," 316.

96 Pugliese, "Canadian Military Weighs Future of ADATS," 16.

97 Agreement between the Government of Canada and the Government of the United States of America on the North American Aerospace Defense Command, May 2006, para. 1.

98 Author discussion with NORTHCOM officials during the NORAD Familiarization Visit, Colorado Springs, 6 October 2008.

99 See, for example, Orvik, "Canadian Security and Defence against Help."

100 Huebert, "Shipping News Part II," 297.

CHAPTER SIX

1 Center for Defense Information, *National Missile Defence*, 2.

2 Cox, "Canada and Ballistic Missile Defence," 242.

3 This means that the satellites stay fixed with respect to their location above Earth.

4 Lindsey, "Potential Contributions by the Canadian Armed Forces to the Defence of North America against Terrorism," 313.

5 Cox, "Canada and Ballistic Missile Defence," 244.

6 Maskell, "Sapphire: Canada's Answer to Space-Based Surveillance of Orbital Objects."

7 Cox, "Canada and Ballistic Missile Defence," 247.

8 Sokolsky, "The Bilateral Defence Relationship with the United States," 179.

9 As quoted in Murray, "NORAD and US Nuclear Operations," 227–8.

10 Sokolsky, "Bilateral Defence Relationship," 183–4.
11 Fergusson, "National Missile Defense, Homeland Defense, and Outer Space," 235.
12 "Airborne Laser Begins Final Proof-of-Concept Test."
13 "President Obama Outlines His Plan for Missile Defense."
14 Shanker, "Missile Defense System Is Up and Running, Military Says."
15 Perry, "Preparing for the Next Attack," 39.
16 Graham, "Missile Defense Agency Faulted on Testing and Accountability."
17 "President Obama Outlines His Plan for Missile Defense."
18 Sherman, "US Navy's Role Soars," 1.
19 Government of Canada, 1994 Defence White Paper, 25.
20 Multiple Independently Targetable Reentry Vehicle, or MIRVed, missiles.
21 Treaty on Principles Governing the Activities of States in the Exploration and Use of Outer Space, Including the Moon and Other Celestial Bodies, January 1967, article 4.
22 Ibid., articles 3 and 4.
23 Jockel, Four US Military Commands, 4–5.
24 Conversations with CF members posted to NORAD headquarters, during the NORAD Familiarization Visit, Colorado Springs, 6 October 2008.
25 For example, Defence Minister Bill Graham as paraphrased in Ward, "Canada-US Amend Defence Pact to Keep Missile Detection within NORAD."
26 Jockel, "A Strong Friend Is a Good Defence."
27 General Gene Renuart, commander of NORTHCOM, as quoted in Blanchfield, "Canada Kept in Loop at NORAD about All Missile Threats."
28 Author conversation with General Gene Renuart, commander of NORTHCOM, during the 2008 NORTHCOM Civic Leader Tour, 10 June 2008.
29 General Renuart, as quoted in Blanchfield, "Canada Kept in Loop."
30 Author conversation with General Renuart, 10 June 2008.
31 Lieutenant General (retired) George MacDonald, former deputy commander of NORAD, as quoted in Thorne, "NORAD Role Could Be Altered."
32 Lieutenant General Charles Bouchard, deputy commander of NORAD, presentation to students in a class on North American security and defence policy, Carleton University, Ottawa, 25 November 2008.
33 Baker, "Missile Defense Endorsed by NATO."

CHAPTER SEVEN

1 Standing Committee on National Defence and Veterans Affairs, *Facing Our Responsibilities*, 23.

2 See, for example, "Define Canada's Global Agenda"; and "Where Paul Martin Should Lead Canada."

3 Governor General of Canada, *Speech from the Throne*, http://pco-bcp. gc.ca/index.asp?lang=eng&page=information&sub=publications& doc=sft-ddt/2004_1-eng.htm (accessed August 2009).

4 Government of Canada, *Canada First Defence Strategy*, 1.

5 Canadian Security Intelligence Service (CSIS), *2001 Public Report*, http://www.csis-scrs.gc.ca/pblctns/nnlrprt/2001/rprt2001-eng.asp (accessed August 2009).

6 CSIS, *2007–2008 Public Report*, 10.

7 For a discussion of US military capabilities for warfighting, stabilization, and counterinsurgency operations, see Sloan, *Military Transformation and Modern Warfare*, chs 2 and 3.

8 See Cordesman, *US Airpower in Iraq and Afghanistan*; and Hanley, "Airpower Bombings Double in Iraq from 2006."

9 Sloan, *Military Transformation and Modern Warfare*, 65.

10 Sloan, *Military Transformation: Key Aspects and Canadian Approaches*, 8.

11 McLean, "Canada's Next Drones Will Carry Bombs."

12 Murray and Scales Jr, *The Iraq War*, 243.

13 Sloan, *Military Transformation: Key Aspects*, 9.

14 Pugliese, "Canada Takes Modular Approach to Future Vessels," 14.

15 British Ministry of Defence, *The Strategic Defence Review*, 16.

16 Sloan, *Military Transformation: Key Aspects*, 6.

17 Independent Panel on Canada's Future Role in Afghanistan, *Report of the Independent Panel on Canada's Future Role in Afghanistan*, 38.

18 Horn, "When Cultures Collide," 3.

19 Scarborough, "Special Ops Steal Show as Successes Mount in Iraq."

20 Sloan, *Military Transformation: Key Aspects*, 2.

21 As quoted in Pugliese, "Canada Expects C-130 to Boost Air Mobility," 14.

22 Smith, "Conquering Canadians Take Stock."

23 Brewster, "DND Looks at Buying Light Tanks to Replace Battered Fleet."

24 Pugliese, "Armoured Vehicles Hit Their Limits."

25 Independent Panel on Canada's Future Role in Afghanistan, *Report*, 38.

26 Sallot, "Graham Defends Joining US Arms Interception Plan."

27 As quoted in Fisher, "Canadian Warships Hunt Modern-Day Pirates."

28 Fisher, "Canadian Warships."

29 Vickers, "LCS Could Bolster Defense against Terror."

30 Vice Admiral Drew Robertson, as quoted in Pugliese, "Canadian Navy Needs More Procurement Specialists," 21.

31 Pugliese, "Need for Supply Ships Strains Canada's Navy, Budget."

32 Richard Gimblett, testimony before the Standing Senate Committee on National Security and Defence, Ottawa, 21 February 2005.

33 Naval officers aboard HMCS *Athabaskan* on exercise off Jacksonville, Florida, conversations with the author, 18–21 February 2005.

34 Binnendijk and Johnson, eds, *Transforming for Stabilization and Reconstruction Operations*, 98.

35 Murray and Scales Jr, *Iraq War*, 97.

36 Sloan, *Military Transformation: Key Aspects*, 9–10.

37 Binnendijk and Johnson, eds, *Transforming for Stabilization*, 8.

38 Graham, "U.S. Directive Prioritizes Post-Conflict Stability," 21, as quoted in Sloan, *Military Transformation and Modern Warfare*, 32.

39 Boot, "The Struggle to Transform the Military," 108, as quoted in Sloan, *Military Transformation and Modern Warfare*, 32.

40 Government of the United States, *Field Manual 3–24, Counterinsurgency*, 1–1.

41 Schultz Jr and Dew, "Counterinsurgency, by the Book."

42 Chief of the Land Staff, *B-GL-323-004/FP-003, Counterinsurgency Operations*, ch. 1, para. 19.

43 Ibid., ch. 1, para. 30.

44 Brewster, "General Says New Army Manual Will Shape the Future of Afghan War."

45 Chief of the Land Staff, *B-GL-323-004/FP-003*, ch. 6, para. 172.

46 Pugliese, "Canada Anticipates Larger Counterinsurgency Role for Armor," 18.

47 Brewster, "General Says."

48 Chief of the Land Staff, *B-GL-323-004/FP-003*, ch. 5, para. 9.

49 Ibid., ch. 5, para. 67.

CHAPTER EIGHT

1 Government of Canada, *Securing an Open Society*, 2.

2 Simon, "The New Terrorism," 22.

3 Falkenrath, "Confronting Nuclear, Biological and Chemical Terrorism," 56.

4 Bowers, "Terror Still a No-Show on US Soil."

5 Johnston and Stout, "Bin Laden Is Said to be Organizing for a US Attack."

6 Perry, "Preparing for the Next Attack," 36.

7 Betts, "Fixing Intelligence," 44.

8 Cronin, "Rethinking Sovereignty," 134.

9 Crocker, "Engaging Failed States," 41.

10 Glaser and Kaufmann, "What Is the Offense-Defense Balance and Can We Measure It?" 64.

11 Van Evera, *Causes of War*, 163.

12 Directorate of Maritime Strategy, unpublished document produced for the Canadian Navy Strategic Advisory Group, 1.

13 Parachini, "Putting WMD Terrorism into Perspective," 40.

14 Ellis, "The Best Defense," 119.

15 Levy, "The Offensive/Defensive Balance of Military Technology," 225.

16 Perry, "Preparing for the Next Attack," 35.

17 Flynn, "The Neglected Home Front," 21.

18 Simon, "New Terrorism," 22.

19 Bowers, "Terror Still a No-Show."

20 Posen, "The Struggle against Terrorism," 46.

21 See Drogin, "U.S. Gets Tough on Canadian Border."

22 Directorate of Maritime Strategy, unpublished document, 12.

Bibliography

Agreement between the Government of Canada and the Government of the United States of America on the North American Aerospace Defense Command, May 2006.

"Airborne Laser Begins Final Proof-of-Concept Test." *Missile Defense Agency News Release*, 24 April 2009.

Alberts, Sheldon. "Napolitano Chided for Linking Canada to 9/11." *Ottawa Citizen*, 22 April 2009.

– "US Report Raises Alarm over Arctic Defence as Ice Melts." *Ottawa Citizen*, 11 May 2007.

"Al Qaeda Claims to Have Bought Nuclear Weapons." *CTV News*, 20 March 2004.

Arend, Anthony Clark. "International Law and the Preemptive Use of Military Force." *Washington Quarterly* 26, no. 2 (2003).

Auditor General of Canada. "National Defence – Upgrading the CF-18 Fighter Aircraft." In *Report of the Auditor General of Canada*. Ottawa: Government of Canada, November 2004.

– *National Security: The 2001 Anti-terrorism Initiative*. Ottawa: Government of Canada, March 2004.

Babington, Charles. "Congress Votes to Renew Patriot Act, with Changes." *Washington Post*, 8 March 2006.

Bailey, Eric, et al. "Sticky Issues for Coast Guard." *Los Angeles Times*, 13 November 2007.

Baker, Peter. "Missile Defense Endorsed by NATO." *Washington Post*, 4 April 2008.

Barnett, Thomas P.M. *The Pentagon's New Map: War and Peace in the Twenty-first Century*. New York: G.P. Putnam's Sons, 2004.

Barrett, Randy. "US Study: Growing Threat from Ballistic Missiles." *Defense News*, 13 October 2003.

Bell, Stewart. "Terrorists Made Plan in Toronto." *National Post*, 22 April 2006.

Bergen, Peter. "Al-Qaeda at 20 ... Dead or Alive?" *Washington Post*, 17 August 2008.

Betts, Richard K. "Fixing Intelligence." *Foreign Affairs* 81, no. 1 (2002).

– "The New Threat of Mass Destruction." *Foreign Affairs* 77, no. 1 (1998).

Binnendijk, Hans, and Stuart Johnson, eds. *Transforming for Stabilization and Reconstruction Operations*. Washington, DC: National Defense University, 2003.

Blair, Denis C. *Annual Threat Assessment of the Intelligence Community*. Testimony before the Senate Select Committee on Intelligence, 12 February 2009.

Blanchfield, Mike. "Canada Kept in Loop at NORAD about All Missile Threats." *Ottawa Citizen*, 10 April 2008.

– "MacKay Touts $60B for New Military Equipment." *Ottawa Citizen*, 28 May 2009.

Bland, Douglas L., ed. *Canada's National Defence*. Vol. 1, *Defence Policy*. Kingston, ON: School of Policy Studies, 1997.

Boot, Max. "The Struggle to Transform the Military." *Foreign Affairs* 84, no. 2 (March-April 2005).

Borgerson, Scott G. "Arctic Meltdown: The Economic and Security Implications of Global Warming." *Foreign Affairs* 87, no. 2 (March-April 2008).

Boswell, Randy. "Arctic Conflict Possible, Russian Report Says." *Ottawa Citizen*, 14 May 2009.

– "CSIS a Model for US Spies, Expert Argues." *Ottawa Citizen*, 1 September 2005.

– "EU Report Warns of Trouble over Arctic Resources." *Ottawa Citizen*, 11 March 2008.

– "NATO Cautions against Division over Arctic." *Ottawa Citizen*, 30 January 2009.

Bowers, Faye. "Terror Still a No-Show on US Soil." *Christian Science Monitor*, 5 January 2004.

Boyer, Dave. "Troops for Border Sought." *Washington Times*, 19 June 2002.

"Breakthrough Technology Brings Air Traffic Surveillance to Hudson Bay." *Nav Canada News Release*, 22 January 2009.

Brewster, Murray. "DND Looks at Buying Light Tanks to Replace Battered Fleet." *Canadian Press*, 26 May 2009.

- "Flying Flag in the Arctic Could Cost Forces $843 Million a Year: Documents." *Winnipeg Free Press*, 22 January 2009.
- "General Says New Army Manual Will Shape the Future of Afghan War." *Canadian Press*, 1 March 2009.

"British Exceptionalism: After the Terror Plot." *Economist*, 19 August 2006.

British Ministry of Defence. *The Strategic Defence Review: A New Chapter*. London, UK: British Ministry of Defence, July 2002.

Bronskill, Jim. "Ports Deemed Soft Touch for Terrorists." *Halifax Chronicle Herald*, 23 March 2007.
- "Spy Agency Sure Bin Laden Intent on Going Nuclear." *Halifax Herald*, 4 November 2004.

Buzan, Barry. *People, States and Fear: An Agenda for International Security Studies in the Post–Cold War Era*. Boulder, CO: Lynne Rienner, 1991.

Canada Border Services Agency. *Departmental Performance Report to the Treasury Board Secretariat, 2007–2008*. http://www.tbs-sct.gc.ca (accessed April 2009).

Canadian Security Intelligence Service (CSIS). *2001 Public Report*. Ottawa: CSIS, 2002.
- *2002 Public Report*. Ottawa: CSIS, 2003.
- *2006–2007 Public Report*. Ottawa: CSIS, 2008.
- *2007–2008 Public Report*. Ottawa: CSIS, 2009.

Carafano, Jay. *Citizen-Soldiers and Homeland Security: A Strategic Assessment*. Arlington, VA: Lexington Institute, March 2004.

Carter, Sara A. "Al Qaeda Eyes Bio Attack from Mexico." *Washington Times*, 3 June 2009.
- "U.S. Strikes More Precise on Al Qaeda." *Washington Times*, 16 January 2009.

Center for Defense Information. *National Missile Defence: What Does It All Mean?* Washington, DC: Center for Defense Information, September 2000.

Center for Naval Analysis. *National Security and the Threat of Climate Change*. Washington, DC: Center for Naval Analysis, 2007.

Chase, Steven. "US Terrorist Advisory Targets Canadian Flights." *Globe and Mail*, 5 September 2003.

Chief of the Land Staff. *B-GL-323-004/FP-003, Counterinsurgency Operations*. Kingston, ON: Army Publishing Office, 2007.

"A Chinese Ghost in the Machine?" *Economist*, 4 April 2009.

Cohen, Andrew. *While Canada Slept: How We Lost Our Place in the World*. Toronto: McClelland and Stewart, 2003.

Commission on the Prevention of WMD Proliferation and Terrorism. *World at Risk*. New York: Vintage Books, 2008.

Conservative Party of Canada. *Stand Up for Canada*. Federal election platform of 2006. Ottawa: Conservative Party of Canada, 2006.

Cooper, Barry. *A Foreign Intelligence Service for Canada*. Calgary: Canadian Defence and Foreign Affairs Institute, 2007.

Cordesman, Anthony H. *US Airpower in Iraq and Afghanistan: 2004–2007*. Washington, DC: Center for Strategic and International Studies, December 2007.

Cox, David. "Canada and Ballistic Missile Defence." In Joel J. Sokolsky and Joseph T. Jockel, eds, *Fifty Years of Canada-United States Security Cooperation*. Lewiston, NY: Edwin Meller Press, 1992.

Crocker, Chester A. "Engaging Failed States." *Foreign Affairs* 82, no. 5 (2003).

Cronin, Audrey Kurth. "Rethinking Sovereignty: American Grand Strategy in the Age of Terrorism." *Survival* 44, no. 2 (2002).

"Cutting through the Red Tape: US Intelligence Reform." *Jane's Defence Weekly*, 23 October 2002.

Dareini, Ali Akbar. "Iran Launches Missile Threat." *Globe and Mail*, 9 July 2008.

de Luce, Dan. "Iran Can Build Nuclear Bomb, Top US Military Officer Says." *Ottawa Citizen*, 2 March 2009.

"Define Canada's Global Agenda." *Toronto Star*, 30 December 2003.

Dewitt, David. "Directions in Canada's International Security Policy." *International Journal* 55, no. 3 (Summer 2000).

– and David Leyton-Brown. "Canada's International Security Policy." In David Dewitt and David Leyton-Brown, eds, *Canada's International Security Policy*. Scarborough, ON: Prentice Hall, 1995.

– and David Leyton-Brown, eds. *Canada's International Security Policy*. Scarborough, ON: Prentice Hall, 1995.

Directorate of Maritime Strategy. Unpublished document produced for the Canadian Navy Strategic Advisory Group. Ottawa: Directorate of Maritime Strategy, June 2009.

Doran, Michael Scott. "Somebody Else's Civil War." *Foreign Affairs* 81, no. 1 (2002).

Drogin, Bob. "U.S. Gets Tough on Canadian Border." *Los Angeles Times*, 10 May 2009.

Duffy, Andrew. "Canada Developing Strategy to Protect against Foreign Hackers." *Ottawa Citizen*, 9 April 2009.

Eayrs, James. *In Defence of Canada: Appeasement and Rearmament.* Toronto: University of Toronto Press, 1965.

Eggen, Dan. "Air Plot Said to Target Cities." *Washington Post,* 2 November 2006.

– "FBI Applies New Rules to Surveillance." *Washington Post,* 13 December 2003.

Eizenstat, Stuart E., and John Edward Porter. "Weak States Are a US Security Threat." *Christian Science Monitor,* 29 June 2004.

Ellis, Jason D. "The Best Defense: Counterproliferation and US National Strategy." *Washington Quarterly* 26, no. 2 (2003).

Evans, Gareth. "When Is It Right to Fight?" *Survival* 46, no. 3 (2004).

"Failed States: Fixing a Broken World." *Economist,* 31 January 2009.

Falkenrath, Richard. "Confronting Nuclear, Biological and Chemical Terrorism." *Survival* 40, no. 3 (1998).

Felicetti, Gary, and John Luce. "The *Posse Comitatus Act*: Liberation from the Lawyers." *Parameters* 34, no. 3 (2004).

"A Fence in the North, Too." *Economist,* 1 March 2008.

Fergusson, James. "National Missile Defense, Homeland Defense, and Outer Space: Policy Dilemmas in the Canada-US Relationship." In Fen Osler Hampson, Norman Hiller, and Maureen Appel Molot, eds, *Canada Among Nations 2001: The Axworthy Legacy.* Toronto: Oxford University Press, 2001.

Fife, Robert. "Terrorism Draws Us Closer to US." *Ottawa Citizen,* 15 October 2004.

Fisher, Matthew. "Canadian Warships Hunt Modern-Day Pirates." *Ottawa Citizen,* 15 July 2008.

Flynn, Stephen E. "The Neglected Home Front." *Foreign Affairs* 83, no. 5 (2004).

Forcier, Vice-Admiral Jean-Yves. "Interview." *Defense News,* 3 May 2004.

Foreign Affairs and International Trade Canada. "Canada and the World: A History." http://www.international.gc.ca (accessed August 2008).

Freeman, Alan. "Hillier Cool to Ottawa's Reserve Plan." *Globe and Mail,* 26 July 2007.

Galloway, Gloria. "No New Agency for Foreign Intelligence, Top Spy Says." *Globe and Mail,* 29 May 2007.

Gardham, Duncan. "Muslim Was Planning Dirty Bomb Attack in UK." *Telegraph,* 13 October 2006.

Garrett, Laurie, "The Nightmare of Bioterrorism." *Foreign Affairs* 80, no. 1 (2001).

Gellman, Barton. "Qaeda Cyberterror Called Real Peril." *International Herald Tribune*, 28 June 2002.

Gertz, Bill. "'Eroded' Al Qaeda Still a Threat." *Washington Times*, 16 January 2004.

Glaser, Charles L., and Chaim Kaufmann. "What Is the Offense-Defense Balance and Can We Measure It?" *International Security* 22, no. 4 (1988).

Glionna, John M. "Neighbors Angry about North Korea's Satellite Launch Plans." *Los Angeles Times*, 14 March 2009.

Goodspeed, Peter. "Canada Seen as Having 'Soft Belly,' Terror Expert Says." *National Post*, 3 November 2005.

Gordon, James. "Avoiding Iraq Has 'Mitigated' Terror Threat." *Ottawa Citizen*, 23 June 2006.

Gosselin, Daniel. "Hellyer's Ghosts: Unification of the Canadian Forces Is 40 Years Old." *Canadian Military Journal* 9, no. 2 (2009).

Government of Canada. "Backgrounder – Expanding Canadian Forces Operations in the Arctic." Press release, 10 August 2007, http://www.pm.gc.ca (accessed August 2007).

– *Canada First Defence Strategy*. Ottawa: Department of National Defence, 2008.

– *Canada's International Policy Statement: Defence*. Ottawa: Government of Canada, 2005.

– *Canada's International Policy Statement: Overview*. Ottawa: Government of Canada, 2005.

– *Canadian Defence Policy*. Ottawa: Department of National Defence, 1992.

– *Challenge and Commitment: A Defence Policy for Canada*. Ottawa: Department of National Defence, June 1987.

– *Defence in the 70s*. Ottawa: Department of National Defence, 1971.

– *Defence Update 1988–89*. Ottawa: Department of National Defence, 1988.

– *1994 Defence White Paper*. Ottawa: Department of National Defence, 1994.

– *Securing an Open Society: Canada's National Security Policy*. Ottawa: Government of Canada, 2004.

– *White Paper on Defence*. Ottawa: Department of National Defence, 1964.

Government of the United States. *Field Manual 3–24, Counterinsurgency*. Washington, DC: Department of the Army, 2006.

– *Quadrennial Defense Review*. Washington, DC: Department of Defense, 1997.

– *Quadrennial Defense Review*. Washington, DC: Department of Defense, 2001.

– *Quadrennial Defense Review*. Washington, DC: Department of Defense, 2006.

– *Strategy for Homeland Defense and Civil Support*. Washington, DC: Department of Defense, 2005.

Governor General of Canada. *Speech from the Throne*. Ottawa: Government of Canada, 2 February 2004.

Graham, Bradley. "Missile Defense Agency Faulted on Testing and Accountability." *Washington Post*, 24 April 2004.

– "U.S. Directive Prioritizes Post-Conflict Stability." *Washington Post*, 1 December 2005.

– "U.S. Urged to Broaden Defense against Terrorist Missiles." *Washington Post*, 19 August 2002.

Grier, Peter. "Al Qaeda Still a Threat to U.S., Intelligence Chiefs Say." *Christian Science Monitor*, 8 February 2008.

Griffiths, Franklin. "The Shipping News: Canada's Arctic Sovereignty Not on Thinning Ice." *International Journal* 58, no. 2 (2003).

"The Growing, and Mysterious, Irrelevance of al-Qaeda." *Economist*, 24 January 2009.

Gutkin, Steven. "Terrorists Pursuing WMD Capability." *Washington Times*, 9 February 2004.

Hall, Mimi. "Passenger Jets Get Anti-Missile Devices." *USA Today*, 4 January 2008.

Hampson, Fen Osler, Norman Hillmer, and Maureen Appel Molot. "The Return to Continentalism in Canadian Foreign Policy." In Fen Osler Hampson, Norman Hiller, and Maureen Appel Molot, eds, *Canada among Nations 2001: The Axworthy Legacy*. Toronto: Oxford University Press, 2001.

Hanley, Charles J. "Airpower Bombings Double in Iraq from 2006." *Associated Press*, 6 June 2007.

Harden, Blaine. "North Korean Nuclear Blast Draws Global Condemnation." *Washington Post*, 26 May 2009.

Harrington, Cailin. "US Pledges More Troops to Northcom." *Jane's Defence Weekly*, 5 September 2008.

Harrold, Max. "Canada to Respond Tit for Tat to Russian Jet Fighter." *Montreal Gazette*, 24 March 2009.

Hashim, Ahmed. "The World According to Usama Bin Laden." *Naval War College Review* 54, no. 4 (2001).

"A Haven for Villains." *Economist*, 15 September 2007.

High-Level Panel on Threats, Challenges and Change. *A More Secure World: Our Shared Responsibility*. New York: United Nations, 2004.

Hildreth, Steven A. *North Korean Ballistic Missile Threat to the United States*. Washington, DC: CRS Report for Congress, 24 January 2008.

Hoffman, Bruce. "Remember Al Qaeda? They're Baaack." *Los Angeles Times*, 20 February 2007.

Homeland Security Council. *National Strategy for Homeland Security*. Washington, DC: Homeland Security Council, 2007.

Horn, Bernd. "When Cultures Collide: The Conventional Military/SOF Chasm." *Canadian Military Journal* 5, no. 3 (2004).

Hsu, Spencer S., and Ann Scott Tyson. "Pentagon to Detail Troops to Bolster Domestic Security." *Washington Post*, 1 December 2008.

– and William Branigin. "Congress Passes Bill to Bolster Homeland Security." *Washington Post*, 28 July 2007.

Huebert, Robert. "Renaissance in Canadian Arctic Security?" *Canadian Military Journal* (Winter 2005–06).

– "The Shipping News Part II: How Canada's Arctic Sovereignty Is on Thinning Ice." *International Journal* 58, no. 3 (2003).

Humphreys, Adrian. "Canada's Troops to Reclaim Arctic." *National Post*, 25 March 2004.

– "Military Revamps Domestic Defence." *National Post*, 5 March 2009.

Huntington, Samuel. "The Clash of Civilizations?" *Foreign Affairs* 72, no. 3 (1993).

Hurst, Lynda. "Canada Listens to World as Partner in Spy System." *Toronto Star*, 7 March 2004.

"Imagining Something Much Worse than London." *Economist*, 16 July 2005.

Independent Panel on Canada's Future Role in Afghanistan. *Report of the Independent Panel on Canada's Future Role in Afghanistan*. Ottawa: Government of Canada, January 2008.

Innes, John. "Terrorists 'Would Use WMD If They Could.'" *Scotsman*, 17 November 2003.

International Institute for Strategic Studies. "US Intelligence Reform." *IISS Strategic Comments* 10, no. 8 (2004).

Ivison, John. "Arctic Hot in More Ways Than One." *National Post*, 24 February 2009.

Jockel, Joseph T. *Four US Military Commands:* NORTHCOM, NORAD, SPACECOM, STRATCOM – *The Canadian Opportunity.* Montreal: Institute for Research on Public Policy, 2003.

– "A Strong Friend Is a Good Defence." *Globe and Mail,* 14 January 2004.

Johnson, Carrie. "FBI Director Warns of Terror Attacks on U.S. Cities." *Washington Post,* 23 February 2009.

Johnston, David, and David Stout. "Bin Laden Is Said to be Organizing for a US Attack." *New York Times,* 9 July 2004.

Krim, Jonathan. "Cyber-Security to Get Higher Profile Leader." *Washington Post,* 13 October 2004.

Lambie, Chris. "Midshore Coast Guard Patrol Vessels Back on Ottawa Radar." *Halifax Chronicle Herald,* 28 February 2009.

Lederer, Edith M. "US Sees Nuclear Network Threat." *Washington Times,* 28 April 2004.

Levy, Jack S. "The Offensive/Defensive Balance of Military Technology: A Theoretical and Historical Analysis." *International Studies Quarterly* 28 (1984).

Lewis, Bernard. "License to Kill." *Foreign Affairs* 77, no. 6 (1998).

– "The Roots of Muslim Rage." *Atlantic Monthly* 266, no. 3 (September 1990).

Lindsey, George. "Canada, North American Security, and NORAD." *International Insights* 2, no. 3 (2004).

– "Canada-U.S. Defence Relations in the Cold War." In Joel J. Sokolsky and Joseph T. Jockel, eds, *Fifty Years of Canada-United States Security Cooperation.* Lewiston, NY: Edwin Meller Press, 1992.

– "Potential Contributions by the Canadian Armed Forces to the Defence of North America against Terrorism." *International Journal* 58, no. 3 (2003).

Linzer, Dafna. "Nuclear Capabilities May Elude Terrorists, Experts Say." *Washington Post,* 29 December 2004.

Ljunggren, David. "Arctic Summer Ice Could Vanish by 2013, Expert Says." *Reuters,* 5 March 2009.

– "Ottawa Vows to Do More to Prevent Attacks on US." *Reuters,* 25 March 2004.

– "Ships to Shun Northwest Passage." *Reuters,* 3 October 2007.

MacLeod, Ian. "Homegrown Terror Rising, RCMP Security Boss Warns." *Ottawa Citizen,* 12 February 2009.

– "Latest Terror Threats 'Scare Us': Senior Mountie." *Ottawa Citizen,* 8 May 2008.

– "Next Wave of 'Thrill Seeking' Terrorists Could Destroy Jihadist Movement: Expert." *Ottawa Citizen*, 11 March 2008.

– "US Revives Cross-Border Talk." *Ottawa Citizen*, 13 February 2008.

Maher, Stephen. "Little News Not Good News for Region." *Halifax Chronicle Herald*, 27 February 2008.

Malone, Julia, and Bob Deans. "Homegrown Terrorists Flying 'Under Radar' Says FBI Chief." *Cox News Service*, 23 June 2006.

Manley, John, Pedro Aspe, and William F. Weld. *Creating a North American Community*. New York: Council on Foreign Relations, Independent Task Force on the Future of North America, March 2005.

Marks, Alexandra. "Hard Work Still ahead for Homeland." *Christian Science Monitor*, 15 July 2005.

Maskell, Paul. "Sapphire: Canada's Answer to Space-Based Surveillance of Orbital Objects." Presentation to the Advanced Maui Optical and Space Surveillance Technologies Conference, 17–19 September 2008, http://appspacesol.com/pdf/sapphire.pdf (accessed May 2009).

Mason, Dwight N. *Canadian Defense Priorities: What Might the United States Like to See?* Policy Papers on the Americas 15, study no. 1. Washington, DC: Center for Strategic and International Studies, 2004.

Matthews, William. "Momentum Builds for Single US Intel Chief." *Defense News*, 23 August 2004.

– "US Lawmakers Push 'Prompt Global Strike': Homeland UAVs, Special Forces Also Winners in 2004 Authorization Bill." *Defense News*, 24 November 2003.

Mayeda, Andrew. "Tories Drop Plan to Build Foreign Spy Agency." *Ottawa Citizen*, 16 May 2007.

Mazarr, Michael. "Extremism, Terror, and the Future of Conflict." *Policy Review* (March 2006).

McCarthy, Shawn. "Arctic Contains 13% of Remaining Oil." *Globe and Mail*, 28 May 2009.

McConnell, J. Michael. *Annual Threat Assessment of the Director of National Intelligence*. Testimony before the Senate Select Committee on Intelligence, 5 February 2008.

McLean, Archie. "Canada's Next Drones Will Carry Bombs." *Edmonton Journal*, 5 March 2009.

Mintz, John. "Bioterrorism Procedures Are Outlined: Bush Directive Specifies Agency Responsibilities." *Washington Post*, 29 April 2004.

– "US Officials Warn of New Tactics by Al Qaeda." *Washington Post*, 5 September 2003.

Morton, Desmond. "'No More Disagreeable or Onerous Duty': Canadians and Military Aid of the Civil Power, Past, Present, Future." In David Dewitt and David Leyton-Brown, eds, *Canada's International Security Policy*. Scarborough, ON: Prentice Hall, 1995.

Mousseau, Michael. "Market Civilization and Its Clash with Terror." *International Security* 27, no. 3 (2002–03).

Murray, Douglas. "NORAD and US Nuclear Operations." In Joel J. Sokolsky and Joseph T. Jockel, eds, *Fifty Years of Canada-United States Security Cooperation*. Lewiston, NY: Edwin Meller Press, 1992.

Murray, Williamson, and Robert H. Scales Jr. *The Iraq War*. Cambridge, MA: Harvard University Press, 2003.

Nakashima, Ellen. "Obama Set to Create a Cybersecurity Czar with Broad Mandate." *Washington Post*, 26 May 2009.

National Commission on Terrorist Attacks upon the United States. *The 9/11 Commission Report*. New York: W.W. Norton and Company, 2004.

National Defense Panel. *Transforming Defense: National Security in the 21st Century*. Washington, DC: National Defense Panel, 1997.

National Intelligence Council. *Global Trends 2025: A Transformed World*. Washington, DC: Office of the Director of National Intelligence, November 2008.

– *National Intelligence Estimate: The Terrorist Threat to the US Homeland*. Washington, DC: Office of the Director of National Intelligence, 2007.

National Security Council. *National Security Strategy for a New Century*. Washington, DC: National Security Council, 1998.

– *The National Security Strategy of the United States*. Washington, DC: National Security Council, 2002.

– *The National Security Strategy of the United States*. Washington, DC: National Security Council, 2006.

Negroponte, John D. *Annual Threat Assessment of the Director of National Intelligence*. Testimony before the Senate Select Committee on Intelligence, 2 February 2006.

– *Annual Threat Assessment of the Director of National Intelligence*. Testimony before the House Permanent Select Committee on Intelligence, 18 January 2007.

"The New Terrorism." *Economist*, 15 August 1998.

"The Next War, They Say." *Economist*, 6 August 1994.

Nickerson, Colin. "US-Canada Security Brings Frustration to Both Sides of Border." *Globe and Mail*, 20 January 2003.

O'Dwyer, Gerard. "NATO's High North Ambitions May Have Russian Input." *Defense News*, 9 March 2009.

Office of Homeland Security. *National Strategy for Homeland Security.* Washington, DC: Office of Homeland Security, 2002.

Office of the Secretary of Defense. *Annual Report to Congress: Military Power of the People's Republic of China.* Washington, DC: Department of Defense, 2008.

"On the March, Not on the Run." *The Economist*, 20 January 2007.

Orvik, Nils. "Canadian Security and Defence against Help." *International Perspectives* (May-June 1983).

"Ottawa to Revive Scrapped High-Tech Coastal Radar." *Toronto Star*, 13 March 2008.

Pape, Robert A. "The Strategic Logic of Suicide Terrorism." *American Political Science Review* 97, no. 3 (2003).

Parachini, John. "Putting WMD Terrorism into Perspective." *Washington Quarterly* 26, no. 4 (2003).

Paraskevas, Joe. "Make Coast Guard an Armed Military Force, Committee Urges." *Ottawa Citizen*, 1 April 2004.

Parformak, Paul W., and John Frittelli. *Maritime Security: Potential Terrorist Attacks and Protection Priorities.* Washington, DC: Congressional Research Service, 9 January 2007.

Passport Canada. *A Year to Remember: Annual Report 2007–2008.* Ottawa: Government of Canada, 2008.

Perry, William. "Preparing for the Next Attack." *Foreign Affairs* 80, no. 6 (November-December 2001).

Phares, Walid. "Future Terrorism Mutant *Jihads.*" *Journal of International Security Affairs*, no. 11 (2006).

"Ports at Risk for Smuggled 'Dirty Bombs.'" *Ottawa Citizen*, 29 November 2007.

Posen, Barry R. "The Struggle against Terrorism: Grand Strategy, Strategy, and Tactics." *International Security* 26, no. 3 (2001–02).

"President Obama Outlines His Plan for Missile Defense." *PR Newswire*, 8 May 2009, http://news.prnewswire.com (accessed May 2009).

President of the United States. *National Security Presidential Directive 66: Arctic Region Policy.* Washington, DC: White House, January 2009.

Pugliese, David. "Armoured Vehicles Hit Their Limits." *Ottawa Citizen*, 6 May 2008.

– "Canada Anticipates Larger Counterinsurgency Role for Armor." *Defense News*, 20 April 2009.

– "Canada Buys Radars, Puts Portable Surveillance on Hold." *Defense News*, 21 July 2008.
– "Canada Expects C-130 to Boost Air Mobility." *Defense News*, 3 November 2008.
– "Canada Plans Long-Range UAV Fleet." *Defense News*, 16 February 2009.
– "Canada Takes Modular Approach to Future Vessels." *Defense News*, 20 October 2008.
– "Canada to Establish Marine Security Centres." *Defense News*, 2 October 2006.
– "Canada to Launch Design Work on Radarsat." *Defense News*, 29 September 2008.
– "Canada to Try UAVs in Arctic." *Defense News*, 2 August 2004.
– "Canadian Military Weighs Future of ADATS." *Defense News*, 6 April 2009.
– "Canadian Navy Needs More Procurement Specialists." *Defense News*, 11 May 2009.
– "Navy Shops around for New Midsized Patrol Vessels." *Ottawa Citizen*, 12 July 2004.
– "Need for Supply Ships Strains Canada's Navy, Budget." *Defense News*, 23 February 2009.
– "Pentagon Looks to Buy Canadian Spy Satellite Technology." *Ottawa Citizen*, 13 September 2008.
– "Reserve Units to Form Core of New Arctic Force." *Ottawa Citizen*, 22 March 2009.
Purdy, Margaret. "Countering Terrorism: The Missing Pillar." *International Journal* 60, no. 1 (2004–05).
Record, Jeffrey. *Bounding the Global War on Terrorism*. Carlisle, PA: Strategic Studies Institute, US Army War College, 2003.
Reid, Tim. "Forty States 'Have Nuclear Capability.'" *Times Online*, 1 November 2003.
Rekai, Peter. *United States and Canadian Immigration Policies: Marching Together to Different Tunes*. Border Paper no. 171. Toronto: CD Howe Institute, 2002.
Revkin, Andrew C. "The Arctic's Alarming Sea Change." *International Herald Tribune*, 2 October 2007.
Rice, Susan E., and Stewart Patrick. *Index of State Weakness in the Developing World*. Washington, DC: Brookings Institution, 2008.
Risen, James. "Ex-government Officials Recommend Intelligence Overhaul." *New York Times*, 9 December 2003.

Rubin, Barry. "The Real Roots of Arab Anti-Americanism." *Foreign Affairs* 81, no. 6 (2002).

Rudner, Martin. "Contemporary Threats, Future Tasks: Canadian Intelligence and the Challenges of Global Security." In Norman Hillmer and Maureen Appel Molot, eds, *Canada among Nations 2002: A Fading Power*. Toronto: Oxford University Press, 2002.

– *Protecting Canada's Energy Infrastructure against Terrorism: Mapping a Proactive Strategy*. Ottawa: Canadian Centre of Intelligence and Security Studies, March 2008.

"Russia Dedicates Force to Arctic." *Globe and Mail*, 27 March 2009.

Sallot, Jeff. "Canada Could Escape Attack, CSIS Says." *Globe and Mail*, 20 June 2006.

– "Graham Defends Joining US Arms Interception Plan." *Globe and Mail*, 17 February 2004.

Sappenfield, Mark. "Disaster Relief? Call in the Marines." *Christian Science Monitor*, 19 September 2005.

Scarborough, Rowan. "Special Ops Steal Show as Successes Mount in Iraq." *Washington Times*, 7 April 2003.

Schultz, Richard H. Jr, and Andrea J. Dew. "Counterinsurgency, by the Book." *New York Times*, 7 August 2006.

Security and Prosperity Partnership of North America. *Report to Leaders*, 27 June 2005, http://www.spp.gov (accessed April 2009).

Segal, Heather. "After So Much Spent on Security, Are We Secure Yet?" *Globe and Mail*, 31 March 2004.

Seper, Jerry. "FBI Director Predicts Terrorists Will Acquire Nukes." *Washington Times*, 12 June 2007.

– "FBI 'Reprioritized' after '01 Terror Attacks, Report Says." *Washington Times*, 5 October 2004.

Shane, Scott. "In New Job, Spymaster Draws Bipartisan Criticism." *New York Times*, 20 April 2006.

– "U.S. Report Predicts Decline for Al Qaeda." *International Herald Tribune*, 20 November 2008.

Shanker, Thom. "Missile Defense System Is Up and Running, Military Says." *New York Times*, 3 October 2007.

Shenon, Philip. "US to Put Inspectors at Muslim Ports." *New York Times*, 12 June 2003.

Sherman, Jason. "US Navy's Role Soars." *Defense News*, 3 March 2003.

Simon, Steven. "The New Terrorism: Securing the Nation against a Messianic Foe." *Brookings Review* 21, no. 1 (2003).

Skerry, Peter. "The American Exception: Homegrown Terrorism in the U.S." *Time Magazine*, 14 August 2006.

Sloan, Elinor. "Continental and Homeland Security: From Bush to Obama." *International Journal* 64, no. 1 (2008–09).

– "Defence and Security." In John C. Courtney and David E. Smith, eds, *Oxford Handbook of Canadian Politics*. New York: Oxford University Press, forthcoming.

– *Military Transformation and Modern Warfare*. Westport, CT: Praeger, 2008.

– *Military Transformation: Key Aspects and Canadian Approaches*. Calgary: Canadian Defence and Foreign Affairs Institute, December 2007.

Slobodian, Linda. "General Sees Reserve Force as Vital for Terror Response." *Calgary Herald*, 22 March 2004.

Smith, Graeme. "Conquering Canadians Take Stock." *Globe and Mail*, 13 September 2006.

Smith, Lewis. "Seizures of Radioactive Materials Fuel 'Dirty Bomb' Fears." *Times Online*, 6 October 2006.

Sokolski, Henry. "Rethinking Bio-chemical Dangers." *Orbis* 44, no. 2 (Spring 2000).

Sokolsky, Joel J. "The Bilateral Defence Relationship with the United States." In David Dewitt and David Leyton-Brown, eds, *Canada's International Security Policy*. Scarborough, ON: Prentice Hall, 1995.

– and Joseph T. Jockel, eds. *Fifty Years of Canada-United States Security Cooperation*. Lewiston, NY: Edwin Meller Press, 1992.

Spotts, Peter N. "US Coast Guard Joins in Arctic Oil Rush." *Christian Science Monitor*, 20 August 2007.

Standing Committee on National Defence and Veterans Affairs. *Facing Our Responsibilities: The State of Readiness of the Canadian Forces*. Ottawa: Government of Canada, May 2002.

Standing Senate Committee on National Security and Defence. *Canadian Security Guide Book: Airports*. Ottawa: Government of Canada, March 2007.

– *Canadian Security Guide Book: Seaports*. Ottawa: Government of Canada, March 2007.

– *Canadian Security and Military Preparedness*. Ottawa: Government of Canada, February 2002.

– *The Longest Under-Defended Borders in the World*. Ottawa: Government of Canada, October 2003.

Stern, Jessica. "The Protean Enemy." *Foreign Affairs* 82, no. 4 (2003).

Sullivan, Eileen. "Homeland Security's 5–Year Threat Picture." *Washington Times*, 25 December 2008.

"Survey of Islam and the West." *Economist*, 13 September 2003.

Taylor, Guy, and Tom Ramstack. "Ridge Adds 5,000 Air Marshals to Help Get 'Surge Capacity.'" *Washington Times*, 3 September 2003.

Tenet, George. *Worldwide Threat – Converging Dangers in a Post 9/11 World*. Testimony before the Senate Armed Services Committee, 19 March 2002.

– *The Worldwide Threat in 2003: Evolving Dangers in a Complex World*. Testimony before the Senate Select Committee on Intelligence, 11 February 2003.

Thorne, Stephen. "NORAD Role Could Be Altered." *Canadian Press*, 24 February 2005.

Tibbetts, Janice. "Our Border 'Not a Conduit for Terrorists.'" *Ottawa Citizen*, 30 April 2003.

Tirpak, John A. "The Space Based Radar Plan." *Air Force Magazine* 85, no. 8 (2002).

Treaty on Principles Governing the Activities of States in the Exploration and Use of Outer Space, Including the Moon and Other Celestial Bodies, January 1967.

Ullman, Richard H. "Redefining Security." *International Security* 8, no. 3 (1983).

United Nations General Assembly. *World Summit Outcome*. New York: United Nations, 2005.

"U.S.-Born Militants Seen as Growing Terror Threat." *Washington Times*, 3 September 2005.

U.S. Commission on National Security/21st Century. *New World Coming*. Washington, DC: U.S. Commission on National Security/21st Century, 1999.

– *Road Map for National Security: Imperative for Change*. Washington, DC: U.S. Commission on National Security/21st Century, 2001.

– *Seeking a National Strategy*. Washington, DC: U.S. Commission on National Security/21st Century, 2000.

US Commission on Weak States and National Security. *On the Brink: Weak States and US National Security*. Washington, DC: Center for Global Development, 2004.

"US Intelligence Community in Poll Position." *Jane's Intelligence Digest*, 31 October 2008.

VanderKlippe, Nathan. "Arctic a Potential Terror Target." *Edmonton Journal*, 19 September 2004.

Van Evera, Stephen. *Causes of War: Power and the Roots of Conflict.* Ithaca: Cornell University Press, 1999.

Vickers, Melana Zyla. "LCS Could Bolster Defense against Terror." *Defense News*, 14 July 2003.

Walt, Stephen. "Beyond Bin Laden." *International Security* 26, no. 3 (2001–02).

Ward, John. "Canada-US Amend Defence Pact to Keep Missile Detection within NORAD." *Ottawa Citizen*, 6 August 2004.

"Warning about WMD." *Washington Times*, 25 June 2004.

Warrick, Joby. "U.S. Cites Big Gains against Al-Qaeda." *Washington Post*, 30 May 2008.

Wattie, Chris. "Reservists Touted as Terrorism Fighters." *National Post*, 27 March 2004.

Weber, Bob. "Arm Icebreakers, Beef Up Rangers to Assert Canadian Control of Arctic: Senate." *Ottawa Citizen*, 6 May 2009.

"Where Paul Martin Should Lead Canada." *Globe and Mail*, 15 December 2003.

White, Patrick. "Unmanned Drone Prowls over the Lonely Prairie." *Globe and Mail*, 18 February 2009.

Williamson, Doug. "1 in 5 Border Guards Fails Shooting Lessons." *Windsor Star*, 26 September 2007.

Index

Index